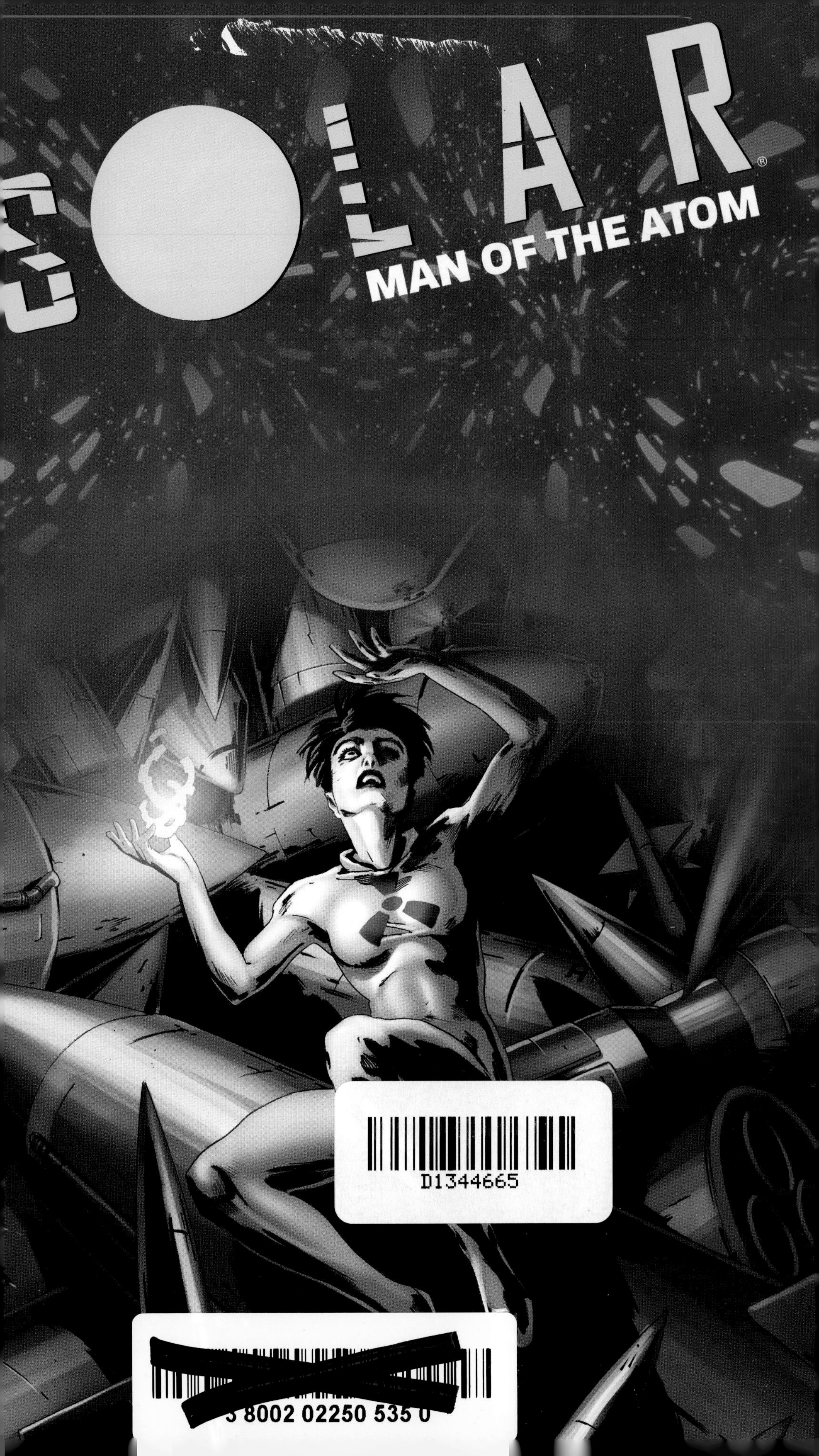
SOLAR®
MAN OF THE ATOM

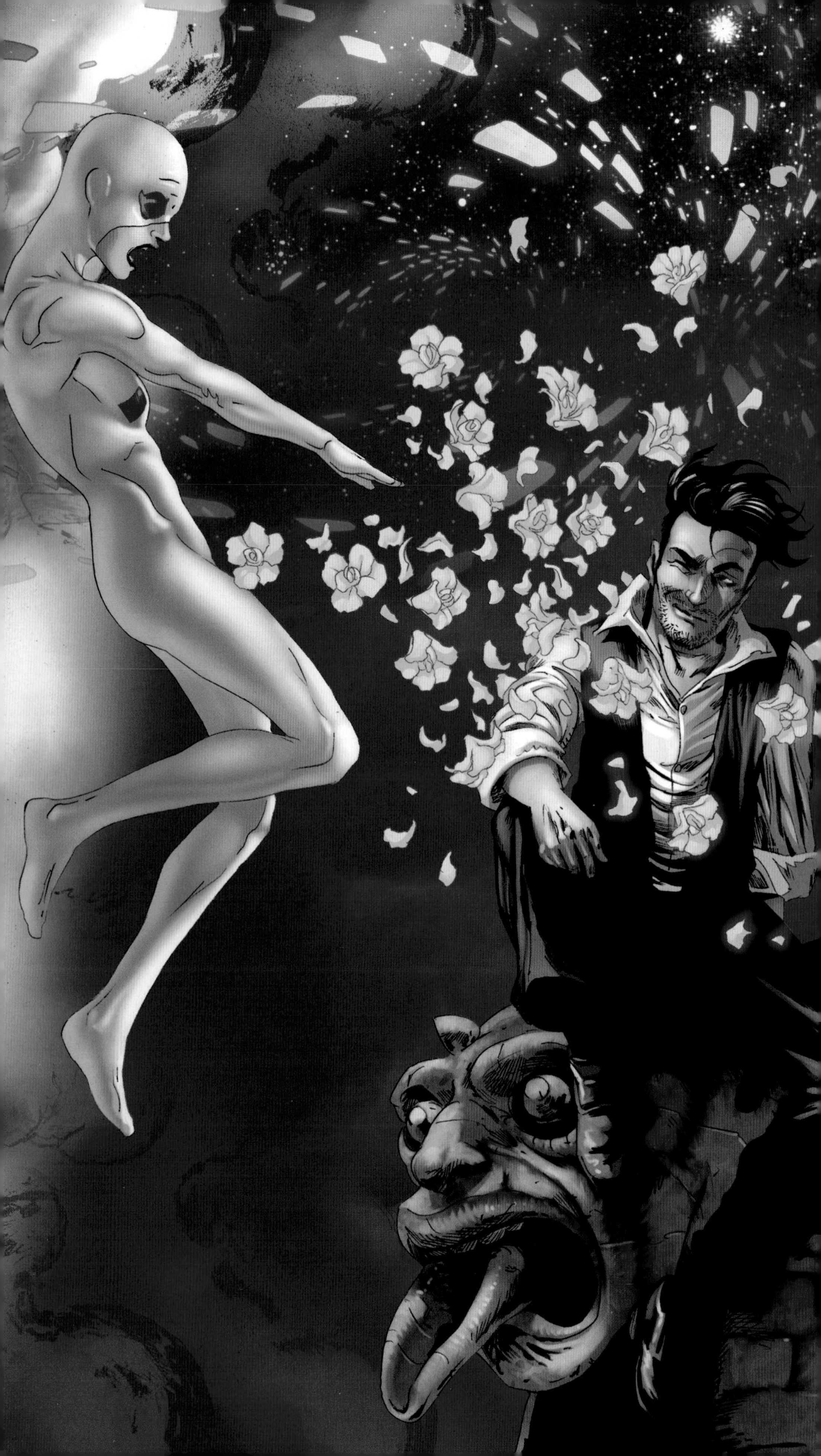

SOLAR
MAN OF THE ATOM
ECLIPSE

WRITTEN BY
FRANK J. BARBIERE

ART BY
JONATHAN LAU
ROBERTO CASTRO
ANTHONY MARQUES

COLORS BY
OMI REMALANTE JR.

LETTERS BY
MARSHALL DILLON

COLLECTION COVER BY
JONATHAN LAU

COLLECTION COVER COLORS BY
IVAN NUNES

COLLECTION DESIGN BY
KATIE HIDALGO

SPECIAL THANKS TO
HANNAH ELDER, TOM ENGLEMAN,
BEN CAWOOD, NICOLE BLAKE,
COLIN MCLAUGHLIN, CHRISTOPHER PREECE,
SIMON BOWLAND AND TOM BRENNAN

PACKAGED AND EDITED BY **NATE COSBY**
OF COSBY AND SONS PRODUCTIONS

THIS VOLUME COLLECTS ISSUES 9-12 OF SOLAR:
MAN OF THE ATOM BY DYNAMITE ENTERTAINMENT.

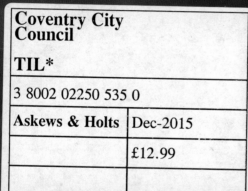

DYNAMITE

ucci, CEO / Publisher
do, President / COO

dt, Senior Editor
der, Associate Editor

meyer, Design Director
lgo, Graphic Designer
kins, Graphic Designer
ano, Digital Associate
bury, Digital Assistant

g, Director Business Development
idsen, Marketing Manager
rl, Sales Associate

Online at www.DYNAMITE.com
On Twitter @dynamitecomics
On Facebook /Dynamitecomics
On YouTube /Dynamitecomics
On Tumblr dynamitecomics.tumblr.com

ISBN-10: 1-60690-736-0   ISBN-13: 978-1-60690-736-8   First Printing   10 9 8 7 6 5 4 3 2 1

For information regarding press, media rights, foreign rights, licensing, promotions, and advertising e-mail:
marketing@dynamite.com

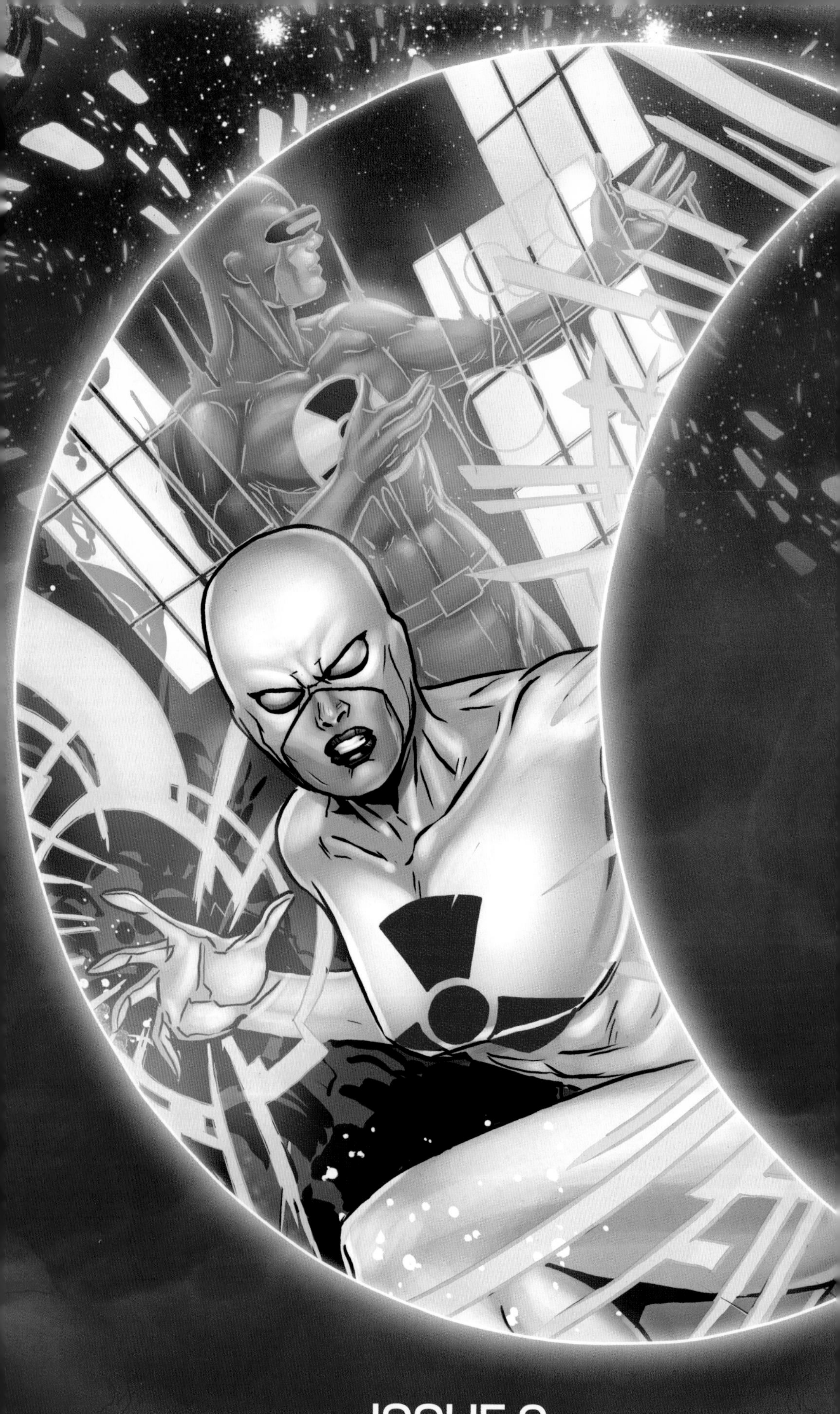

ISSUE 9

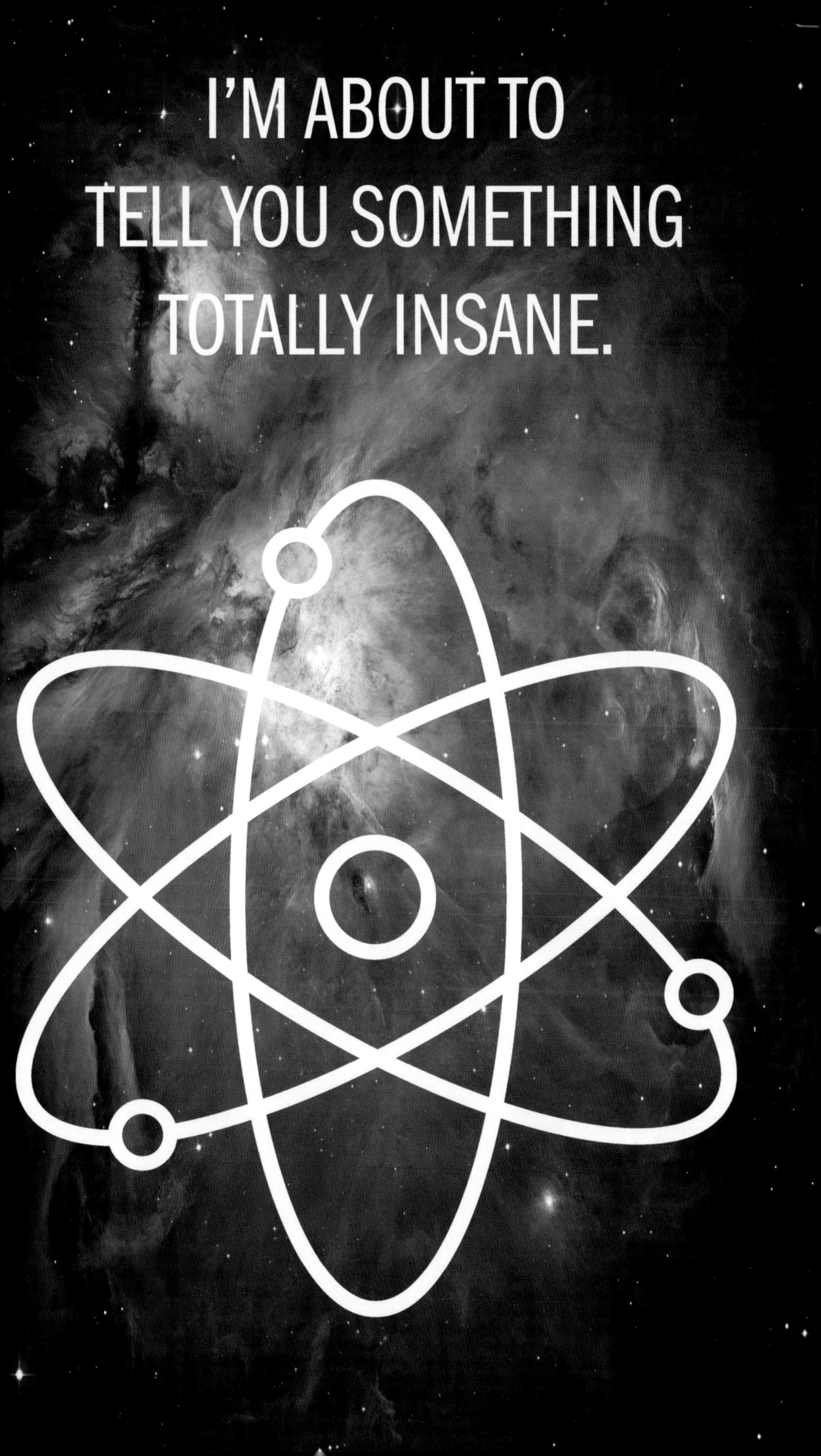
I'M ABOUT TO
TELL YOU SOMETHING
TOTALLY INSANE.

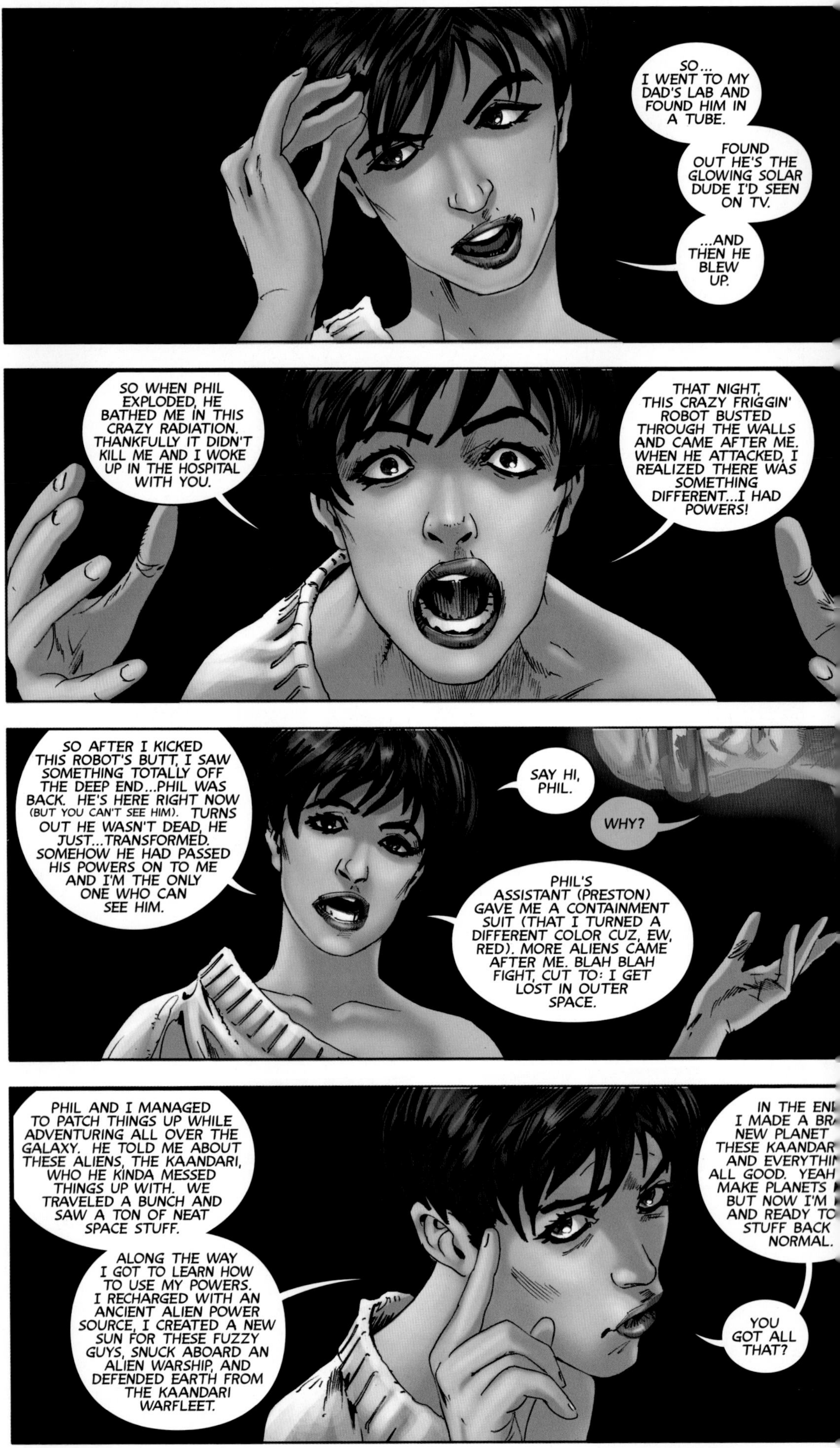
SO... I WENT TO MY DAD'S LAB AND FOUND HIM IN A TUBE.
FOUND OUT HE'S THE GLOWING SOLAR DUDE I'D SEEN ON TV.
...AND THEN HE BLEW UP.
SO WHEN PHIL EXPLODED, HE BATHED ME IN THIS CRAZY RADIATION. THANKFULLY IT DIDN'T KILL ME AND I WOKE UP IN THE HOSPITAL WITH YOU.
THAT NIGHT, THIS CRAZY FRIGGIN' ROBOT BUSTED THROUGH THE WALLS AND CAME AFTER ME. WHEN HE ATTACKED, I REALIZED THERE WAS SOMETHING DIFFERENT...I HAD POWERS!
SO AFTER I KICKED THIS ROBOT'S BUTT, I SAW SOMETHING TOTALLY OFF THE DEEP END...PHIL WAS BACK. HE'S HERE RIGHT NOW (BUT YOU CAN'T SEE HIM). TURNS OUT HE WASN'T DEAD, HE JUST...TRANSFORMED. SOMEHOW HE HAD PASSED HIS POWERS ON TO ME AND I'M THE ONLY ONE WHO CAN SEE HIM.
SAY HI, PHIL.
WHY?
PHIL'S ASSISTANT (PRESTON) GAVE ME A CONTAINMENT SUIT (THAT I TURNED A DIFFERENT COLOR CUZ, EW, RED). MORE ALIENS CAME AFTER ME. BLAH BLAH FIGHT, CUT TO: I GET LOST IN OUTER SPACE.
PHIL AND I MANAGED TO PATCH THINGS UP WHILE ADVENTURING ALL OVER THE GALAXY. HE TOLD ME ABOUT THESE ALIENS, THE KAANDARI, WHO HE KINDA MESSED THINGS UP WITH. WE TRAVELED A BUNCH AND SAW A TON OF NEAT SPACE STUFF.
ALONG THE WAY I GOT TO LEARN HOW TO USE MY POWERS. I RECHARGED WITH AN ANCIENT ALIEN POWER SOURCE, I CREATED A NEW SUN FOR THESE FUZZY GUYS, SNUCK ABOARD AN ALIEN WARSHIP, AND DEFENDED EARTH FROM THE KAANDARI WARFLEET.
IN THE EN I MADE A BR NEW PLANET THESE KAANDAR AND EVERYTHI ALL GOOD. YEAH MAKE PLANETS BUT NOW I'M AND READY TO STUFF BACK NORMAL.
YOU GOT ALL THAT?

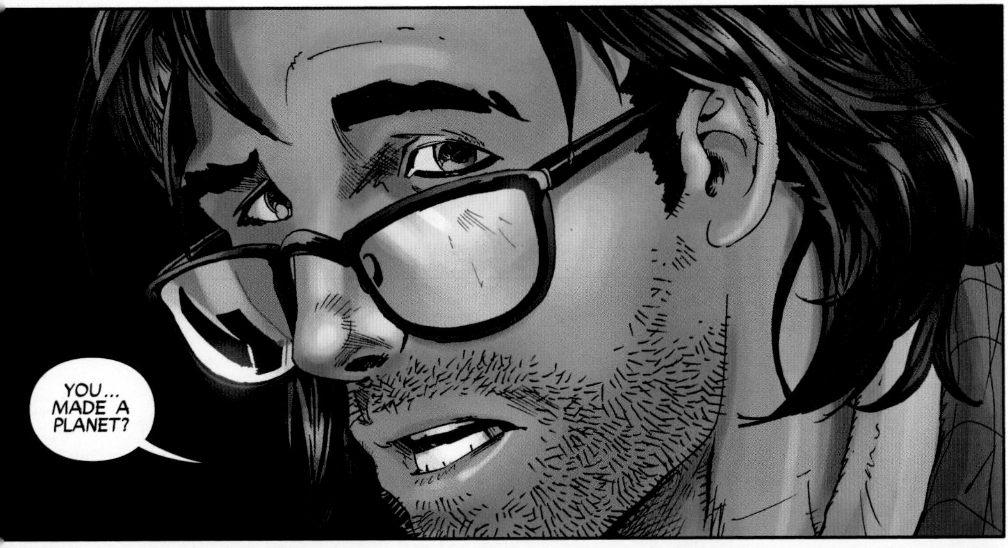
YOU... MADE A PLANET?

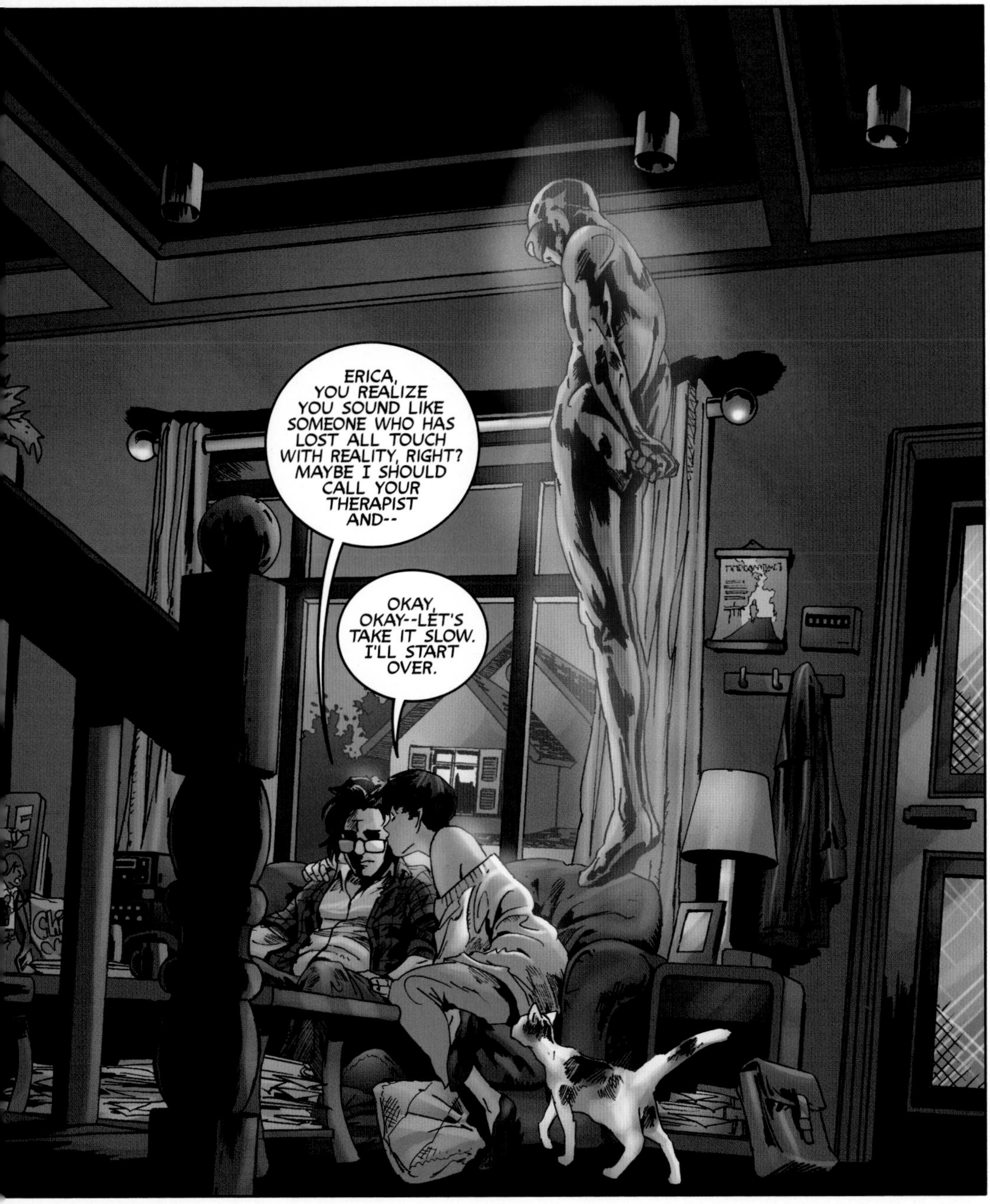
ERICA, YOU REALIZE YOU SOUND LIKE SOMEONE WHO HAS LOST ALL TOUCH WITH REALITY, RIGHT? MAYBE I SHOULD CALL YOUR THERAPIST AND--
OKAY, OKAY--LET'S TAKE IT SLOW. I'LL START OVER.

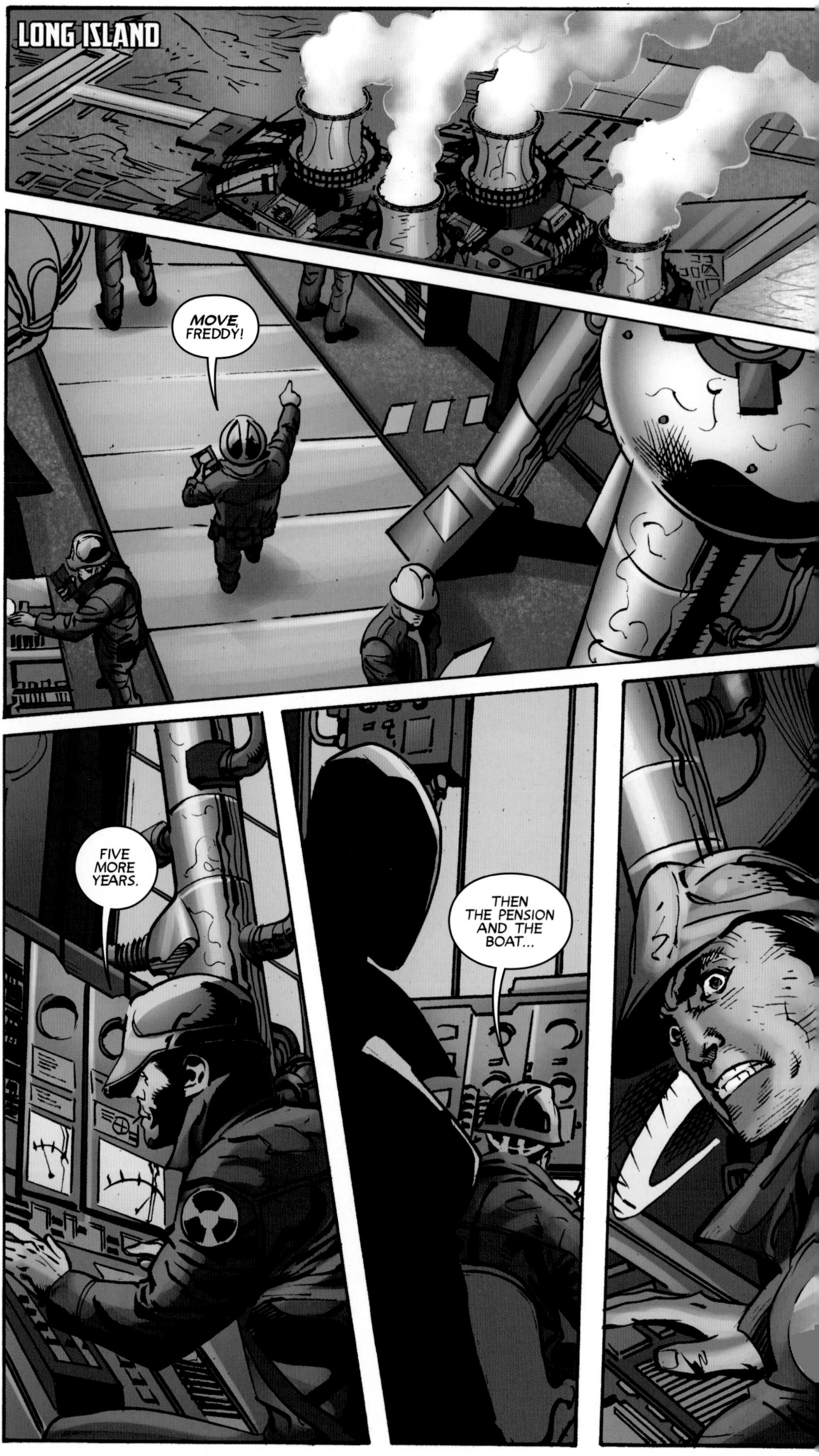
LONG ISLAND
MOVE, FREDDY!
FIVE MORE YEARS.
THEN THE PENSION AND THE BOAT...

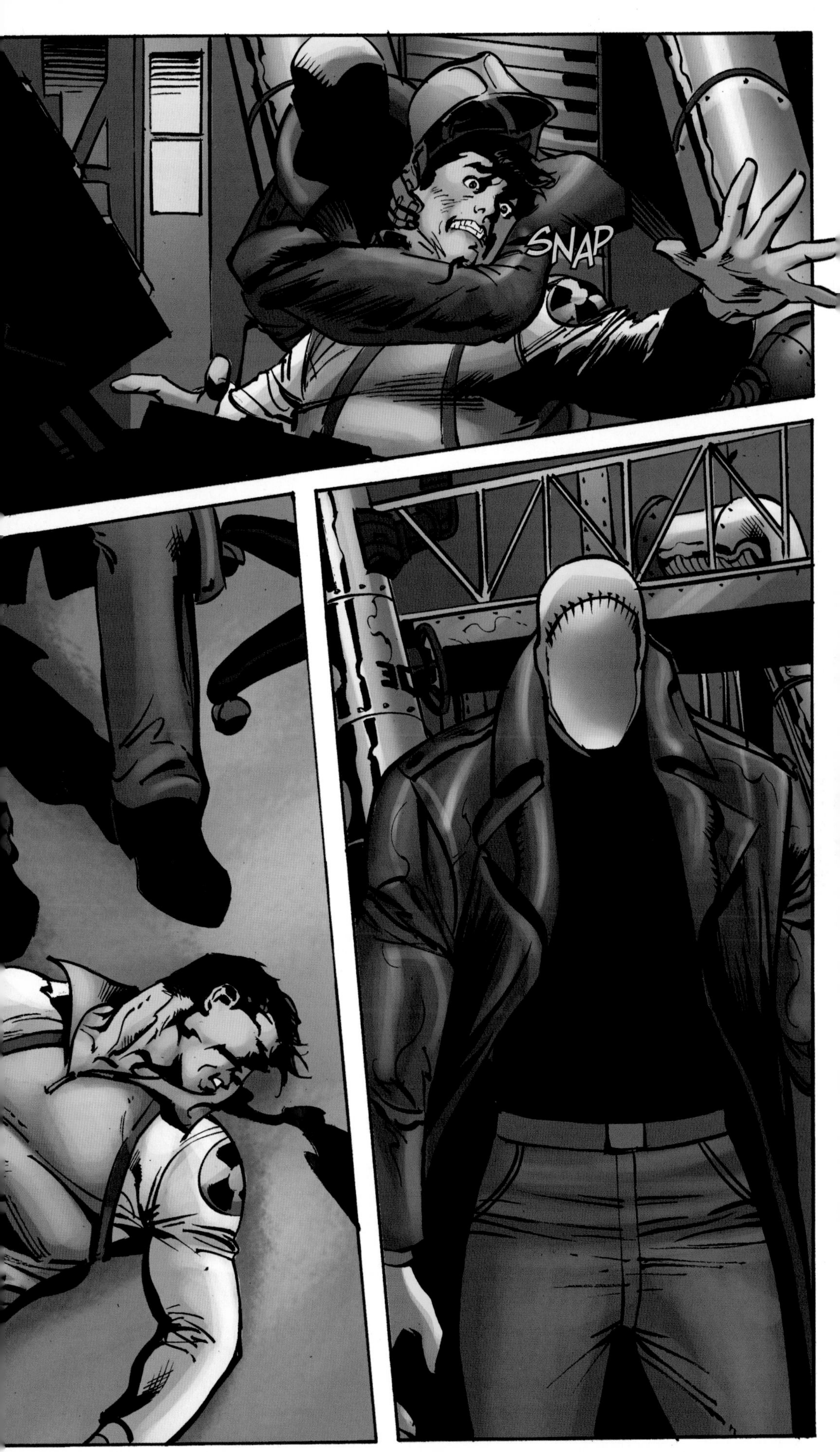
SNAP

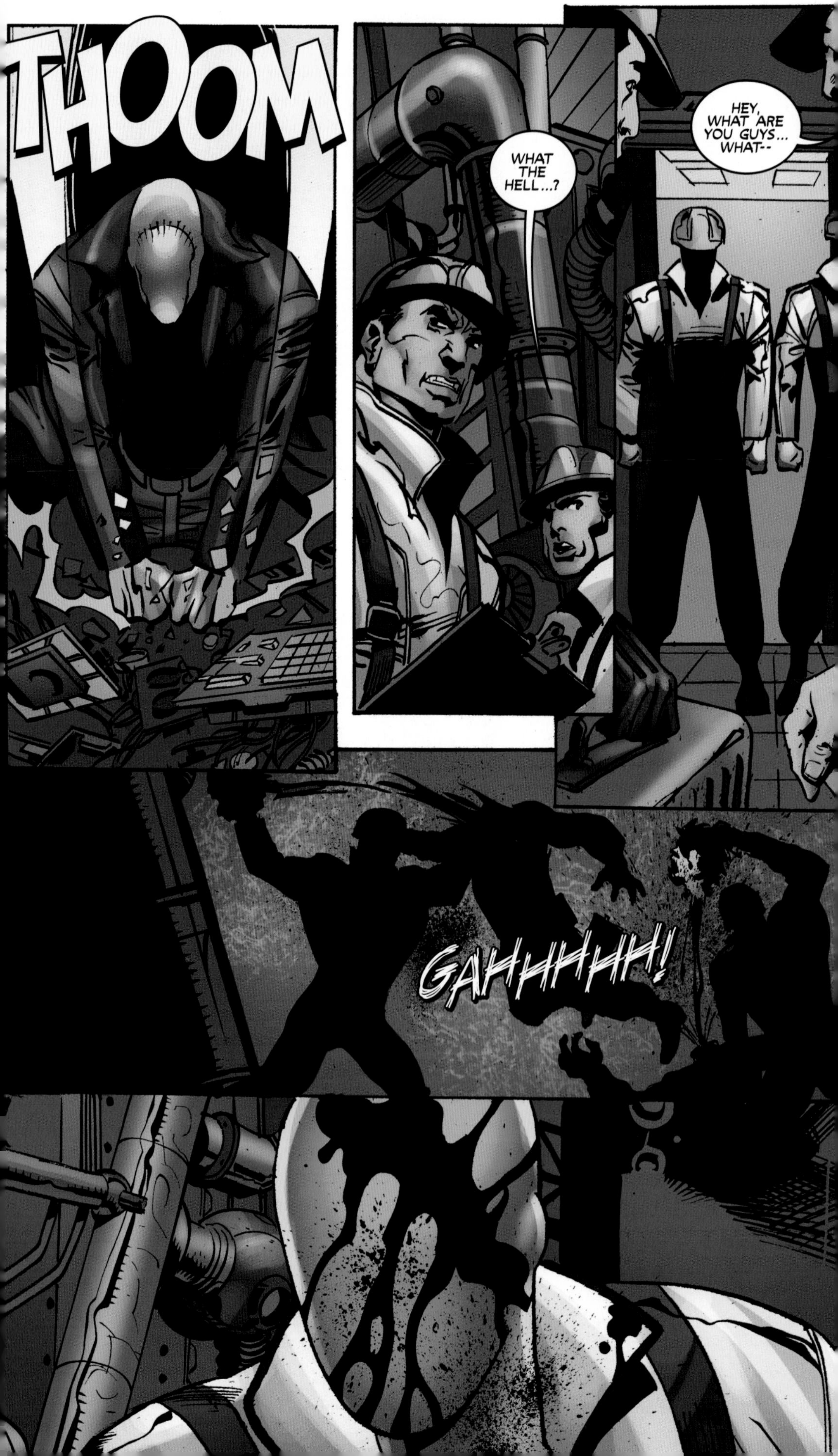
THOOM
WHAT THE HELL...?
HEY, WHAT ARE YOU GUYS... WHAT--
GAHHHHH!

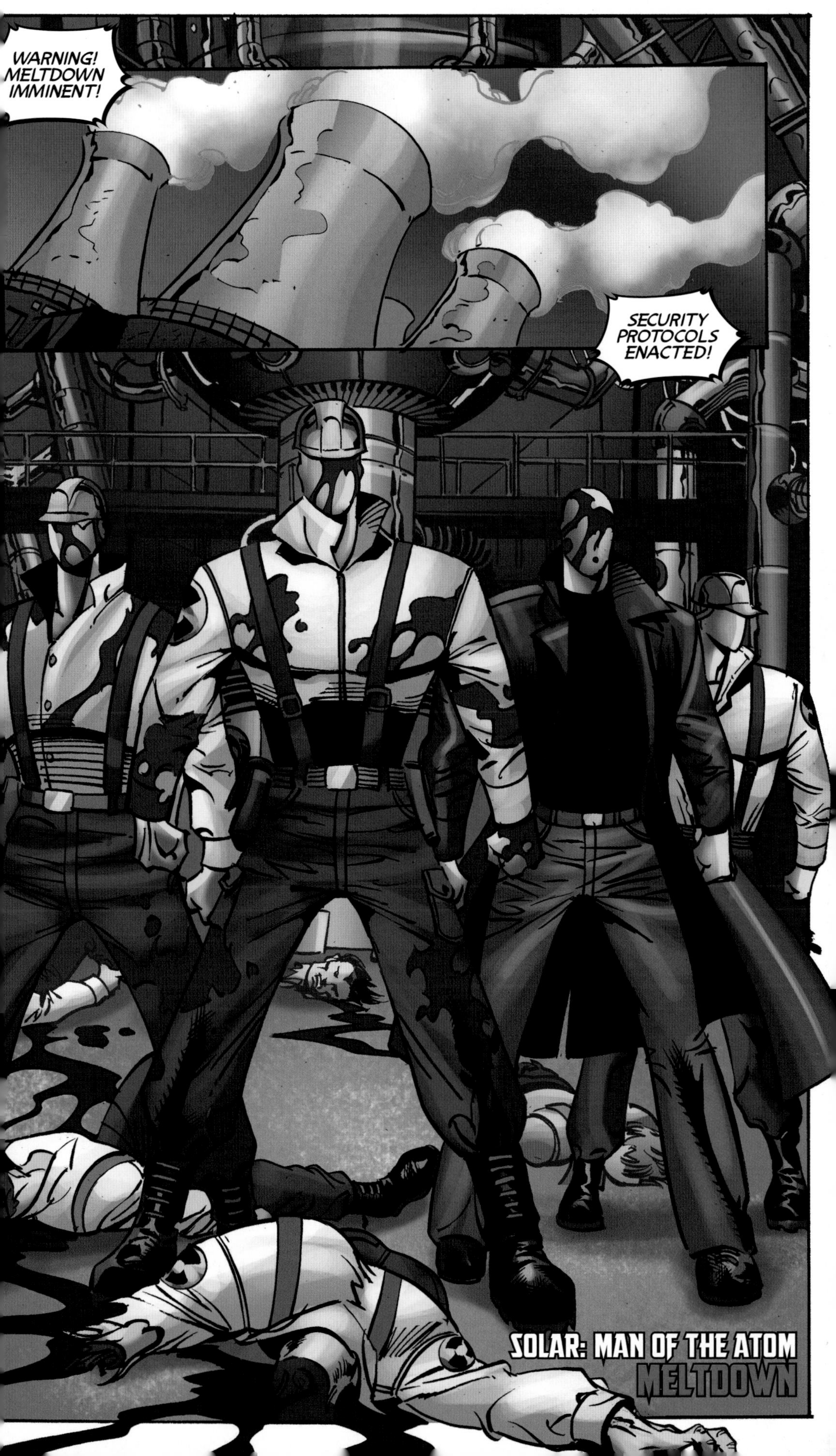
WARNING! MELTDOWN IMMINENT!
SECURITY PROTOCOLS ENACTED!
SOLAR: MAN OF THE ATOM
MELTDOWN

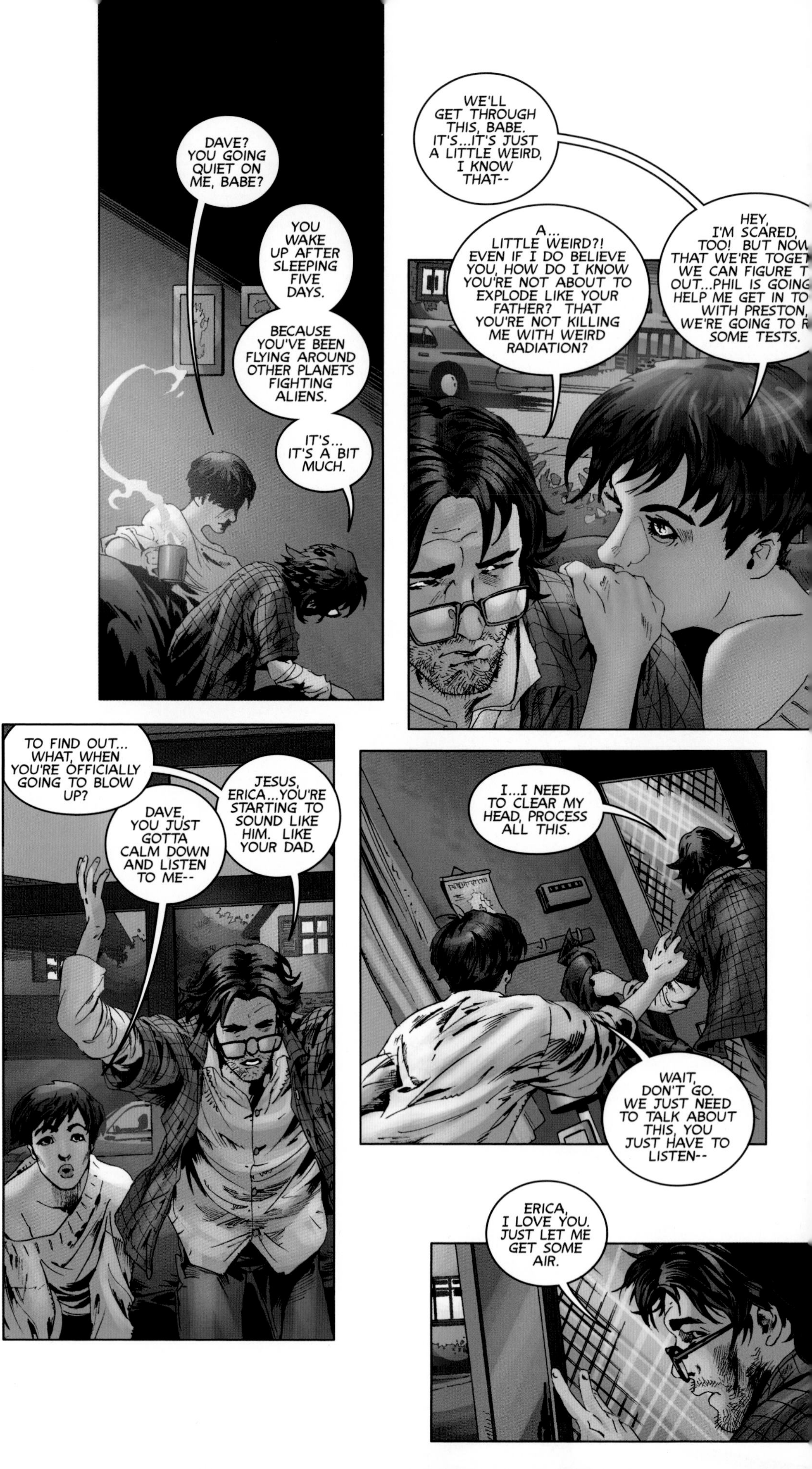
DAVE? YOU GOING QUIET ON ME, BABE?
YOU WAKE UP AFTER SLEEPING FIVE DAYS.
BECAUSE YOU'VE BEEN FLYING AROUND OTHER PLANETS FIGHTING ALIENS.
IT'S... IT'S A BIT MUCH.
WE'LL GET THROUGH THIS, BABE. IT'S...IT'S JUST A LITTLE WEIRD, I KNOW THAT--
A... LITTLE WEIRD?! EVEN IF I DO BELIEVE YOU, HOW DO I KNOW YOU'RE NOT ABOUT TO EXPLODE LIKE YOUR FATHER? THAT YOU'RE NOT KILLING ME WITH WEIRD RADIATION?
HEY, I'M SCARED, TOO! BUT NOW THAT WE'RE TOGET WE CAN FIGURE T OUT...PHIL IS GOING HELP ME GET IN TO WITH PRESTON, WE'RE GOING TO R SOME TESTS.
TO FIND OUT... WHAT, WHEN YOU'RE OFFICIALLY GOING TO BLOW UP?
JESUS, ERICA...YOU'RE STARTING TO SOUND LIKE HIM. LIKE YOUR DAD.
DAVE, YOU JUST GOTTA CALM DOWN AND LISTEN TO ME--
I...I NEED TO CLEAR MY HEAD, PROCESS ALL THIS.
WAIT, DON'T GO. WE JUST NEED TO TALK ABOUT THIS, YOU JUST HAVE TO LISTEN--
ERICA, I LOVE YOU. JUST LET ME GET SOME AIR.

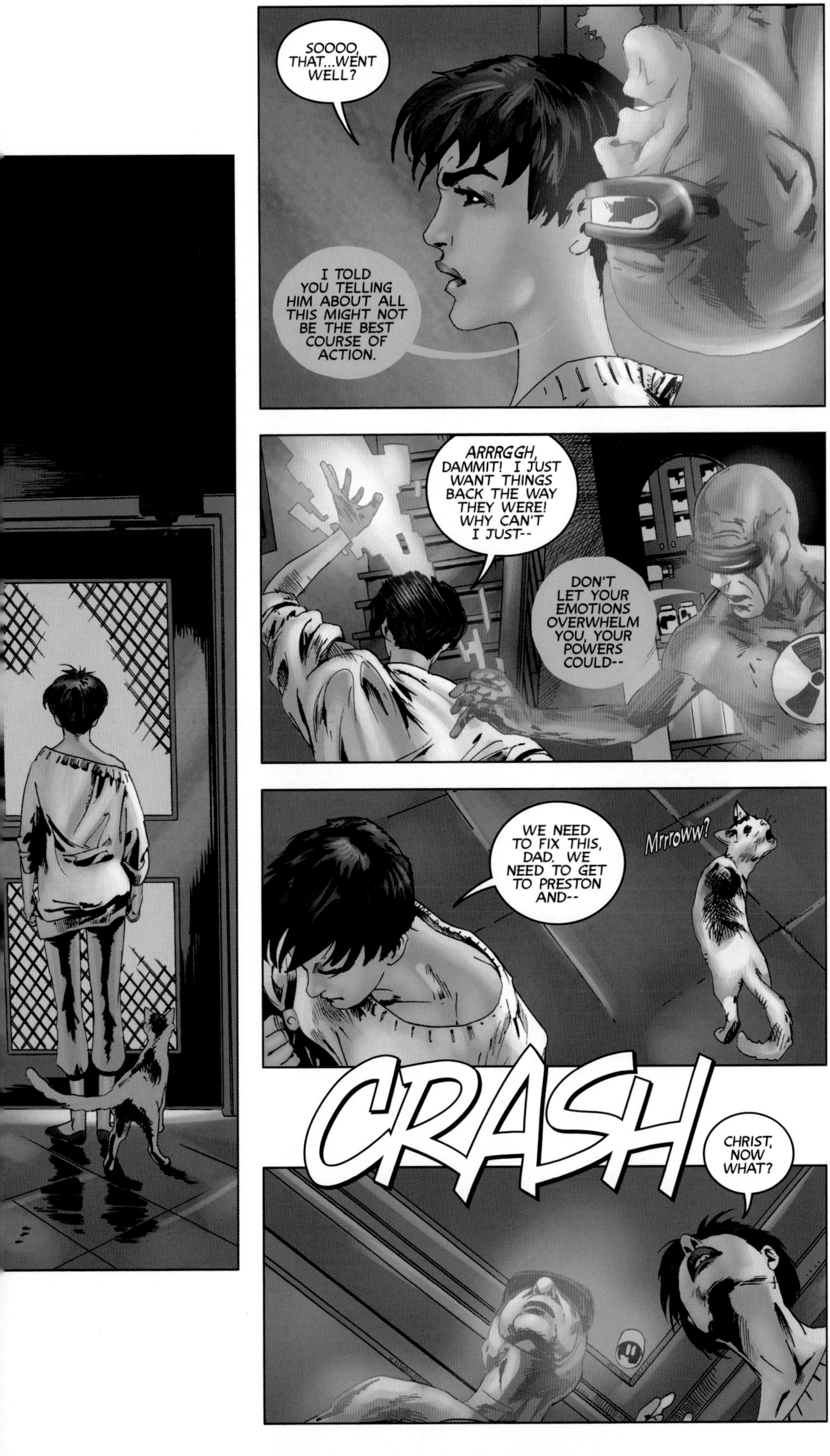
SOOOO, THAT...WENT WELL?
I TOLD YOU TELLING HIM ABOUT ALL THIS MIGHT NOT BE THE BEST COURSE OF ACTION.
ARRRGGH, DAMMIT! I JUST WANT THINGS BACK THE WAY THEY WERE! WHY CAN'T I JUST--
DON'T LET YOUR EMOTIONS OVERWHELM YOU, YOUR POWERS COULD--
WE NEED TO FIX THIS, DAD. WE NEED TO GET TO PRESTON AND--
Mrrroww?
CRASH
CHRIST, NOW WHAT?

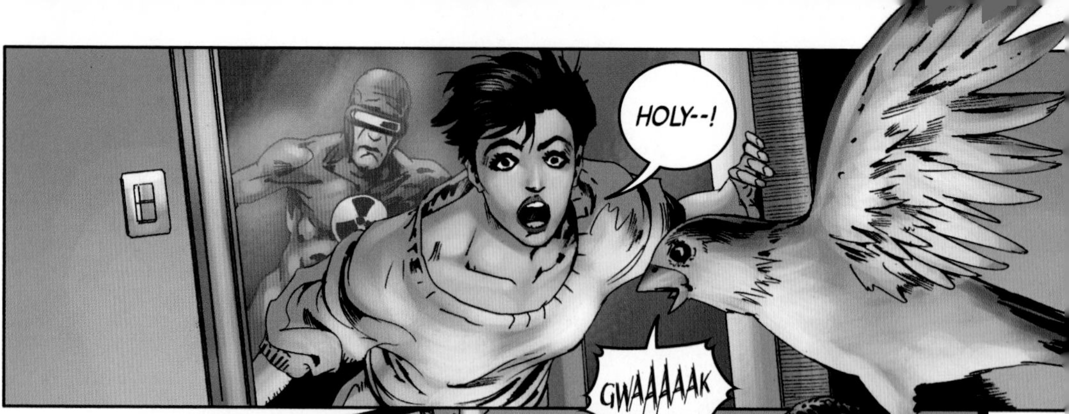
HOLY--!
GWAAAAAK

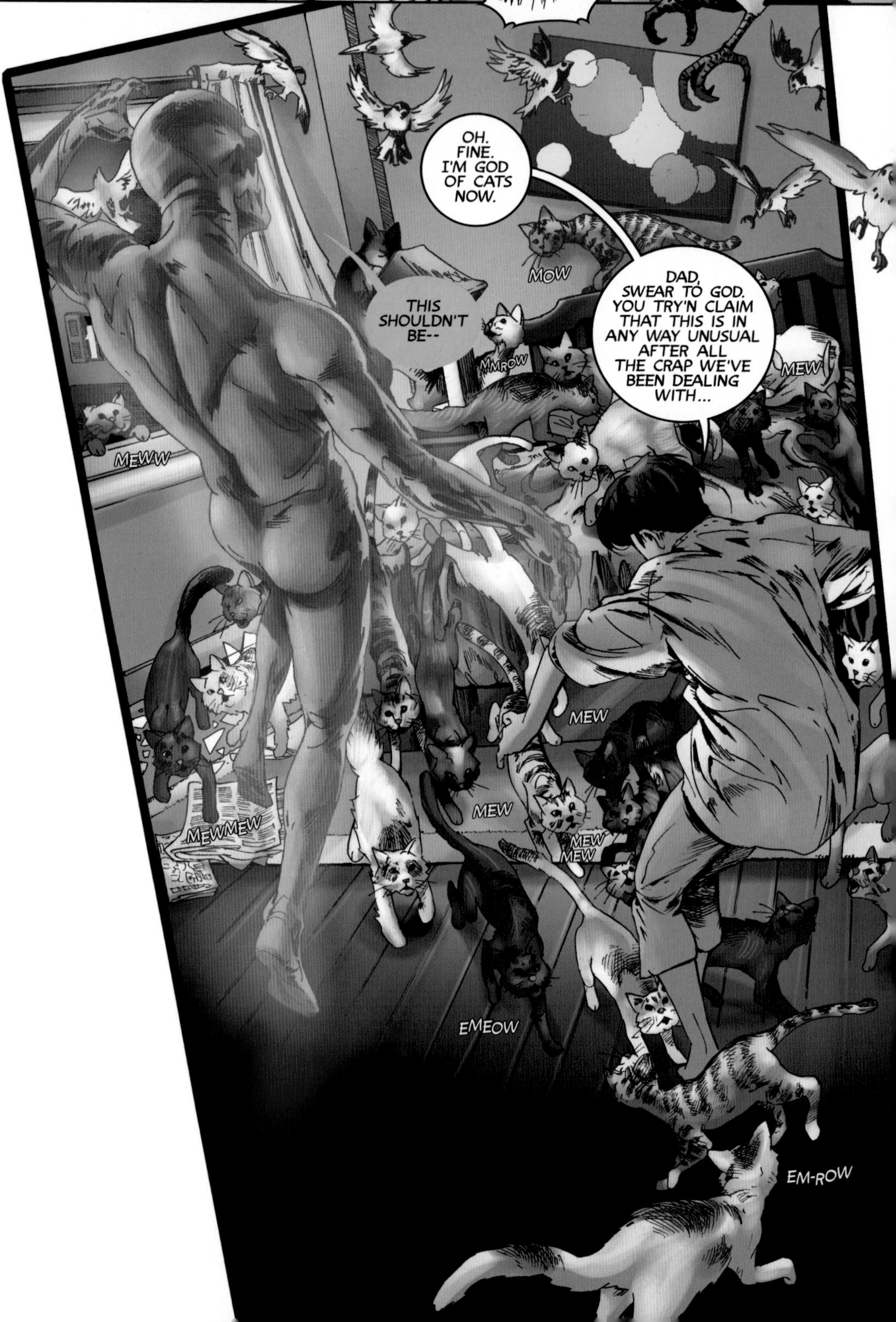
OH. FINE. I'M GOD OF CATS NOW.
DAD, SWEAR TO GOD. YOU TRY'N CLAIM THAT THIS IS IN ANY WAY UNUSUAL AFTER ALL THE CRAP WE'VE BEEN DEALING WITH...
THIS SHOULDN'T BE--
MOW
MMROW
MEW
MEWW
MEW
MEW
MEWMEW
MEW MEW
EMEOW
EM-ROW

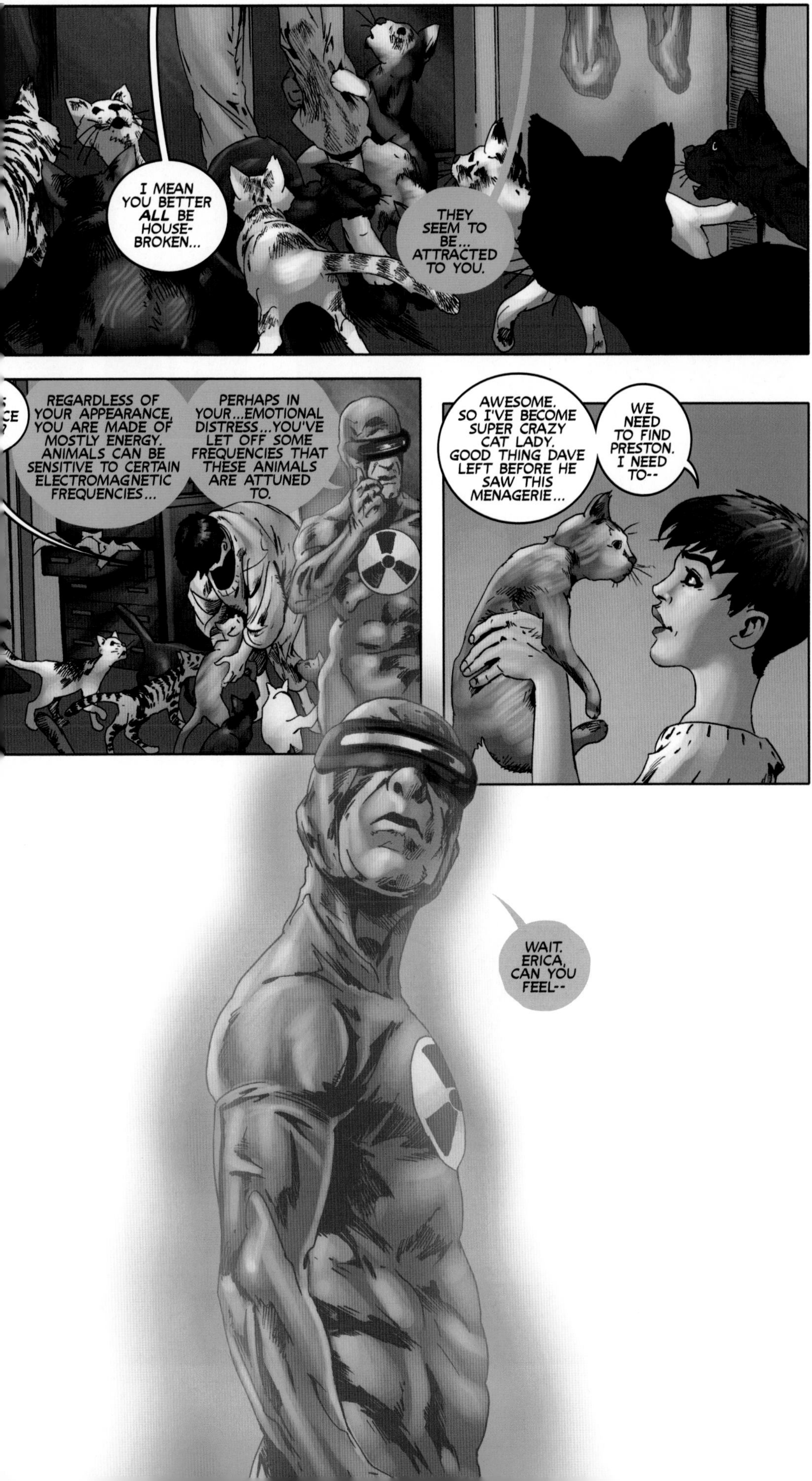
I MEAN YOU BETTER ***ALL*** BE HOUSE-BROKEN...
THEY SEEM TO BE... ATTRACTED TO YOU.
REGARDLESS OF YOUR APPEARANCE, YOU ARE MADE OF MOSTLY ENERGY. ANIMALS CAN BE SENSITIVE TO CERTAIN ELECTROMAGNETIC FREQUENCIES...
PERHAPS IN YOUR...EMOTIONAL DISTRESS...YOU'VE LET OFF SOME FREQUENCIES THAT THESE ANIMALS ARE ATTUNED TO.
AWESOME. SO I'VE BECOME SUPER CRAZY CAT LADY. GOOD THING DAVE LEFT BEFORE HE SAW THIS MENAGERIE...
WE NEED TO FIND PRESTON. I NEED TO--
WAIT. ERICA, CAN YOU FEEL--

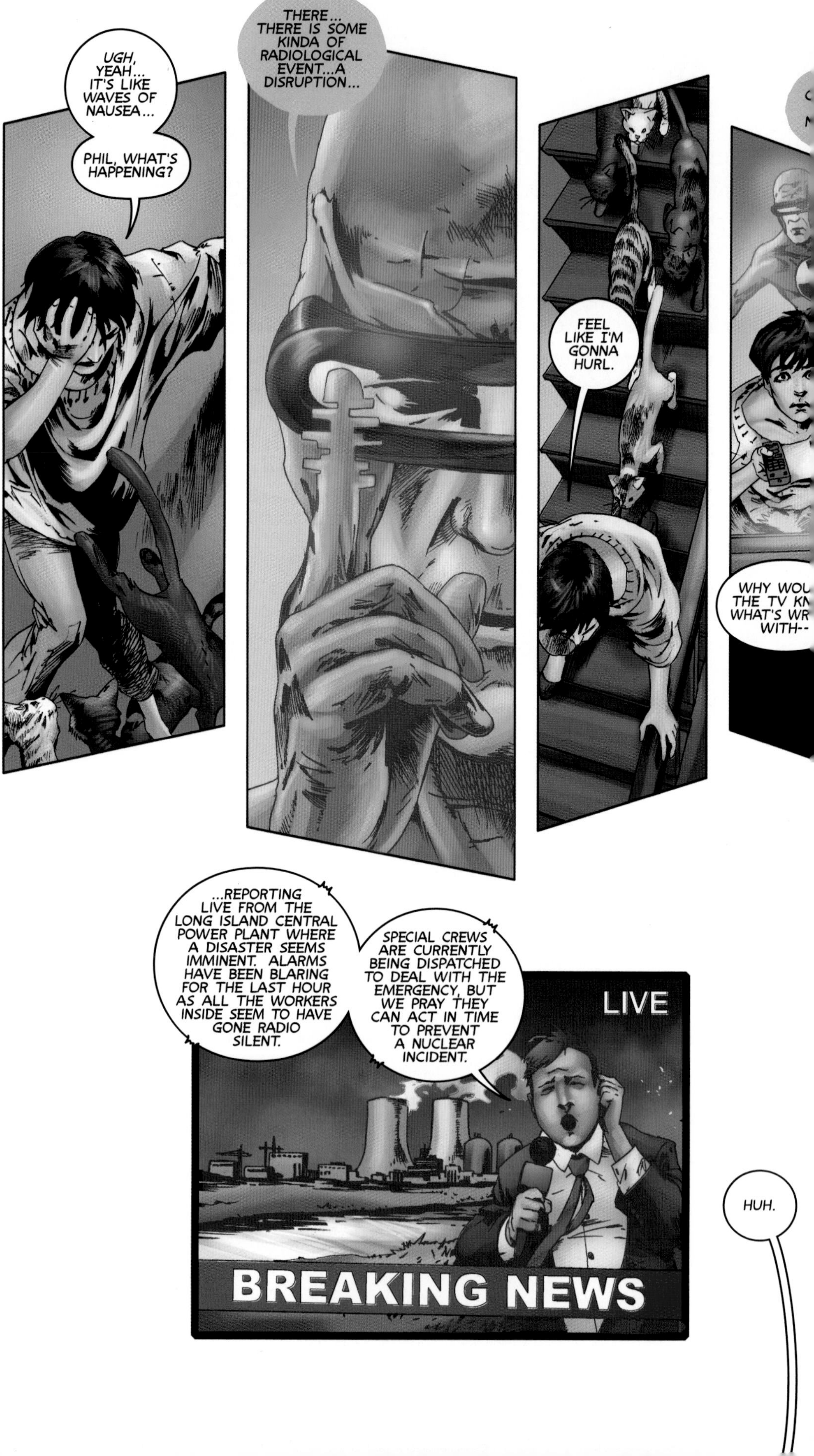
UGH, YEAH... IT'S LIKE WAVES OF NAUSEA...
PHIL, WHAT'S HAPPENING?
THERE... THERE IS SOME KINDA OF RADIOLOGICAL EVENT...A DISRUPTION...
FEEL LIKE I'M GONNA HURL.
WHY WOU THE TV KN WHAT'S WR WITH--
...REPORTING LIVE FROM THE LONG ISLAND CENTRAL POWER PLANT WHERE A DISASTER SEEMS IMMINENT. ALARMS HAVE BEEN BLARING FOR THE LAST HOUR AS ALL THE WORKERS INSIDE SEEM TO HAVE GONE RADIO SILENT.
SPECIAL CREWS ARE CURRENTLY BEING DISPATCHED TO DEAL WITH THE EMERGENCY, BUT WE PRAY THEY CAN ACT IN TIME TO PREVENT A NUCLEAR INCIDENT.
LIVE
BREAKING NEWS
HUH.

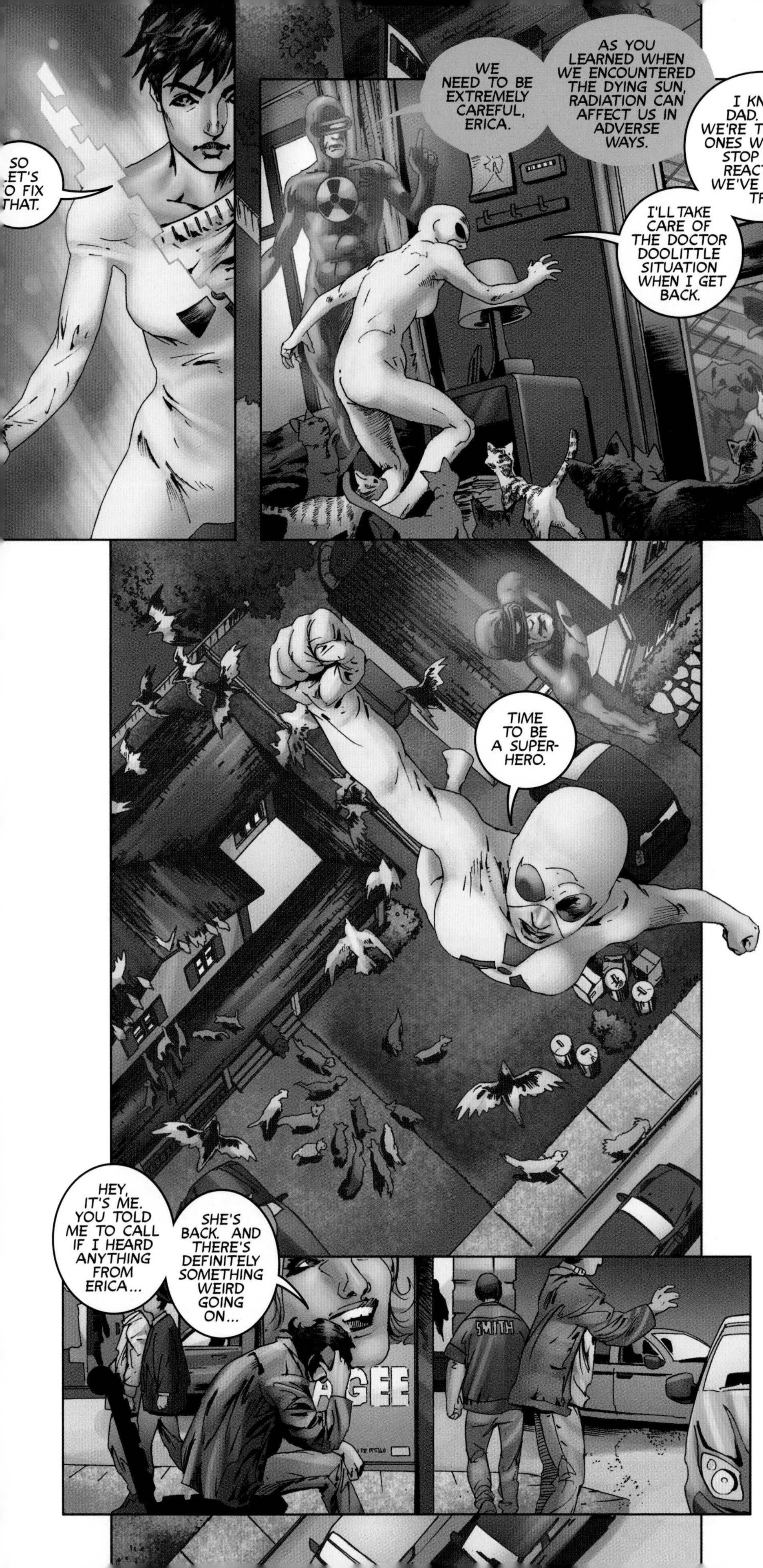
SO LET'S GO FIX THAT.
WE NEED TO BE EXTREMELY CAREFUL, ERICA.
AS YOU LEARNED WHEN WE ENCOUNTERED THE DYING SUN, RADIATION CAN AFFECT US IN ADVERSE WAYS.
I KNOW, DAD. BUT WE'RE THE ONLY ONES WHO CAN STOP THAT REACTOR... WE'VE GOTTA TRY.
I'LL TAKE CARE OF THE DOCTOR DOOLITTLE SITUATION WHEN I GET BACK.
TIME TO BE A SUPER-HERO.
HEY, IT'S ME. YOU TOLD ME TO CALL IF I HEARD ANYTHING FROM ERICA...
SHE'S BACK. AND THERE'S DEFINITELY SOMETHING WEIRD GOING ON...
SMITH
GEE

Y'KNOW, I COULD GET USED TO THIS...

KEEP FOCUSED. WE DON'T KNOW WHAT'S HAPPENING IN HERE.

YEAH, YEAH... SAME OL' BUZZKILL PHIL AS USUAL.

...AND HERE WE ARE. PRESTO.

DON'T GET COCKY. YOU'VE DEFINITELY GOTTEN BETTER WITH YOUR POWERS, BUT THIS RADIATION...

GOD, LET ME JUST ENJOY IT FOR A MINUTE, DAD.

WARNING: CORE MELTDOWN IMMINENT

PERFECTEST OF TIMING...

WE HAVE T[O] GET TO T[HE] REACTO[R] CORE--

HOLD UP. THERE ARE PEOPLE IN HERE!

HEY, BUDDY! YOU'VE GOTTA GET--

YEAAAAGHHH!

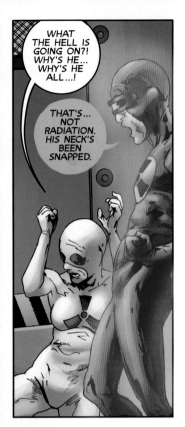

WHAT THE HELL IS GOING ON?! WHY'S HE... WHY'S HE ALL...!

THAT'S... NOT RADIATION. HIS NECK'S BEEN SNAPPED.

I'VE JUST...I'VE NEVER SEEN A DEAD BODY... THIS...

YOU HAVE TO FOCUS--

THERE.

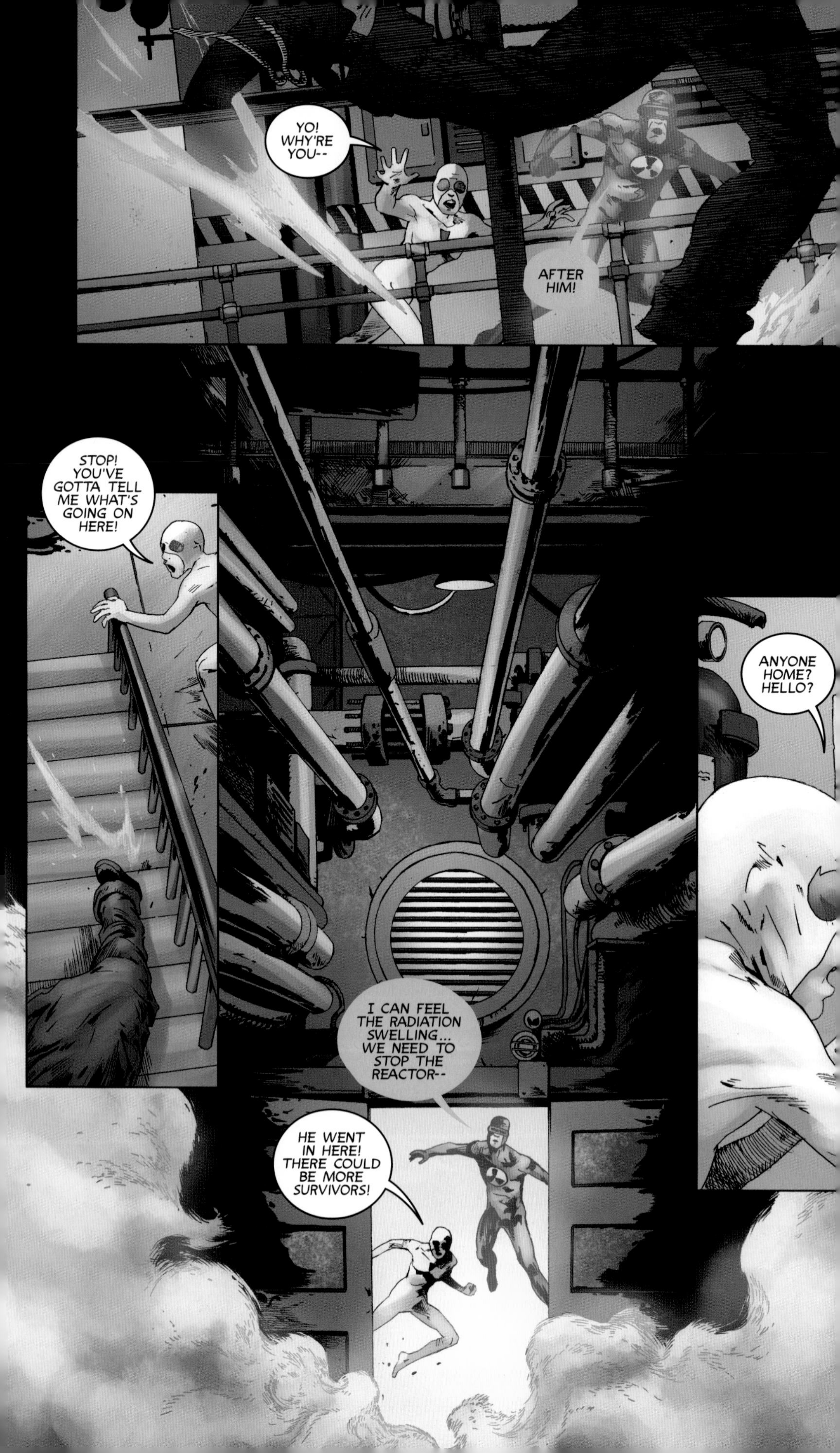
YO! WHY'RE YOU--
AFTER HIM!
STOP! YOU'VE GOTTA TELL ME WHAT'S GOING ON HERE!
ANYONE HOME? HELLO?
I CAN FEEL THE RADIATION SWELLING... WE NEED TO STOP THE REACTOR--
HE WENT IN HERE! THERE COULD BE MORE SURVIVORS!

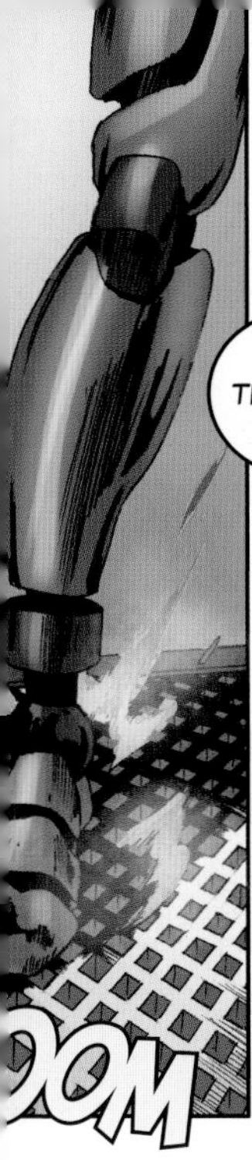
DOOM

WHAT THE HELL WAS--

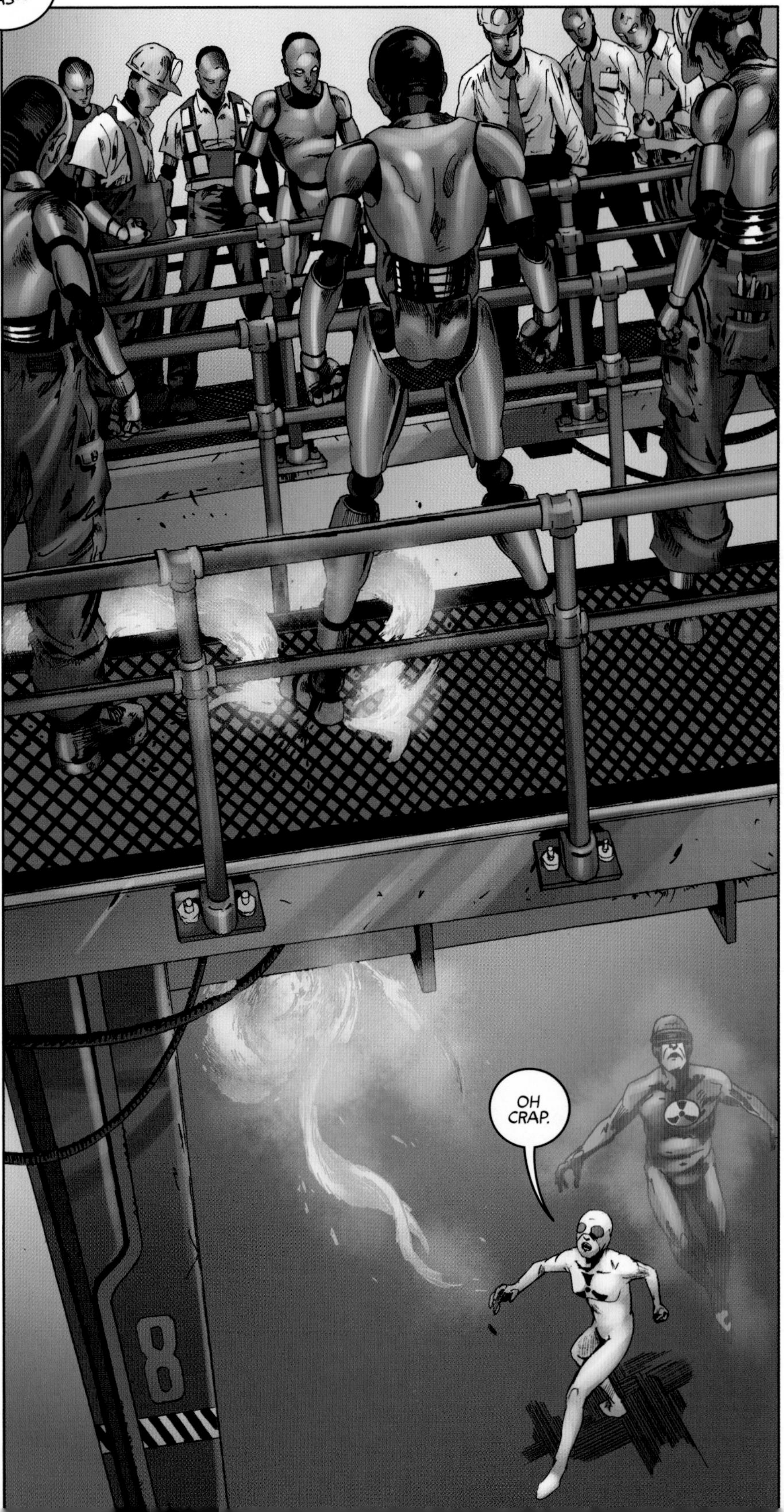
OH CRAP.

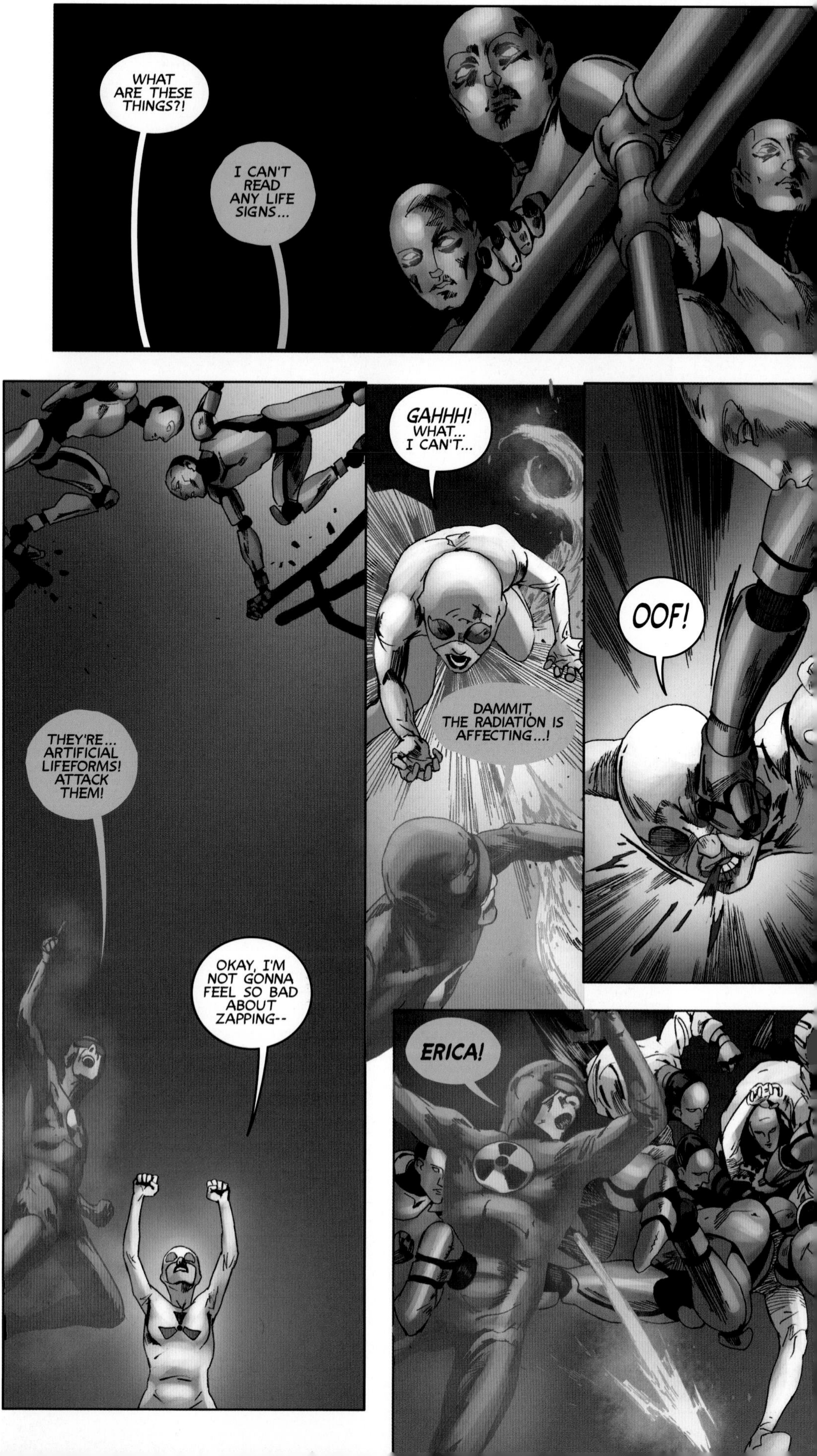

WHAT ARE THESE THINGS?!
I CAN'T READ ANY LIFE SIGNS...
THEY'RE... ARTIFICIAL LIFEFORMS! ATTACK THEM!
OKAY, I'M NOT GONNA FEEL SO BAD ABOUT ZAPPING--
GAHHH! WHAT... I CAN'T...
DAMMIT, THE RADIATION IS AFFECTING...!
OOF!
ERICA!

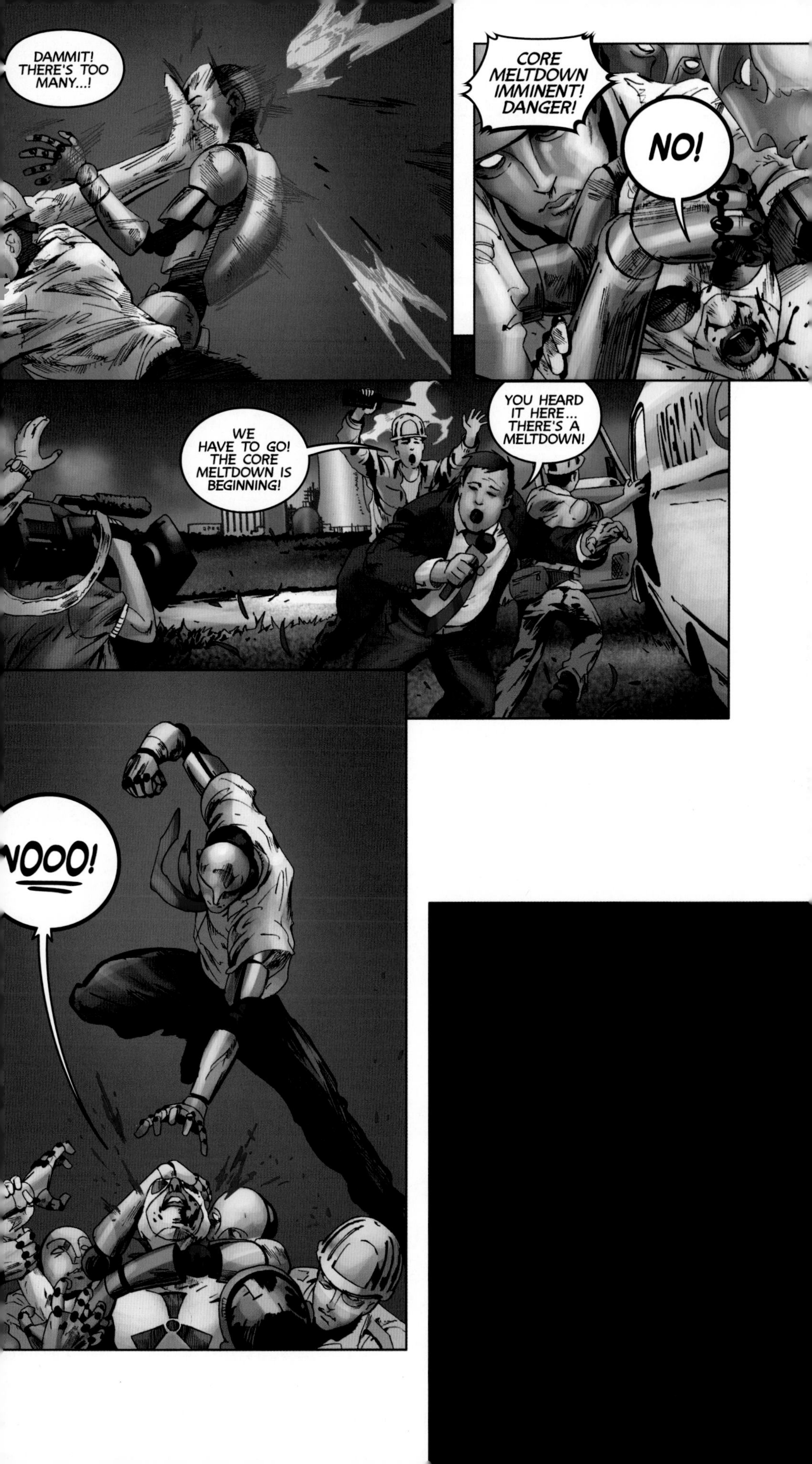
DAMMIT! THERE'S TOO MANY...!
CORE MELTDOWN IMMINENT! DANGER!
NO!
WE HAVE TO GO! THE CORE MELTDOWN IS BEGINNING!
YOU HEARD IT HERE... THERE'S A MELTDOWN!
NOOO!

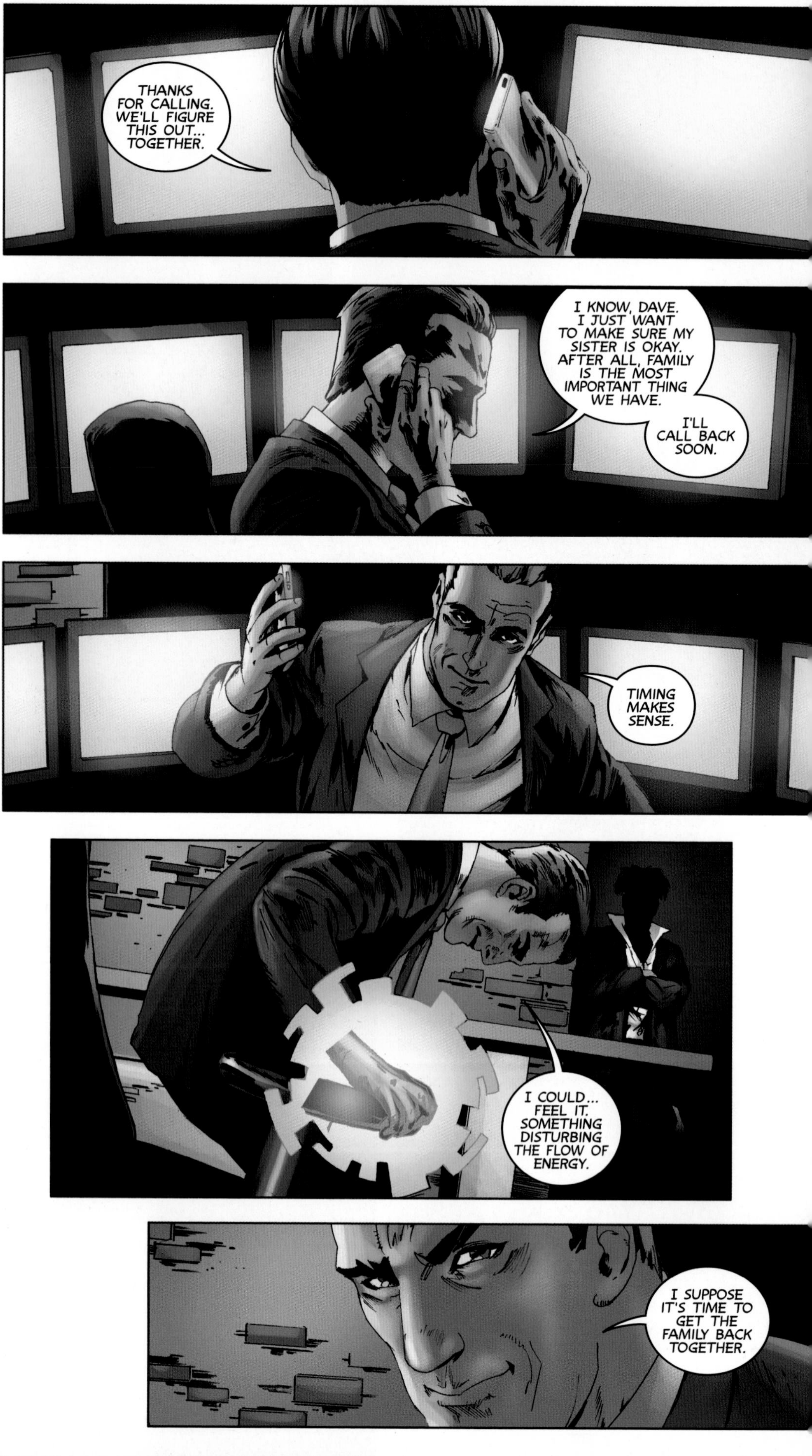
THANKS FOR CALLING. WE'LL FIGURE THIS OUT... TOGETHER.
I KNOW, DAVE. I JUST WANT TO MAKE SURE MY SISTER IS OKAY. AFTER ALL, FAMILY IS THE MOST IMPORTANT THING WE HAVE.
I'LL CALL BACK SOON.
TIMING MAKES SENSE.
I COULD... FEEL IT. SOMETHING DISTURBING THE FLOW OF ENERGY.
I SUPPOSE IT'S TIME TO GET THE FAMILY BACK TOGETHER.

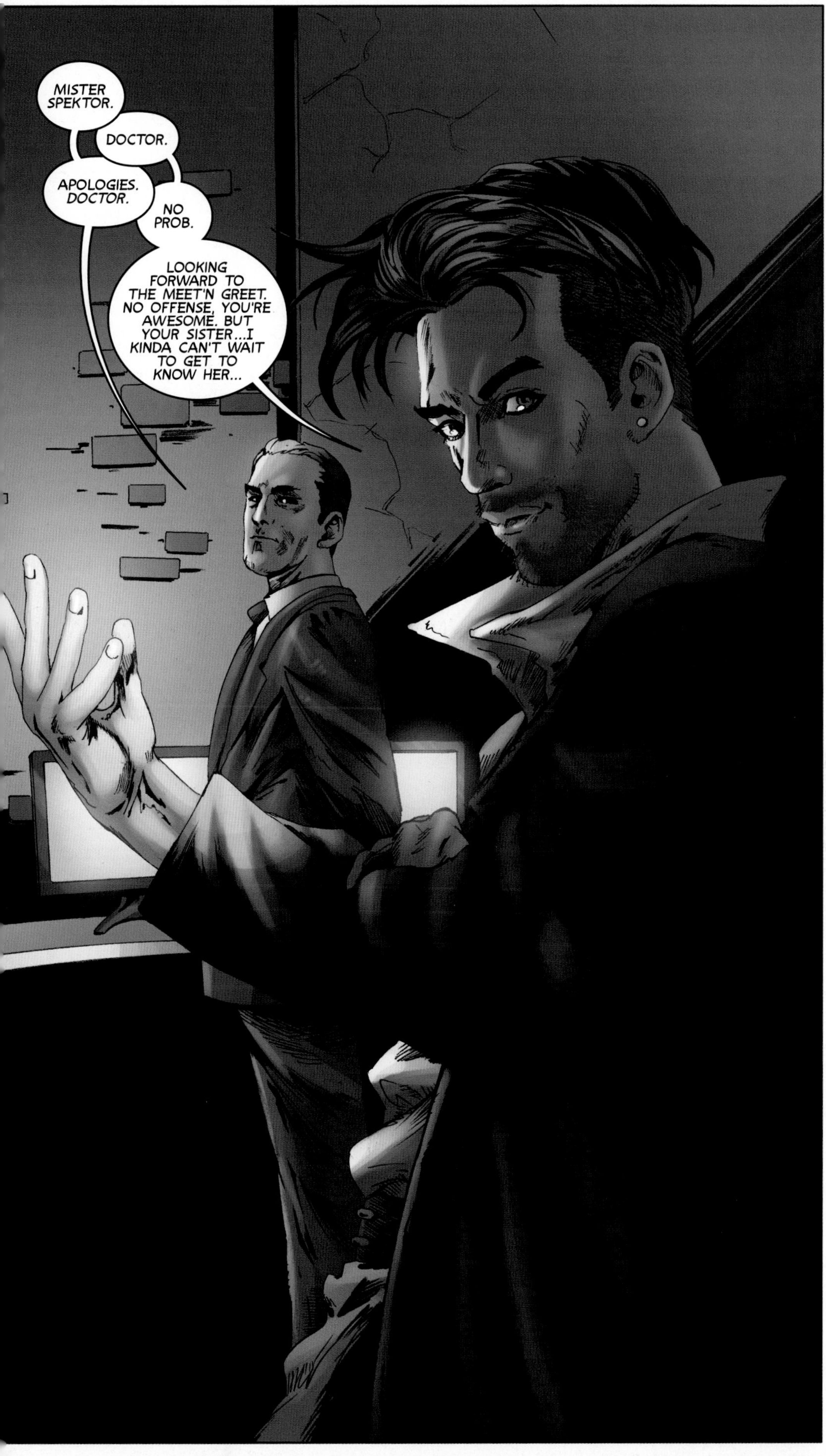
MISTER SPEKTOR.
DOCTOR.
APOLOGIES. DOCTOR.
NO PROB.
LOOKING FORWARD TO THE MEET'N GREET. NO OFFENSE, YOU'RE AWESOME. BUT YOUR SISTER...I KINDA CAN'T WAIT TO GET TO KNOW HER...

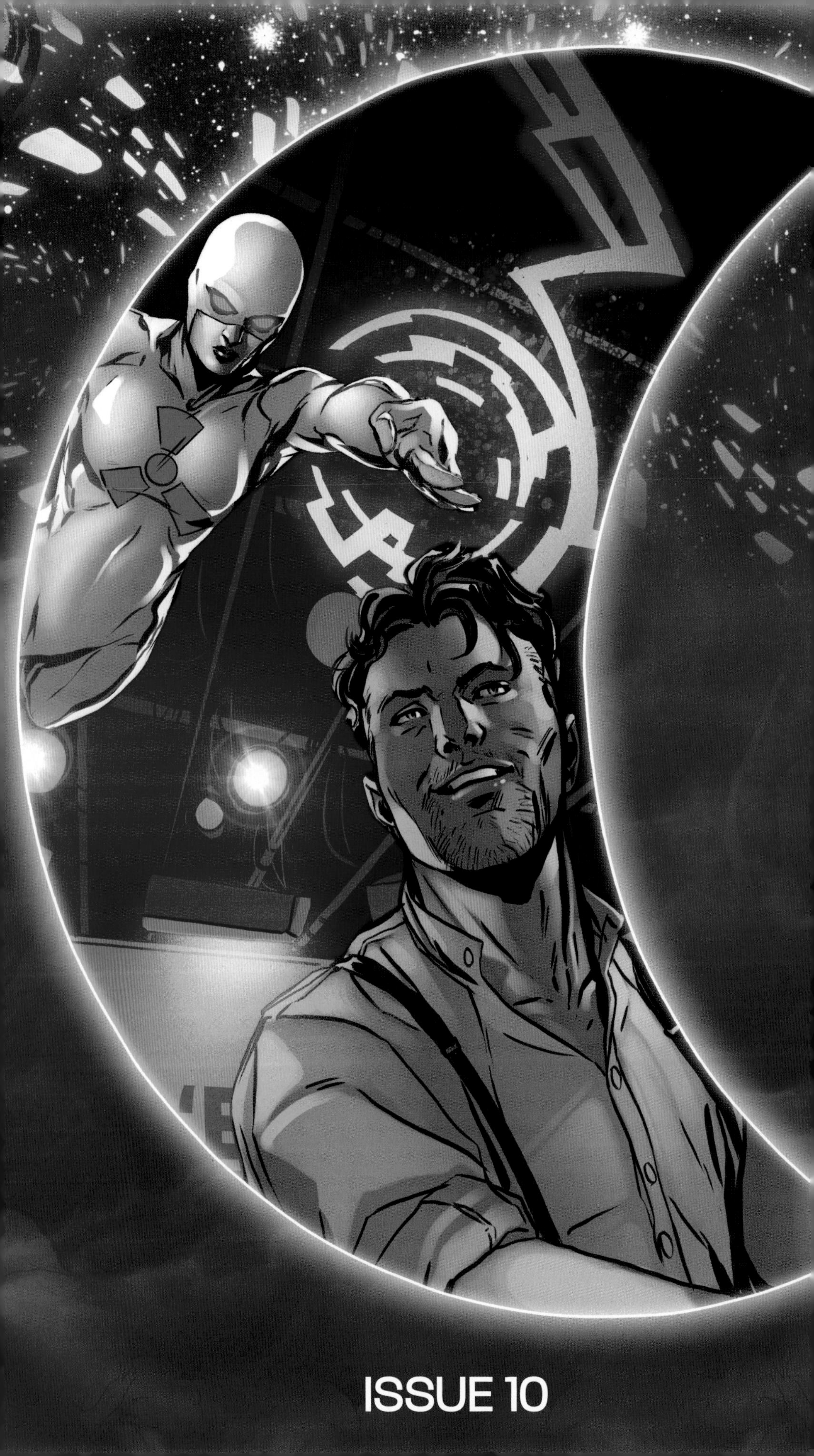
ISSUE 10

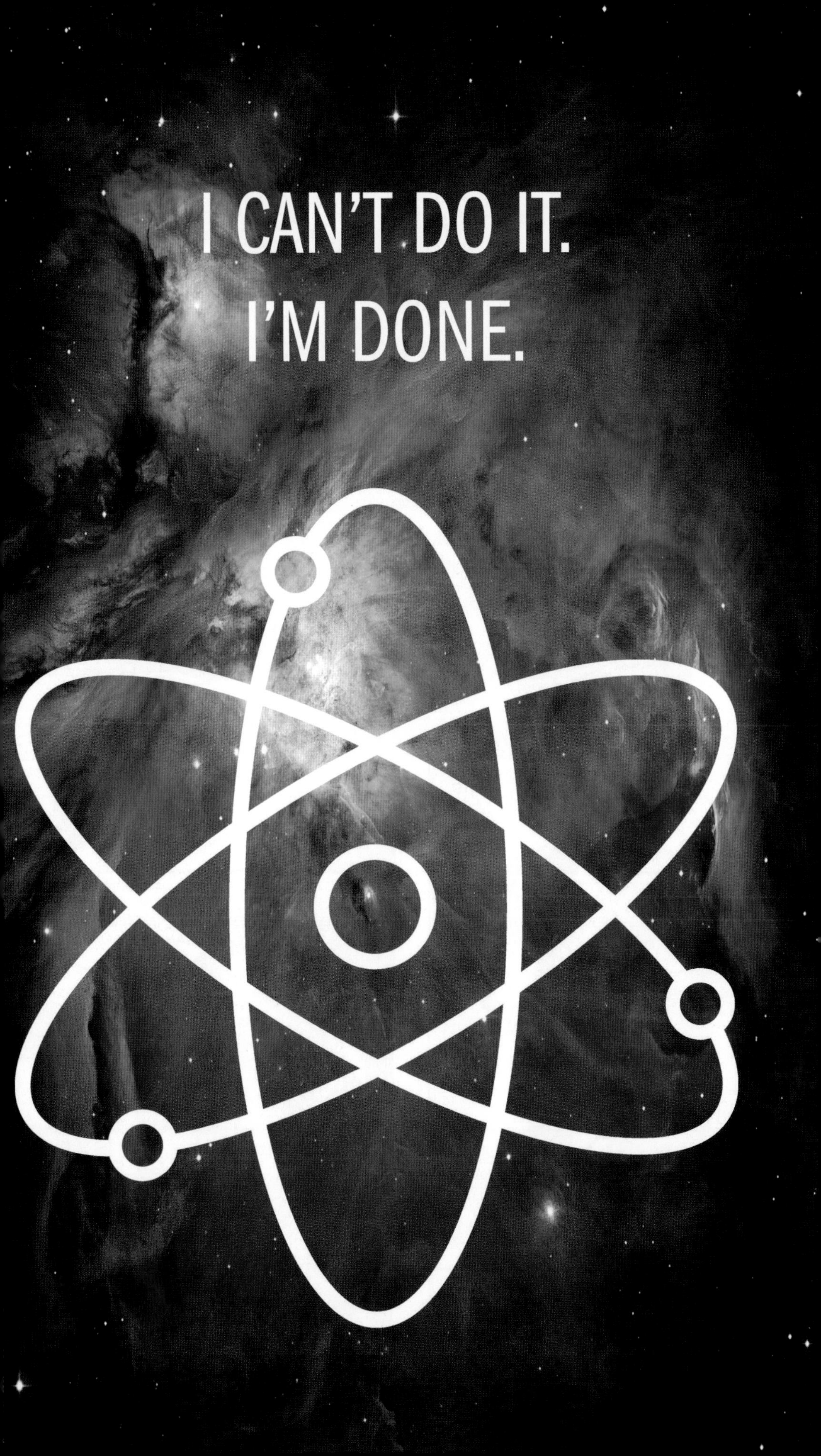
I CAN'T DO IT.
I'M DONE.

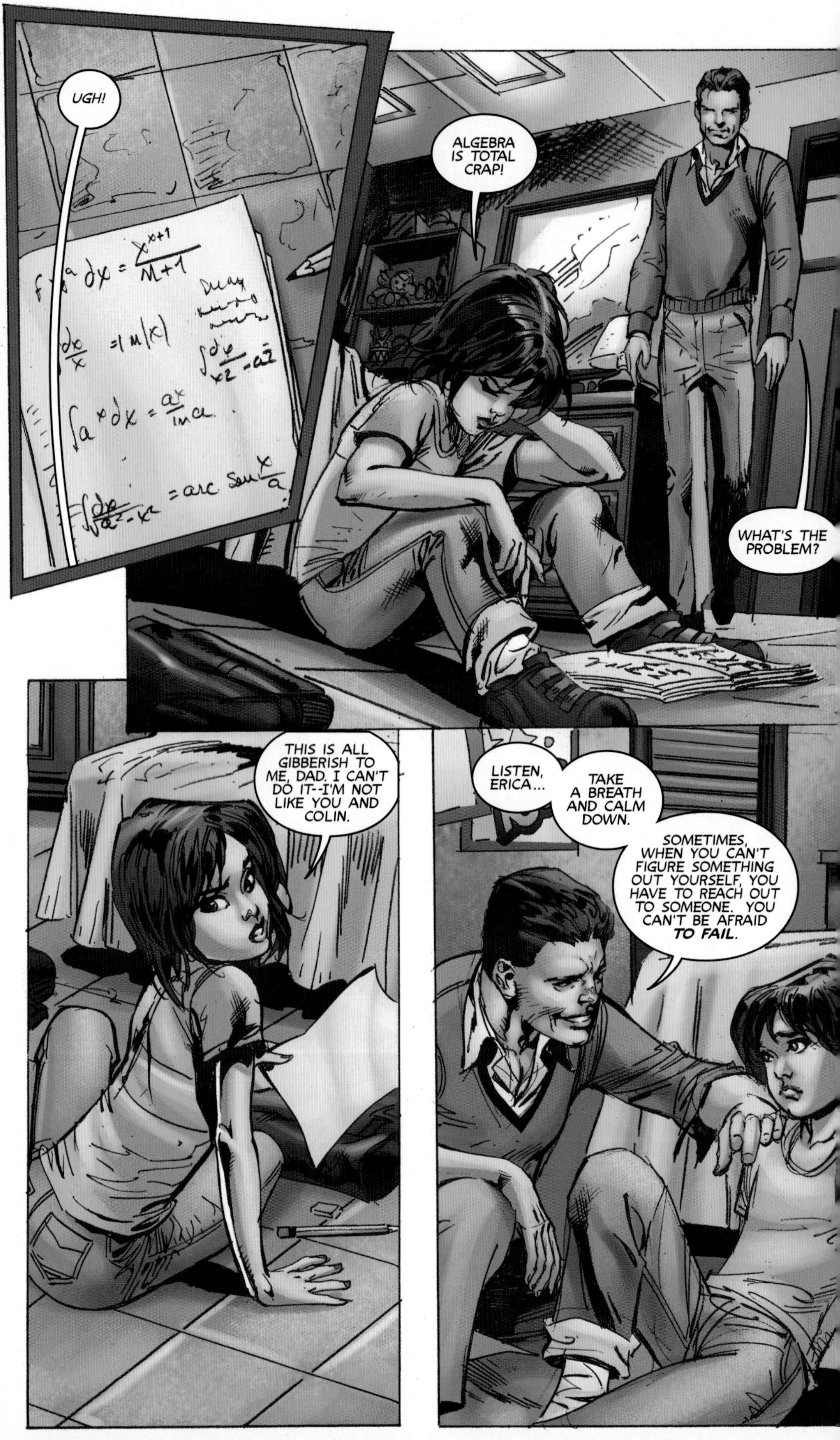
UGH!
ALGEBRA IS TOTAL CRAP!
WHAT'S THE PROBLEM?
THIS IS ALL GIBBERISH TO ME, DAD. I CAN'T DO IT--I'M NOT LIKE YOU AND COLIN.
LISTEN, ERICA...
TAKE A BREATH AND CALM DOWN.
SOMETIMES, WHEN YOU CAN'T FIGURE SOMETHING OUT YOURSELF, YOU HAVE TO REACH OUT TO SOMEONE. YOU CAN'T BE AFRAID TO FAIL.

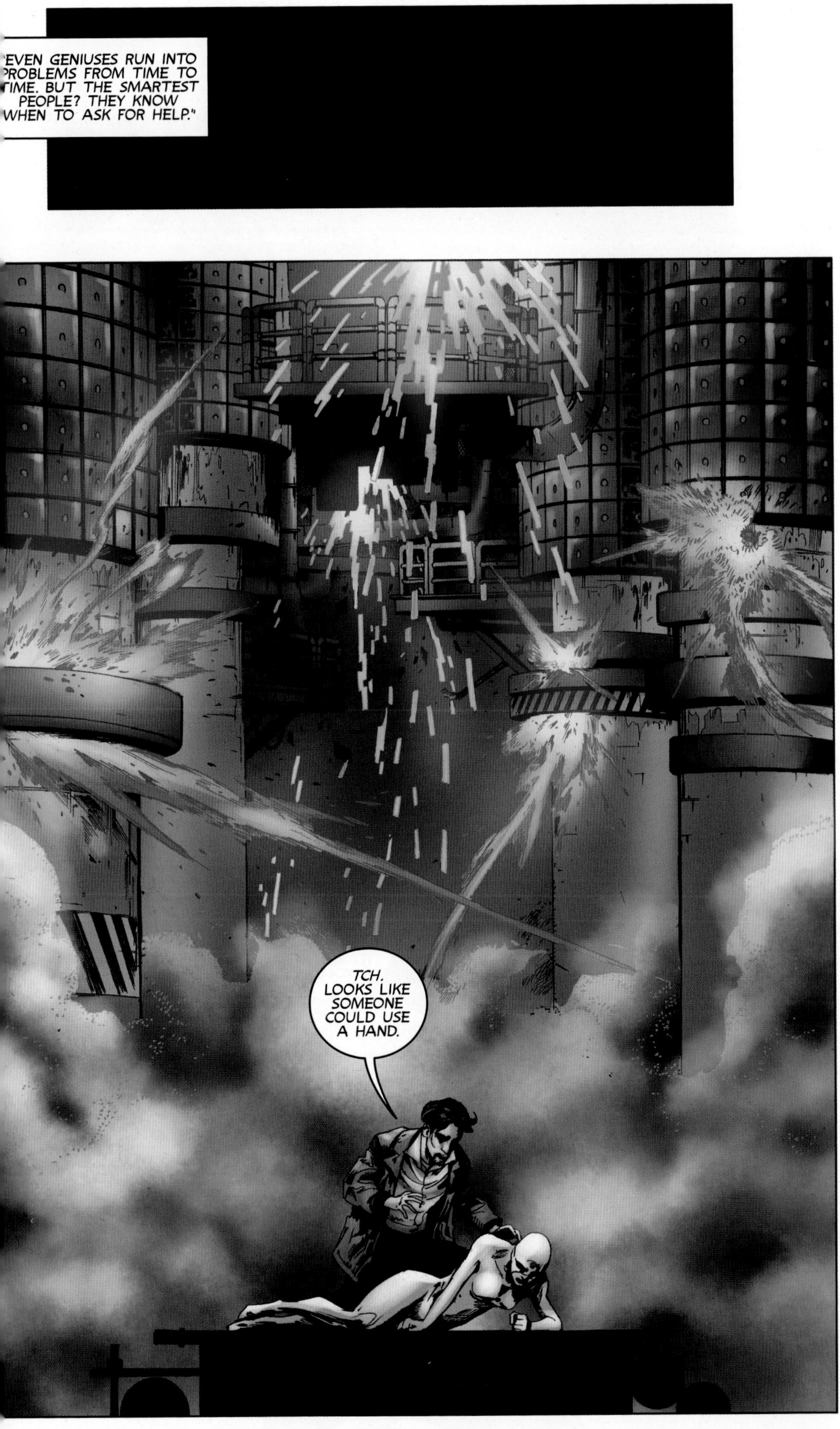
"EVEN GENIUSES RUN INTO PROBLEMS FROM TIME TO TIME. BUT THE SMARTEST PEOPLE? THEY KNOW WHEN TO ASK FOR HELP."
TCH. LOOKS LIKE SOMEONE COULD USE A HAND.

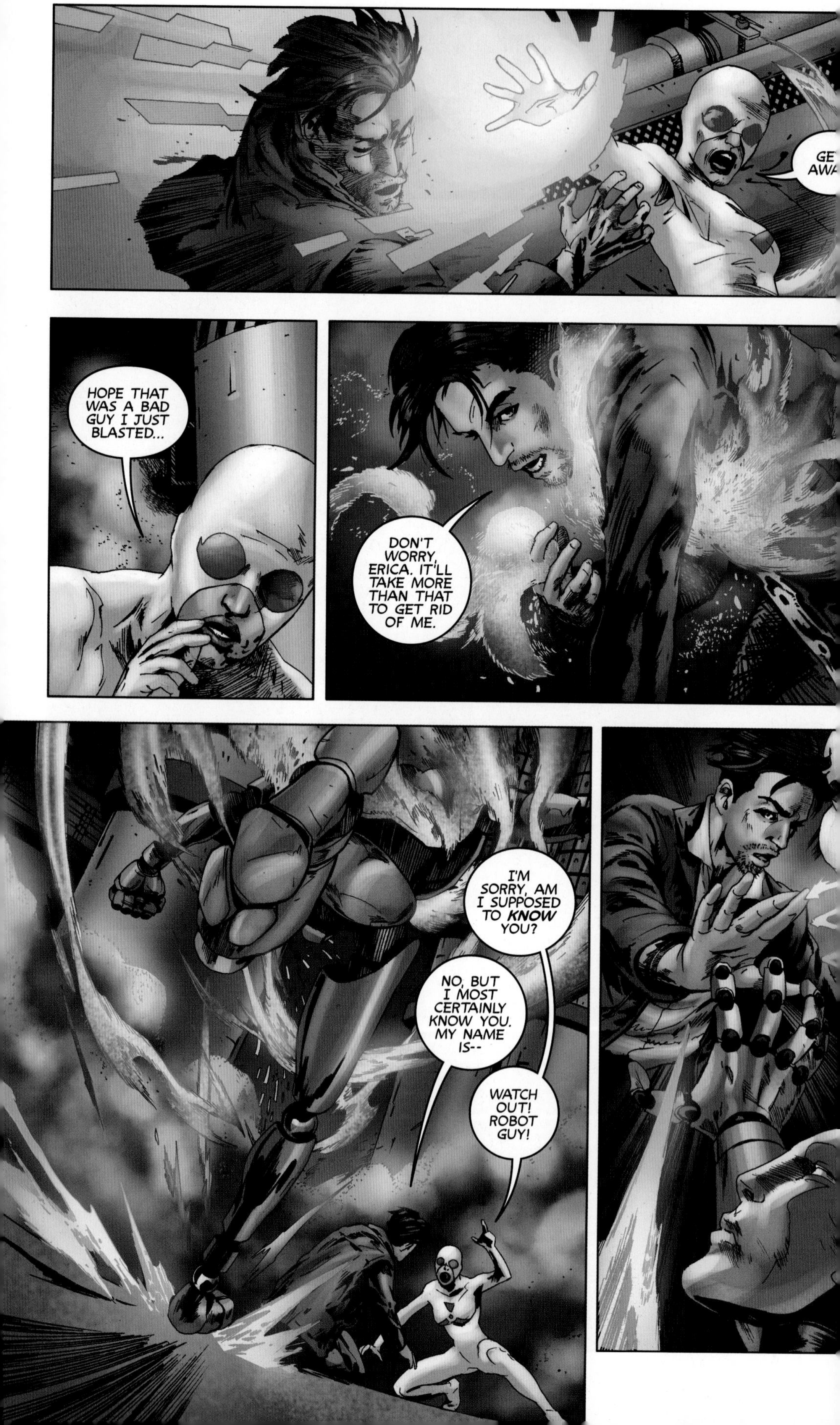
GE
AWA
HOPE THAT WAS A BAD GUY I JUST BLASTED...
DON'T WORRY, ERICA. IT'LL TAKE MORE THAN THAT TO GET RID OF ME.
I'M SORRY, AM I SUPPOSED TO *KNOW* YOU?
NO, BUT I MOST CERTAINLY KNOW YOU. MY NAME IS--
WATCH OUT! ROBOT GUY!

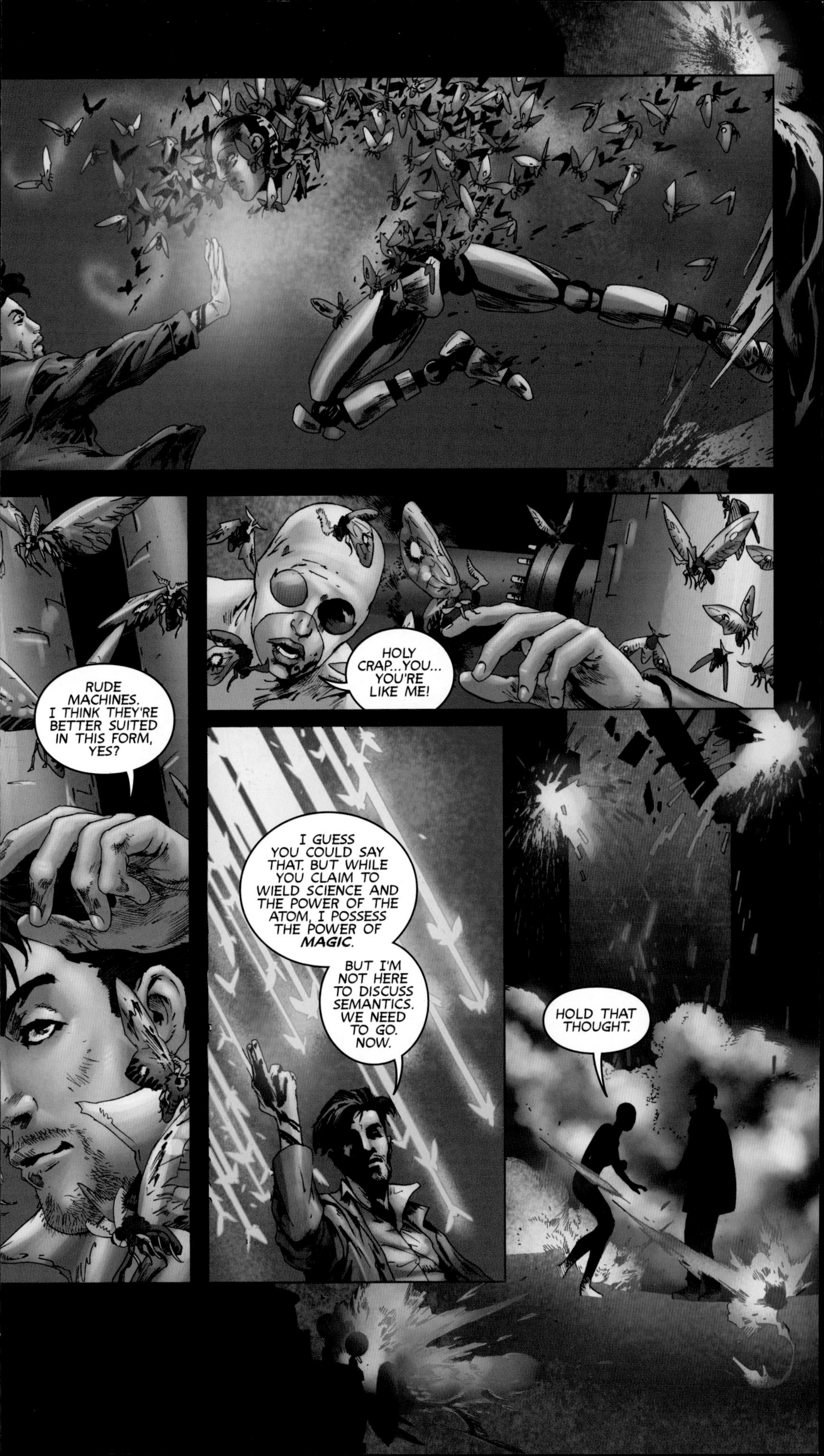
HOLY CRAP...YOU... YOU'RE LIKE ME!
RUDE MACHINES. I THINK THEY'RE BETTER SUITED IN THIS FORM, YES?
I GUESS YOU COULD SAY THAT. BUT WHILE YOU CLAIM TO WIELD SCIENCE AND THE POWER OF THE ATOM, I POSSESS THE POWER OF ***MAGIC***.
BUT I'M NOT HERE TO DISCUSS SEMANTICS. WE NEED TO GO. NOW.
HOLD THAT THOUGHT.

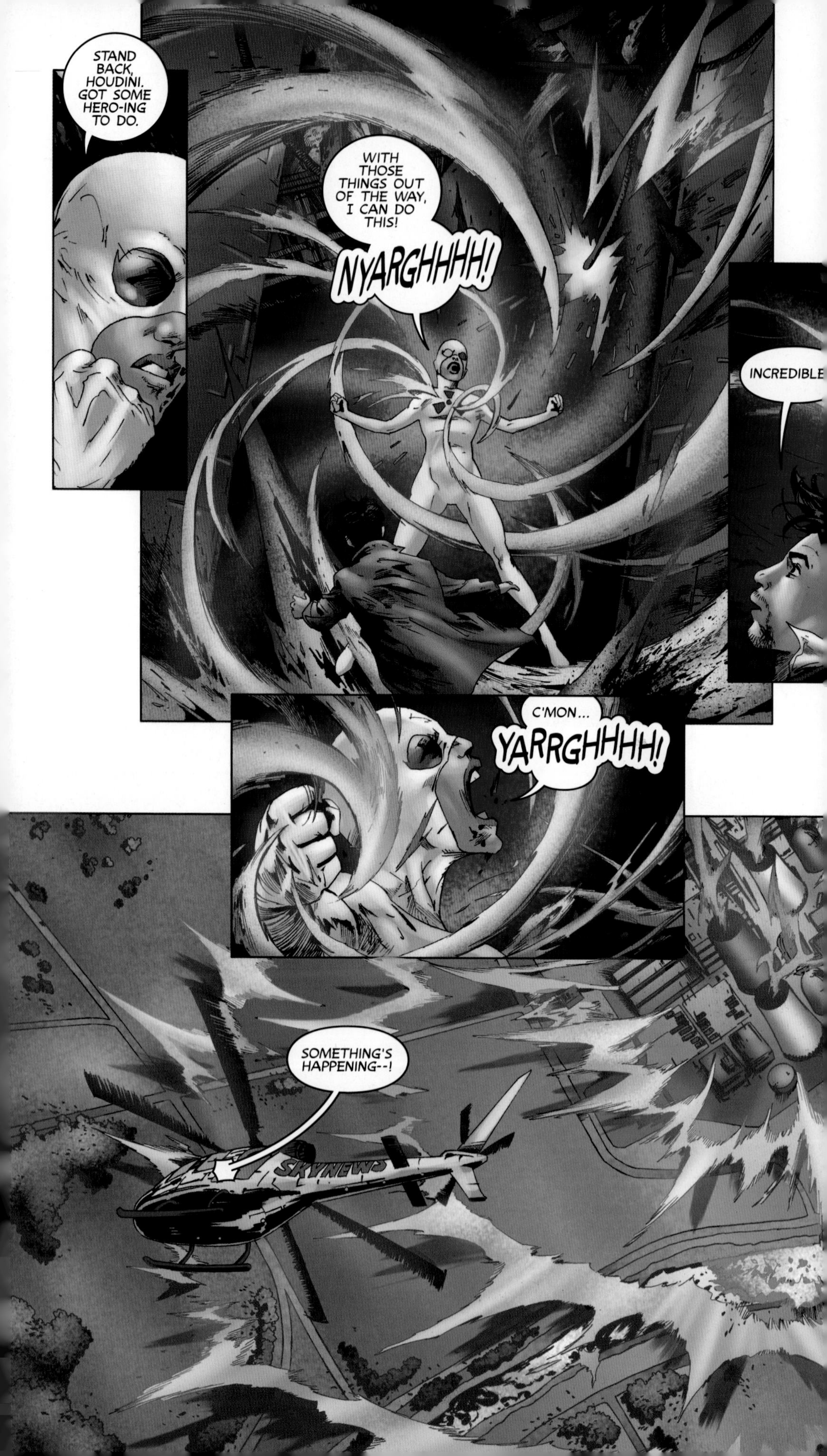
STAND BACK, HOUDINI. GOT SOME HERO-ING TO DO.
WITH THOSE THINGS OUT OF THE WAY, I CAN DO THIS!
NYARGHHHH!
INCREDIBLE
C'MON...
YARRGHHHH!
SOMETHING'S HAPPENING--!
SKYNEWS

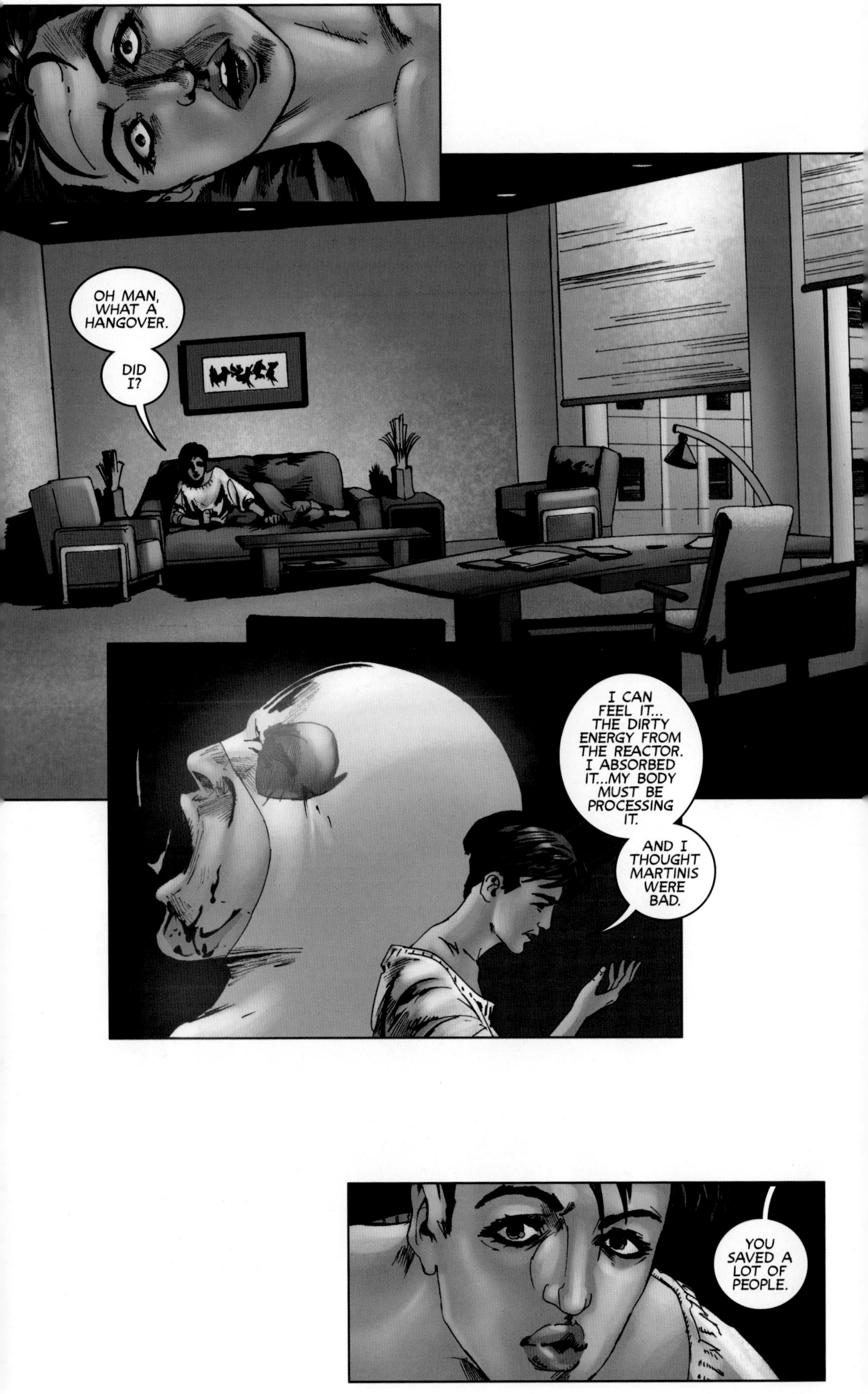
OH MAN, WHAT A HANGOVER.
DID I?
I CAN FEEL IT... THE DIRTY ENERGY FROM THE REACTOR. I ABSORBED IT...MY BODY MUST BE PROCESSING IT.
AND I THOUGHT MARTINIS WERE BAD.
YOU SAVED A LOT OF PEOPLE.

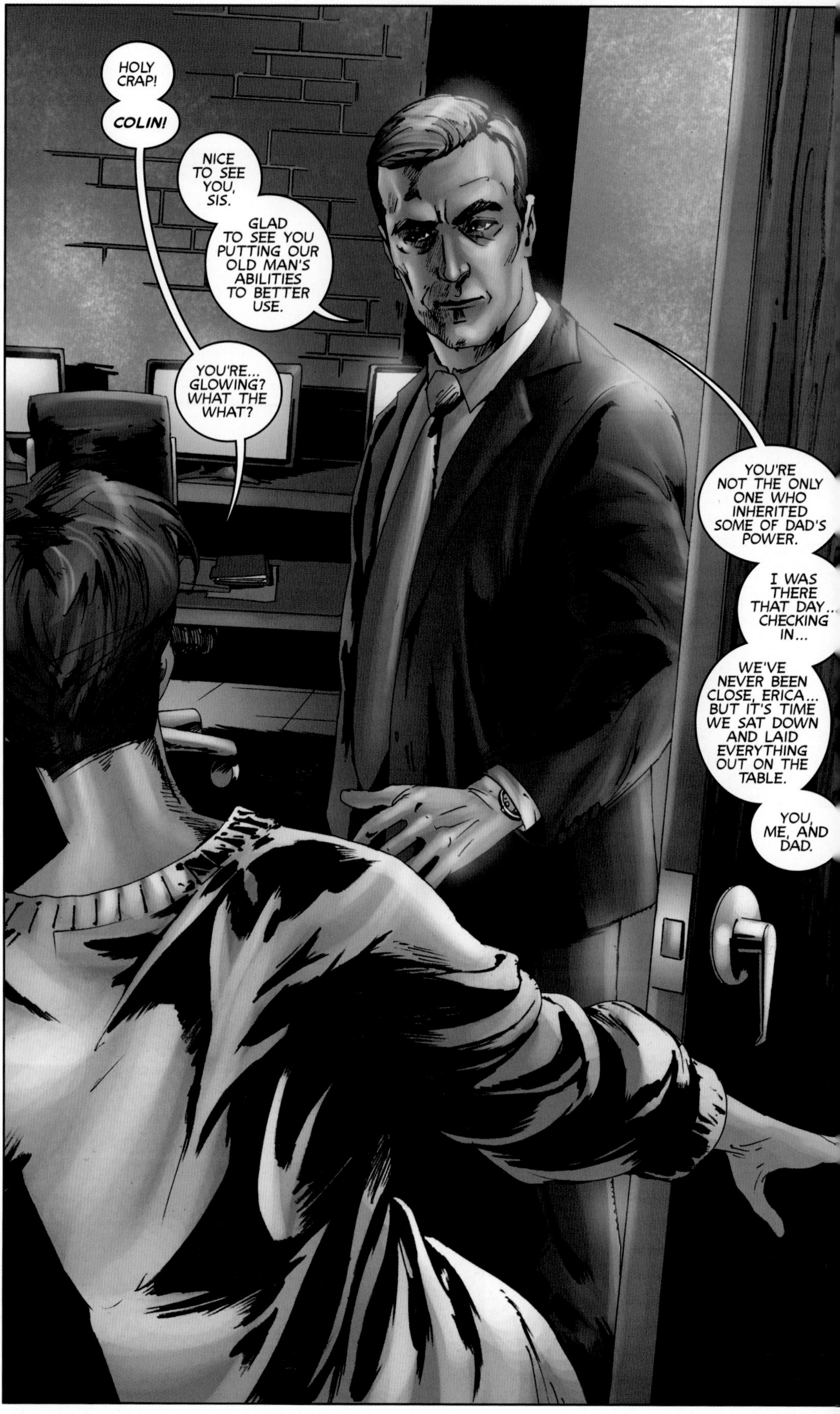
HOLY CRAP!
COLIN!
NICE TO SEE YOU, SIS.
GLAD TO SEE YOU PUTTING OUR OLD MAN'S ABILITIES TO BETTER USE.
YOU'RE... GLOWING? WHAT THE WHAT?
YOU'RE NOT THE ONLY ONE WHO INHERITED SOME OF DAD'S POWER.
I WAS THERE THAT DAY... CHECKING IN...
WE'VE NEVER BEEN CLOSE, ERICA... BUT IT'S TIME WE SAT DOWN AND LAID EVERYTHING OUT ON THE TABLE.
YOU, ME, AND DAD.

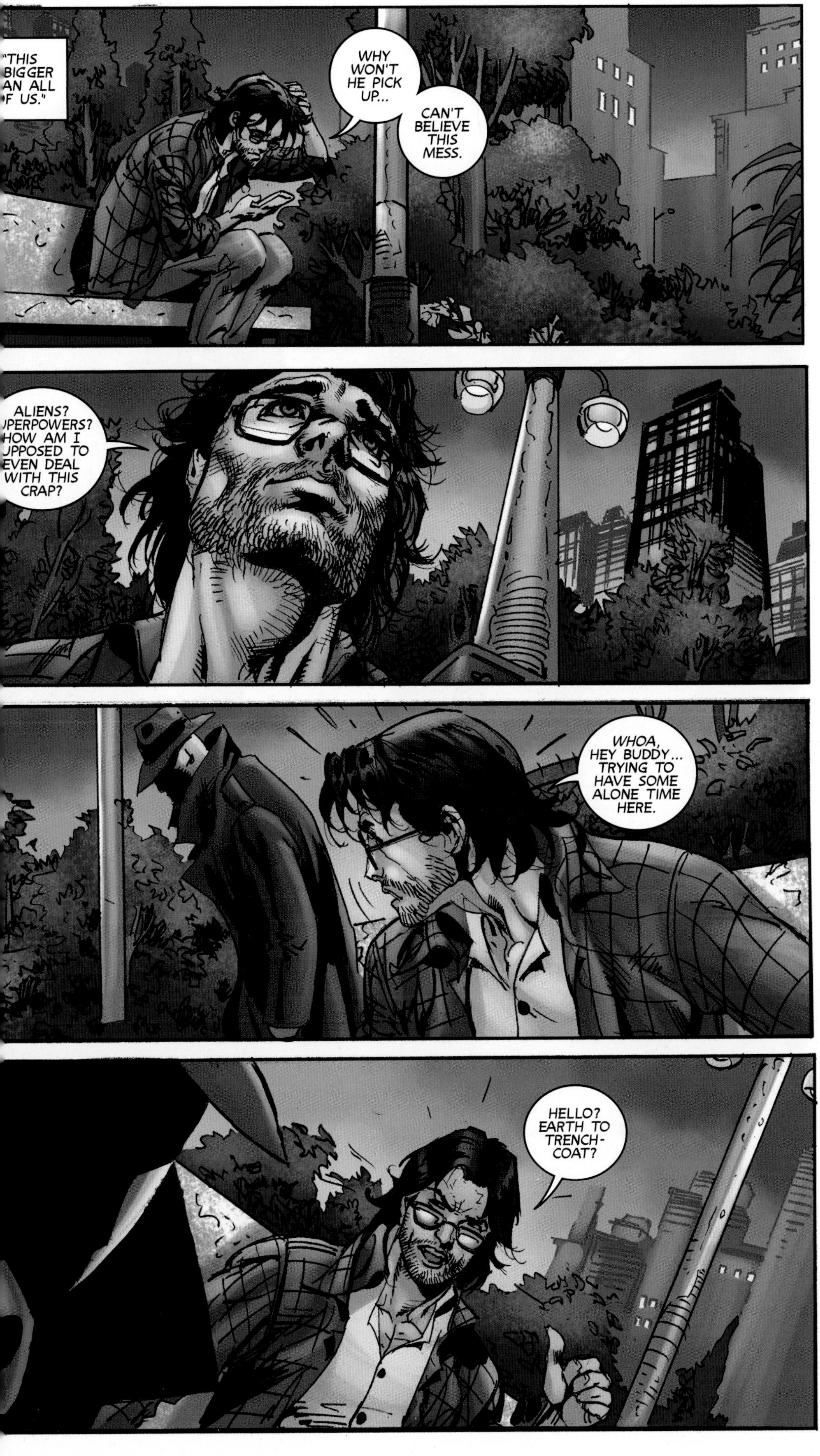
"THIS BIGGER AN ALL F US."
WHY WON'T HE PICK UP...
CAN'T BELIEVE THIS MESS.
ALIENS? UPERPOWERS? HOW AM I UPPOSED TO EVEN DEAL WITH THIS CRAP?
WHOA, HEY BUDDY... TRYING TO HAVE SOME ALONE TIME HERE.
HELLO? EARTH TO TRENCH-COAT?

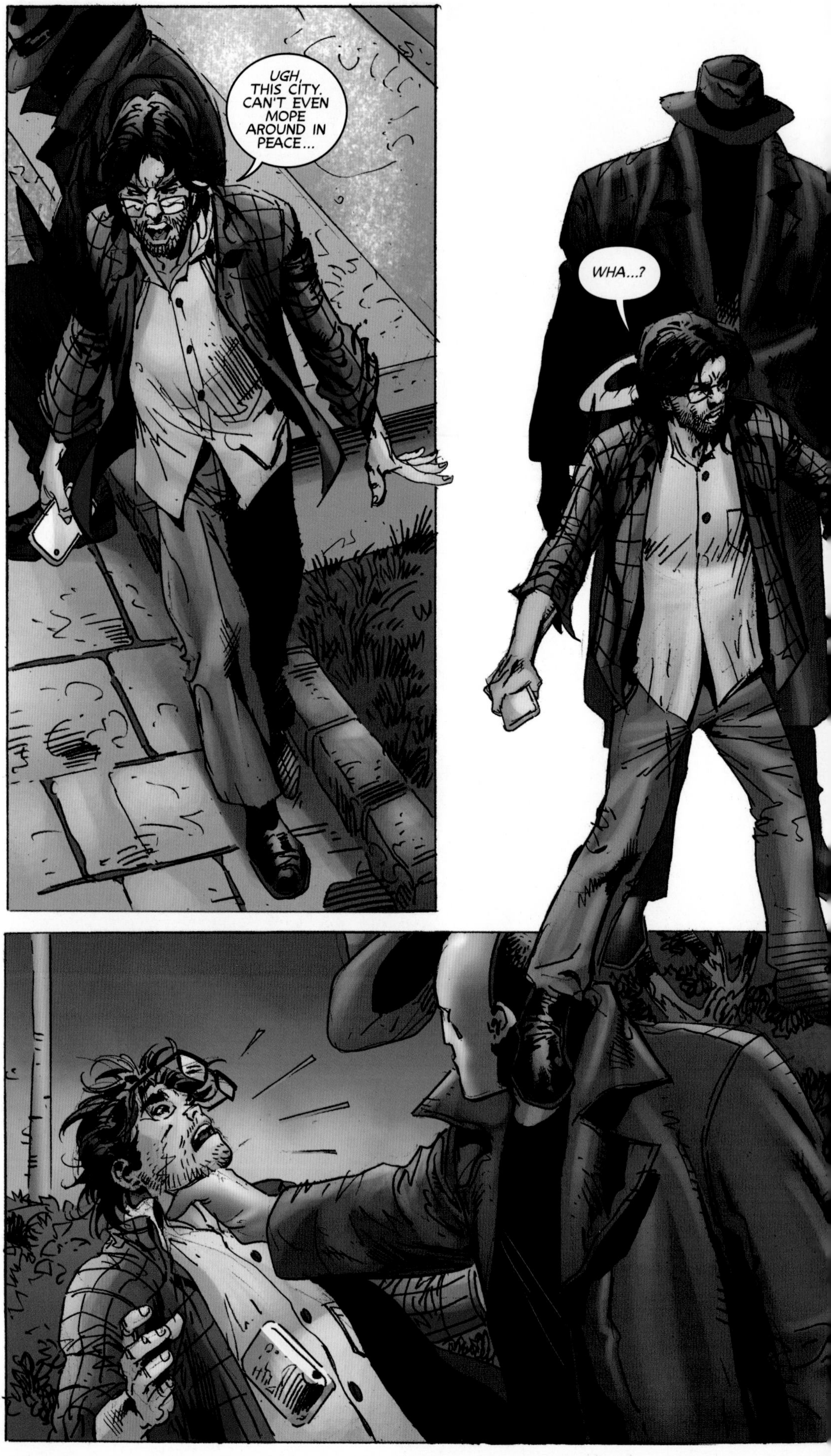
UGH, THIS CITY. CAN'T EVEN MOPE AROUND IN PEACE...
WHA...?

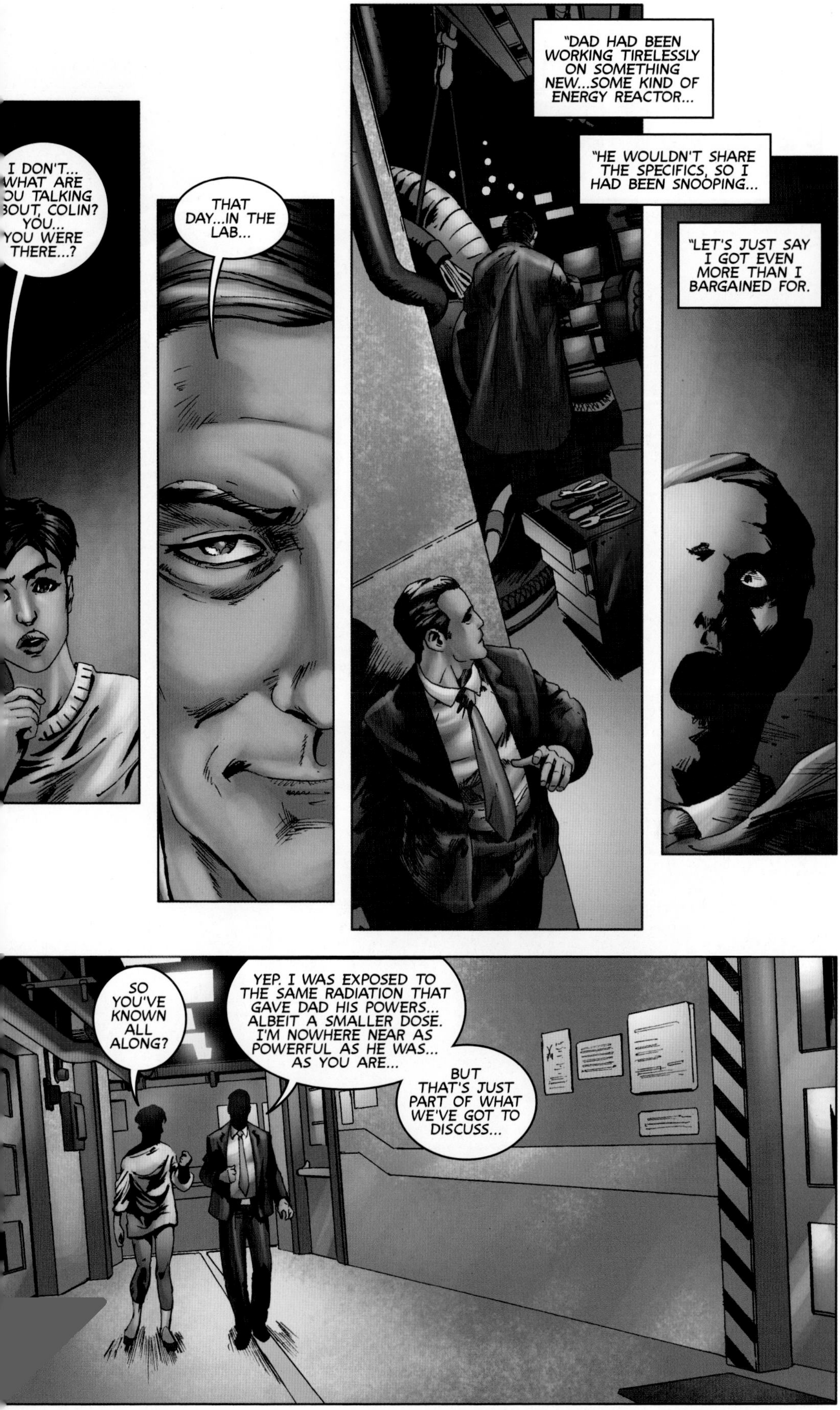
I DON'T... WHAT ARE OU TALKING BOUT, COLIN? YOU... YOU WERE THERE...?
THAT DAY...IN THE LAB...
"DAD HAD BEEN WORKING TIRELESSLY ON SOMETHING NEW...SOME KIND OF ENERGY REACTOR...
"HE WOULDN'T SHARE THE SPECIFICS, SO I HAD BEEN SNOOPING...
"LET'S JUST SAY I GOT EVEN MORE THAN I BARGAINED FOR.
SO YOU'VE KNOWN ALL ALONG?
YEP. I WAS EXPOSED TO THE SAME RADIATION THAT GAVE DAD HIS POWERS... ALBEIT A SMALLER DOSE. I'M NOWHERE NEAR AS POWERFUL AS HE WAS... AS YOU ARE...
BUT THAT'S JUST PART OF WHAT WE'VE GOT TO DISCUSS...

SOLAR: MAN OF THE ATOM
FAMILY REUNION

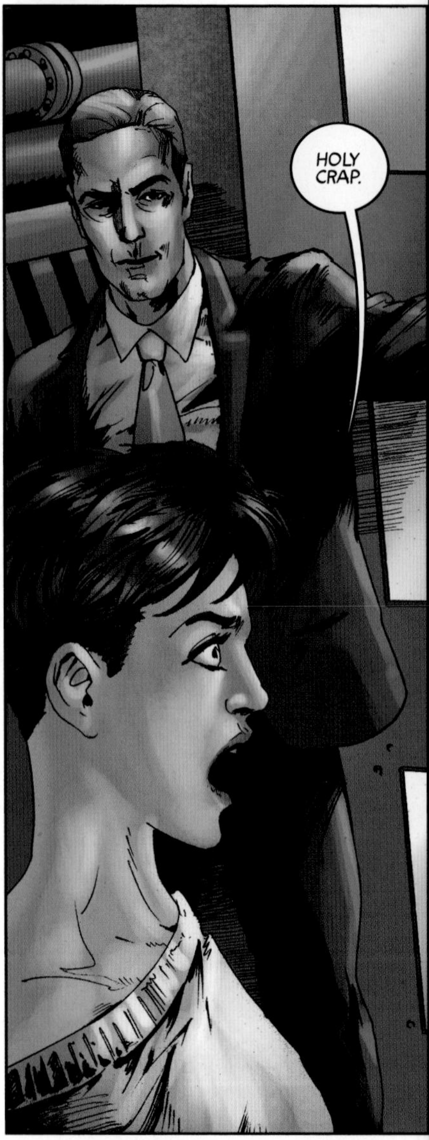

HOLY CRAP.

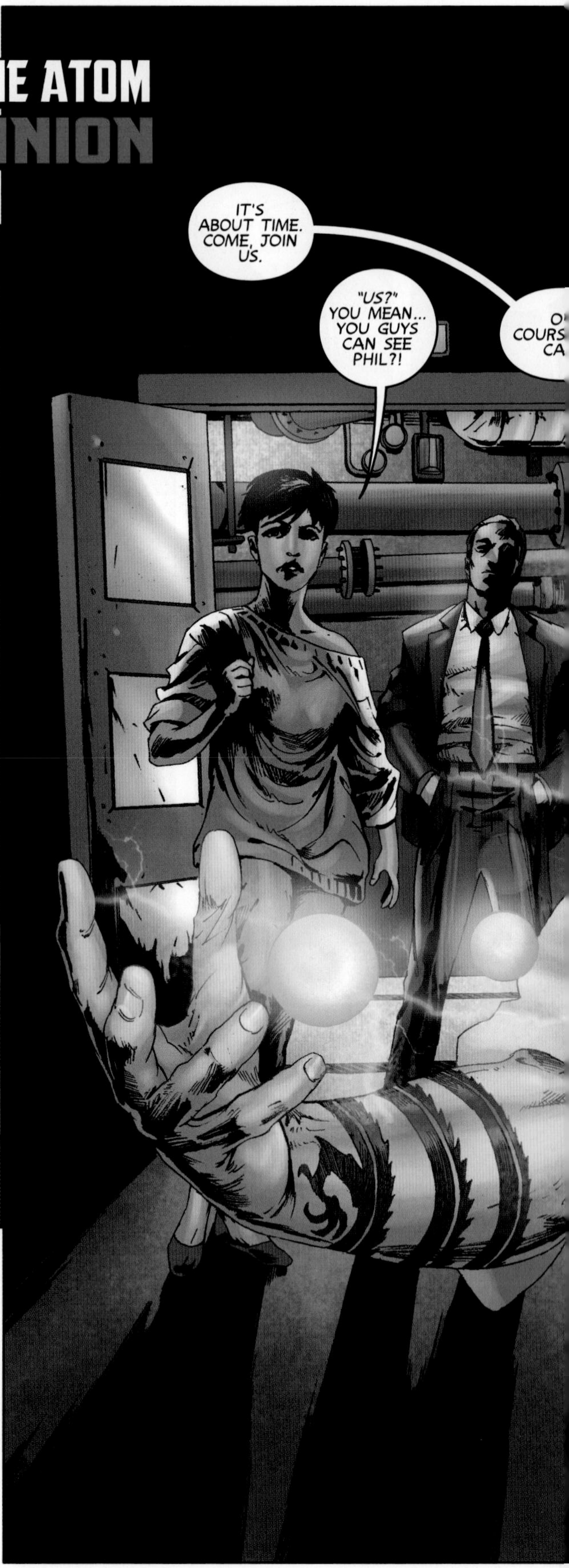

IT'S ABOUT TIME. COME, JOIN US.
"US?" YOU MEAN... YOU GUYS CAN SEE PHIL?!

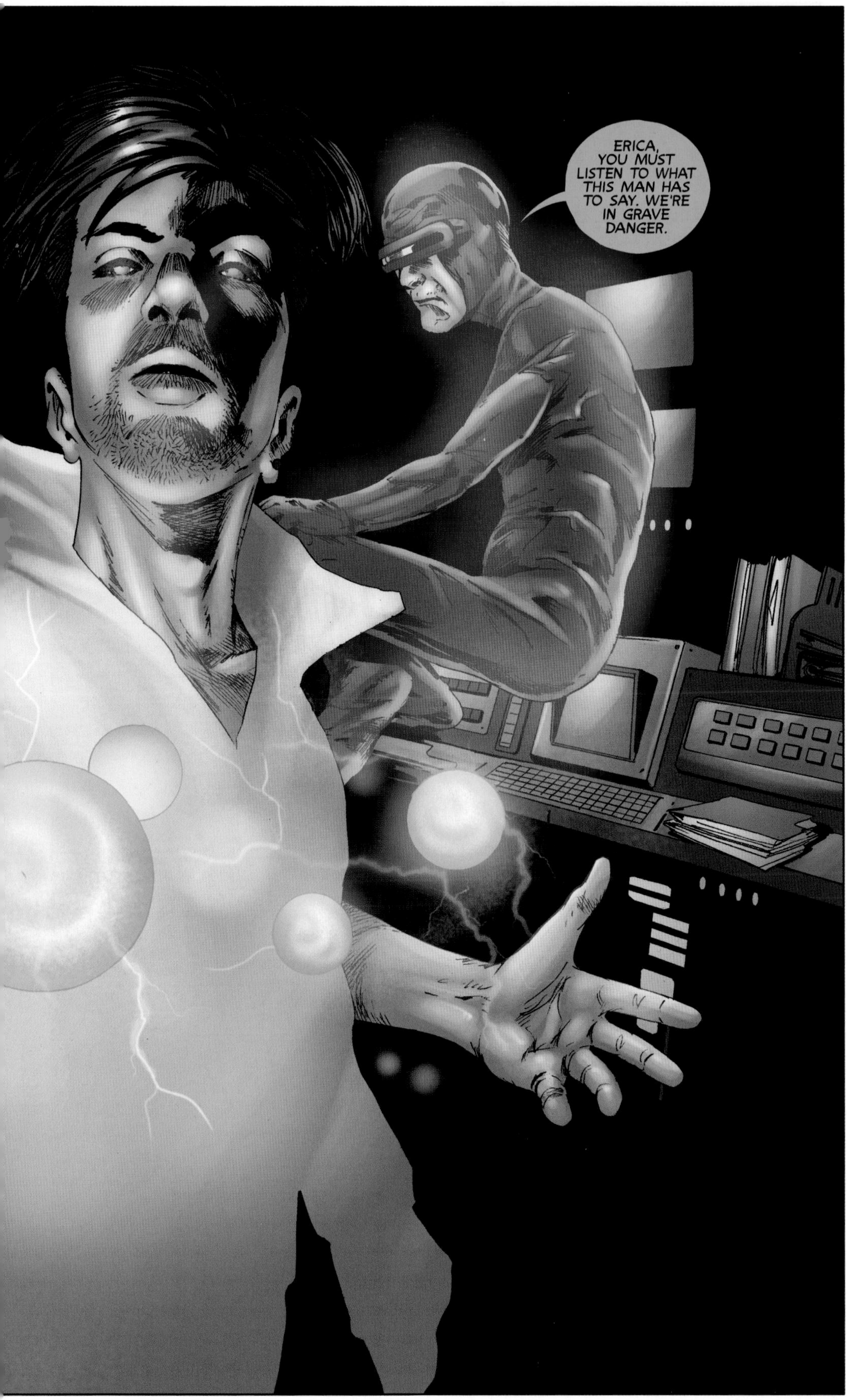
ERICA, YOU MUST LISTEN TO WHAT THIS MAN HAS TO SAY. WE'RE IN GRAVE DANGER.

YUP, I'VE OFFICIALLY SNAPPED. I'VE LOST MY DAMN MIND.

THIS IS NO TIME FOR JOKES. YOU MUST LISTEN...ALL OF THIS HAS BEEN CONNECTED, AND IT'S COMING TO AN END.

ALL RIGHT, YODA. CHILL OUT AND I'LL PULL UP A CHAIR.

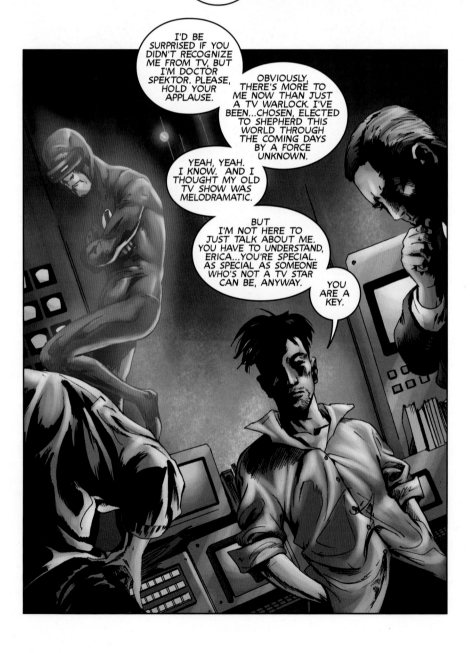

I'D BE SURPRISED IF YOU DIDN'T RECOGNIZE ME FROM TV, BUT I'M DOCTOR SPEKTOR. PLEASE, HOLD YOUR APPLAUSE.

OBVIOUSLY, THERE'S MORE TO ME NOW THAN JUST A TV WARLOCK. I'VE BEEN...CHOSEN, ELECTED TO SHEPHERD THIS WORLD THROUGH THE COMING DAYS BY A FORCE UNKNOWN.

YEAH, YEAH. I KNOW. AND I THOUGHT MY OLD TV SHOW WAS MELODRAMATIC.

BUT I'M NOT HERE TO JUST TALK ABOUT ME. YOU HAVE TO UNDERSTAND, ERICA...YOU'RE SPECIAL. AS SPECIAL AS SOMEONE WHO'S NOT A TV STAR CAN BE, ANYWAY.

YOU ARE A KEY.

WE ALL KNOW THE SCORE--YOU WERE EXPOSED TO RADIATION, BLAH, BLAH, BLAH.

BUT I THINK YOU'VE FIGURED OUT THAT THERE'S SOMETHING MORE GOING ON. WHAT YOU WERE EXPOSED TO...IT WASN'T JUST SIMPLE RADIATION.

THERE'S A COSMIC POWER BEYOND YOUR UNDERSTANDING AT PLAY, AND IT'S AFFECTED US ALL.

AND IF WE'VE GOT ANY CHANCE TO SURVIVE THE COMING DAYS, THEN A PROPHECY MUST BE FULFILLED.

I KNOW, HOW EXCITING.

BUT THE THREE MUST BECOME ONE.

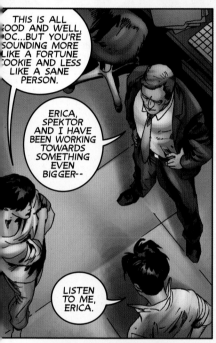

THIS IS ALL GOOD AND WELL, DOC...BUT YOU'RE SOUNDING MORE LIKE A FORTUNE COOKIE AND LESS LIKE A SANE PERSON.

ERICA, SPEKTOR AND I HAVE BEEN WORKING TOWARDS SOMETHING EVEN BIGGER--

LISTEN TO ME, ERICA.

YOU KNOW HOW THESE THINGS USUALLY GO. JUST AS YOU HAVE BECOME THE LIGHT, ANOTHER HAS BECOME THE DARK.

ENERGY... MAGIC...IT'S ALL POWER. AND IT'S BEING MANIPULATED AROUND US AS WE SPEAK.

WHEN I SAVED YOU, YOU WERE ALREADY UNDER ATTACK. YOU FELT THE PRESENCE ALL AROUND YOU.

...THE REACTOR.

NOW YOU'RE SEEING IT. IT'S ALL CONNECTED.

IT ALL STARTED WITH PHIL AND HIS RESEARCH. HE TAPPED INTO SOMETHING FAR STRONGER...AND STRANGER THAN HE COULD'VE IMAGINED.

(WAY TO GO, DOC).

IT...EXPLAINS MUCH OF WHAT I'VE FELT. MY RESEARCH INTO ENERGY MANIPULATION COULD NEVER HAVE TRANSFORMED ME...THERE WAS ALWAYS ANOTHER VARIABLE.

PHIL, ARE YOU REALLY TELLING ME YOU BELIEVE WE'VE ALL BEEN...

POWERED UP BY *MAGIC*? YOU? MR. SCIENCE?

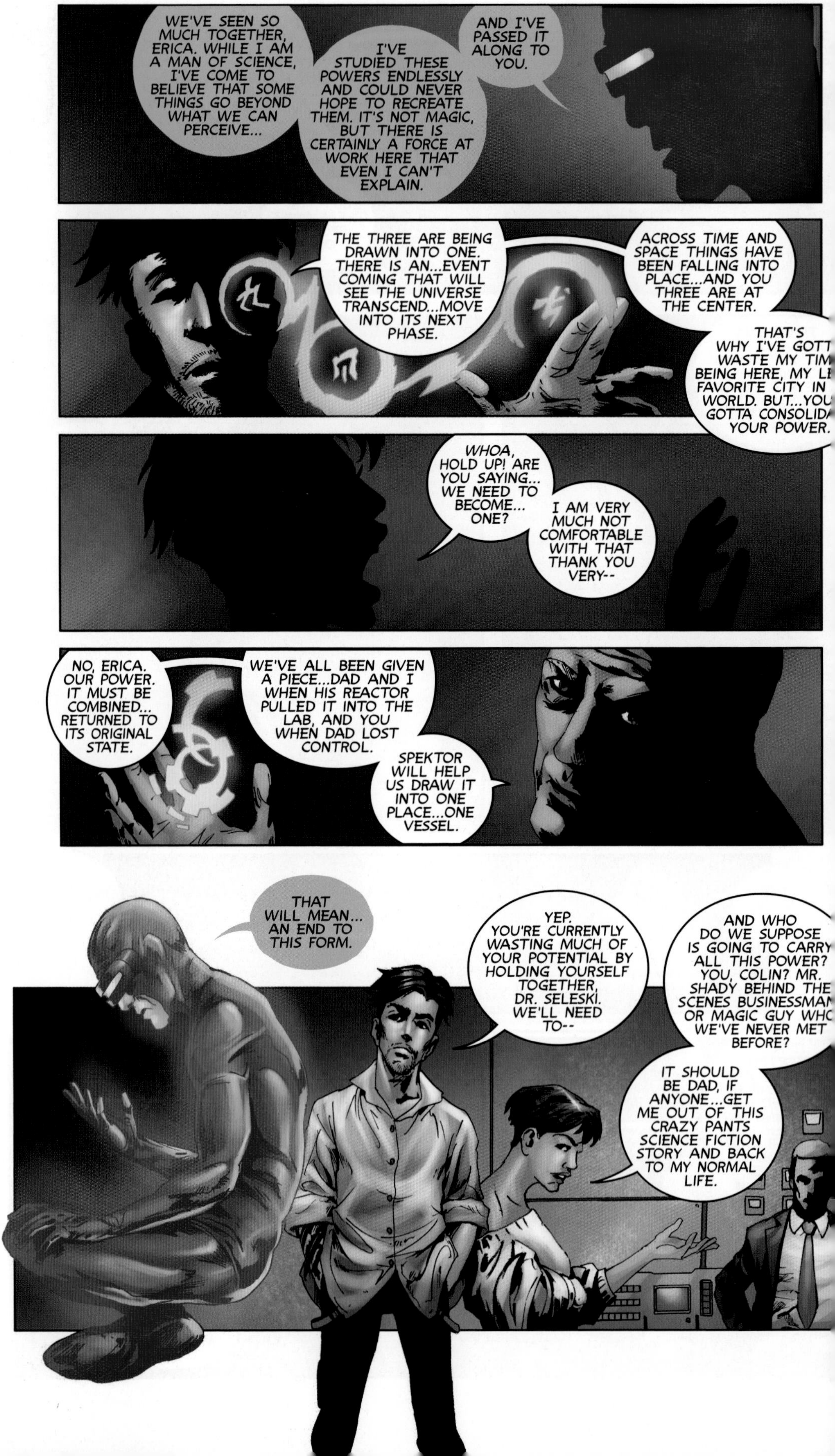
WE'VE SEEN SO MUCH TOGETHER, ERICA. WHILE I AM A MAN OF SCIENCE, I'VE COME TO BELIEVE THAT SOME THINGS GO BEYOND WHAT WE CAN PERCEIVE...
I'VE STUDIED THESE POWERS ENDLESSLY AND COULD NEVER HOPE TO RECREATE THEM. IT'S NOT MAGIC, BUT THERE IS CERTAINLY A FORCE AT WORK HERE THAT EVEN I CAN'T EXPLAIN.
AND I'VE PASSED IT ALONG TO YOU.
THE THREE ARE BEING DRAWN INTO ONE. THERE IS AN...EVENT COMING THAT WILL SEE THE UNIVERSE TRANSCEND...MOVE INTO ITS NEXT PHASE.
ACROSS TIME AND SPACE THINGS HAVE BEEN FALLING INTO PLACE...AND YOU THREE ARE AT THE CENTER.
THAT'S WHY I'VE GOTT WASTE MY TIM BEING HERE, MY LE FAVORITE CITY IN WORLD. BUT...YOU GOTTA CONSOLIDA YOUR POWER.
WHOA, HOLD UP! ARE YOU SAYING... WE NEED TO BECOME... ONE?
I AM VERY MUCH NOT COMFORTABLE WITH THAT THANK YOU VERY--
NO, ERICA. OUR POWER. IT MUST BE COMBINED... RETURNED TO ITS ORIGINAL STATE.
WE'VE ALL BEEN GIVEN A PIECE...DAD AND I WHEN HIS REACTOR PULLED IT INTO THE LAB, AND YOU WHEN DAD LOST CONTROL.
SPEKTOR WILL HELP US DRAW IT INTO ONE PLACE...ONE VESSEL.
THAT WILL MEAN... AN END TO THIS FORM.
YEP. YOU'RE CURRENTLY WASTING MUCH OF YOUR POTENTIAL BY HOLDING YOURSELF TOGETHER, DR. SELESKI. WE'LL NEED TO--
AND WHO DO WE SUPPOSE IS GOING TO CARRY ALL THIS POWER? YOU, COLIN? MR. SHADY BEHIND THE SCENES BUSINESSMAN OR MAGIC GUY WHO WE'VE NEVER MET BEFORE?
IT SHOULD BE DAD, IF ANYONE...GET ME OUT OF THIS CRAZY PANTS SCIENCE FICTION STORY AND BACK TO MY NORMAL LIFE.

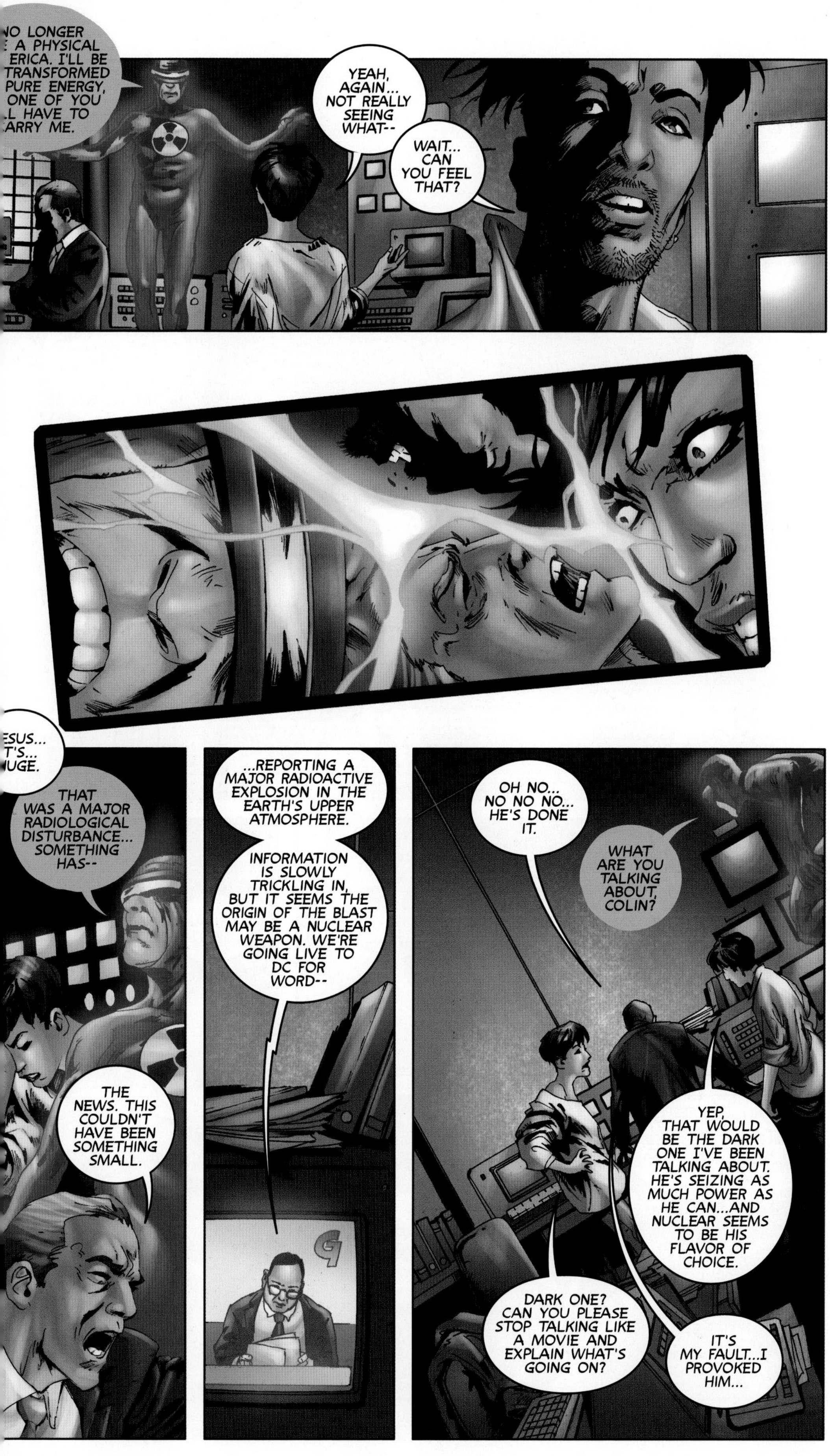

NO LONGER E A PHYSICAL ERICA. I'LL BE TRANSFORMED PURE ENERGY, ONE OF YOU L HAVE TO ARRY ME.
YEAH, AGAIN... NOT REALLY SEEING WHAT--
WAIT... CAN YOU FEEL THAT?
ESUS... T'S... UGE.
THAT WAS A MAJOR RADIOLOGICAL DISTURBANCE... SOMETHING HAS--
THE NEWS. THIS COULDN'T HAVE BEEN SOMETHING SMALL.
...REPORTING A MAJOR RADIOACTIVE EXPLOSION IN THE EARTH'S UPPER ATMOSPHERE.
INFORMATION IS SLOWLY TRICKLING IN, BUT IT SEEMS THE ORIGIN OF THE BLAST MAY BE A NUCLEAR WEAPON. WE'RE GOING LIVE TO DC FOR WORD--
OH NO... NO NO NO... HE'S DONE IT.
WHAT ARE YOU TALKING ABOUT, COLIN?
YEP, THAT WOULD BE THE DARK ONE I'VE BEEN TALKING ABOUT. HE'S SEIZING AS MUCH POWER AS HE CAN...AND NUCLEAR SEEMS TO BE HIS FLAVOR OF CHOICE.
DARK ONE? CAN YOU PLEASE STOP TALKING LIKE A MOVIE AND EXPLAIN WHAT'S GOING ON?
IT'S MY FAULT...I PROVOKED HIM...

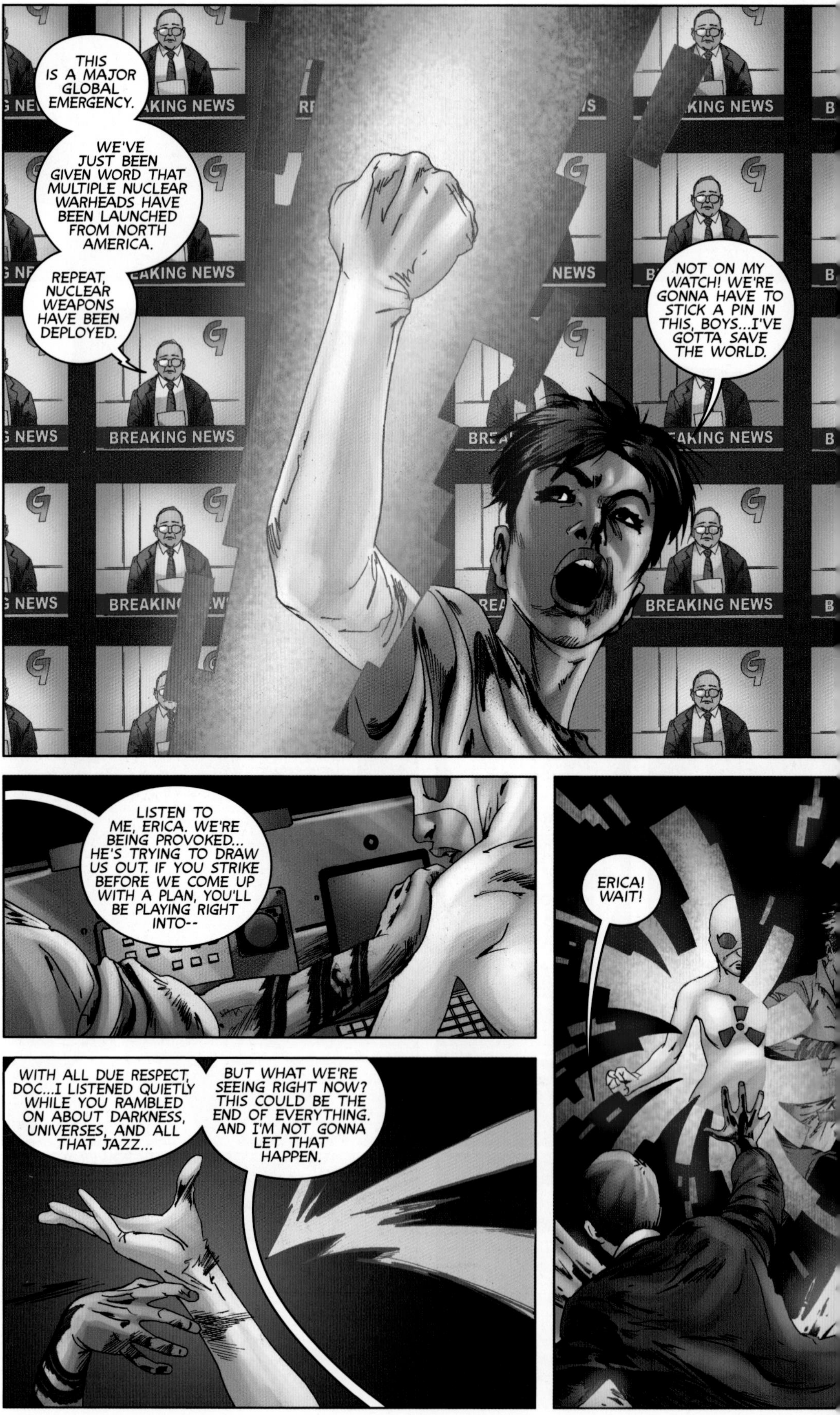

THIS IS A MAJOR GLOBAL EMERGENCY.
WE'VE JUST BEEN GIVEN WORD THAT MULTIPLE NUCLEAR WARHEADS HAVE BEEN LAUNCHED FROM NORTH AMERICA.
REPEAT, NUCLEAR WEAPONS HAVE BEEN DEPLOYED.
BREAKING NEWS
NOT ON MY WATCH! WE'RE GONNA HAVE TO STICK A PIN IN THIS, BOYS...I'VE GOTTA SAVE THE WORLD.
LISTEN TO ME, ERICA. WE'RE BEING PROVOKED... HE'S TRYING TO DRAW US OUT. IF YOU STRIKE BEFORE WE COME UP WITH A PLAN, YOU'LL BE PLAYING RIGHT INTO--
WITH ALL DUE RESPECT, DOC...I LISTENED QUIETLY WHILE YOU RAMBLED ON ABOUT DARKNESS, UNIVERSES, AND ALL THAT JAZZ...
BUT WHAT WE'RE SEEING RIGHT NOW? THIS COULD BE THE END OF EVERYTHING. AND I'M NOT GONNA LET THAT HAPPEN.
ERICA! WAIT!

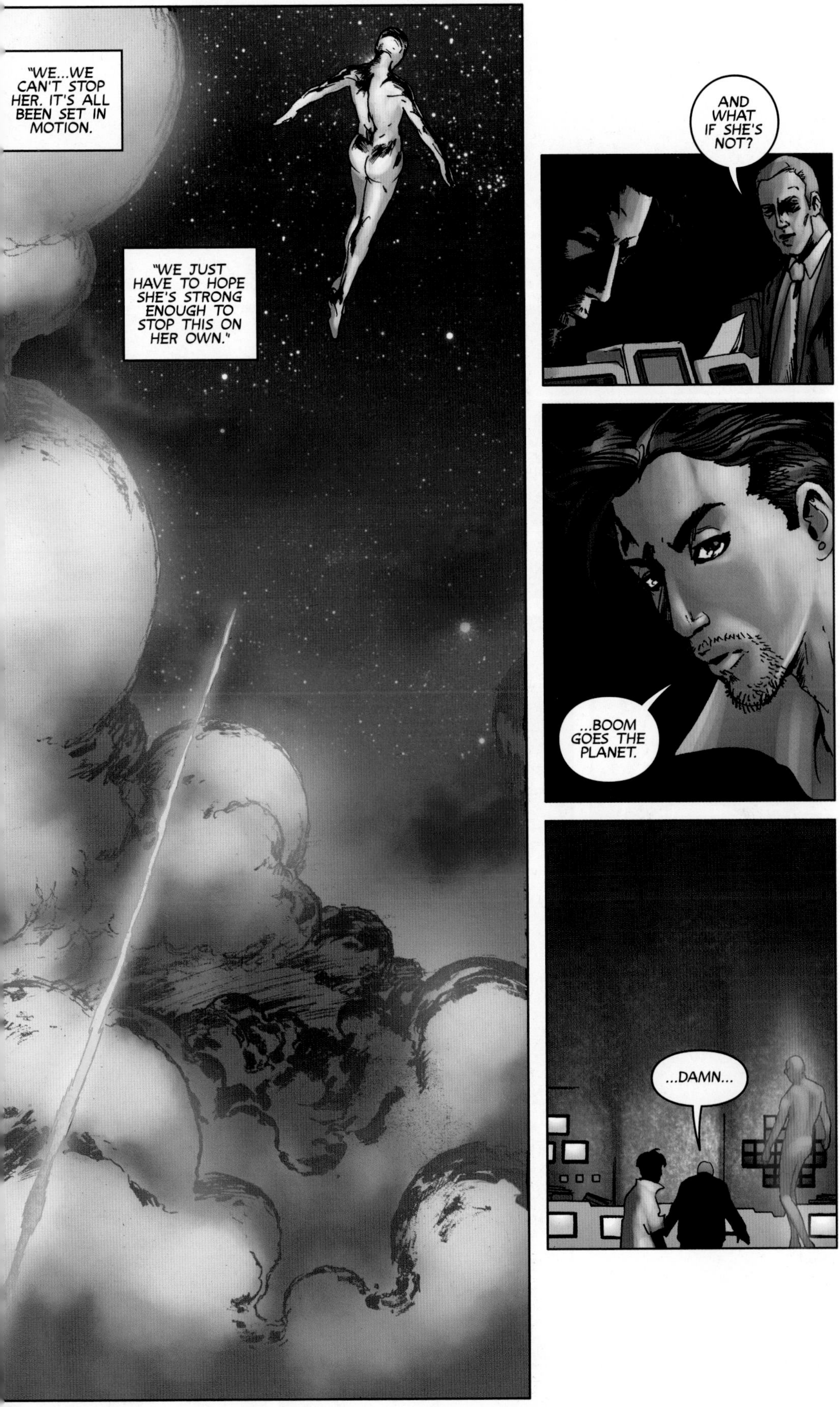
"WE...WE CAN'T STOP HER. IT'S ALL BEEN SET IN MOTION.
"WE JUST HAVE TO HOPE SHE'S STRONG ENOUGH TO STOP THIS ON HER OWN."
AND WHAT IF SHE'S NOT?
...BOOM GOES THE PLANET.
...DAMN...

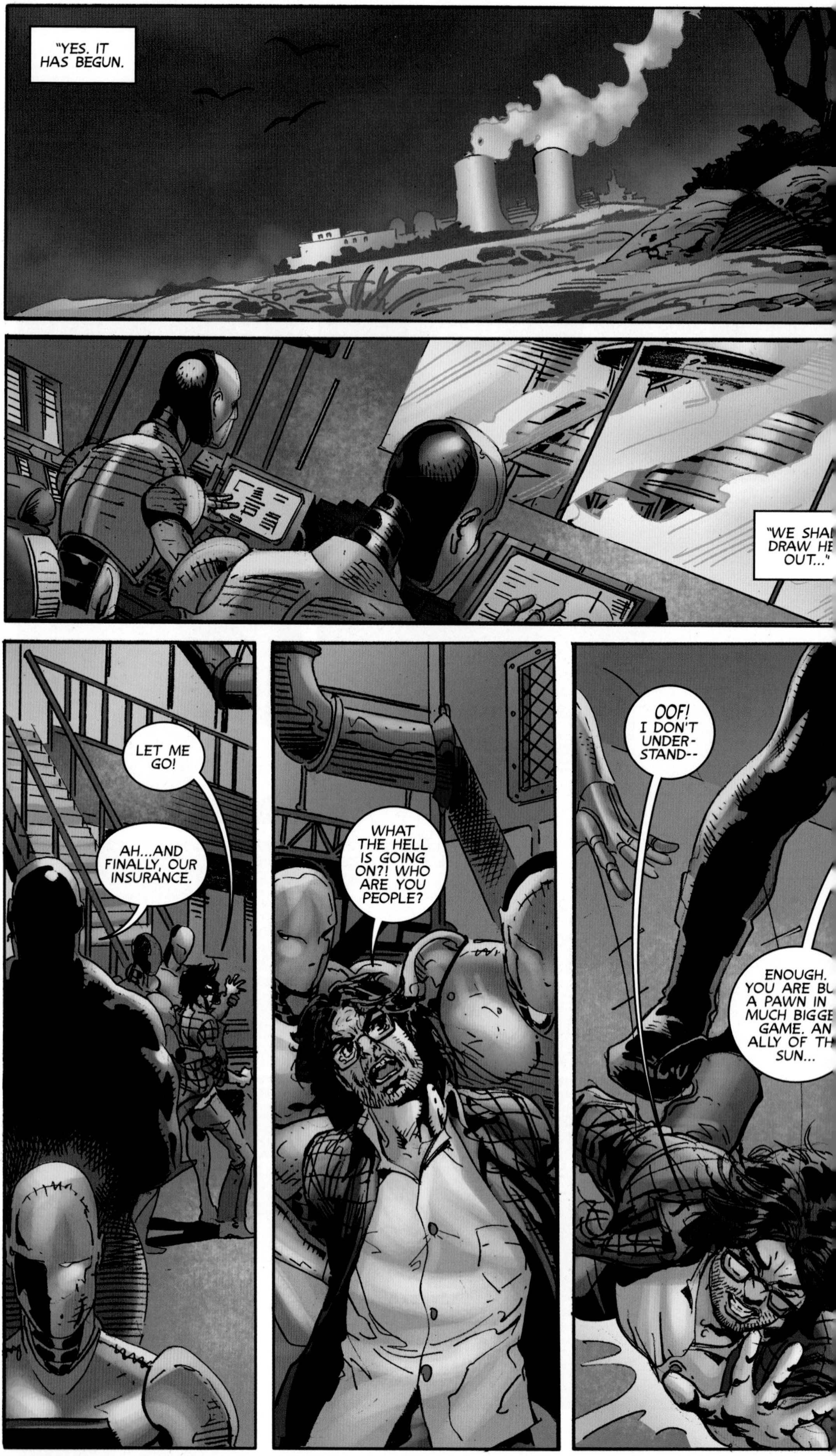
"YES. IT HAS BEGUN.
"WE SHAL DRAW HE OUT..."
LET ME GO!
AH...AND FINALLY, OUR INSURANCE.
WHAT THE HELL IS GOING ON?! WHO ARE YOU PEOPLE?
OOF! I DON'T UNDER-STAND--
ENOUGH. YOU ARE BU A PAWN IN MUCH BIGGE GAME. AN ALLY OF TH SUN...

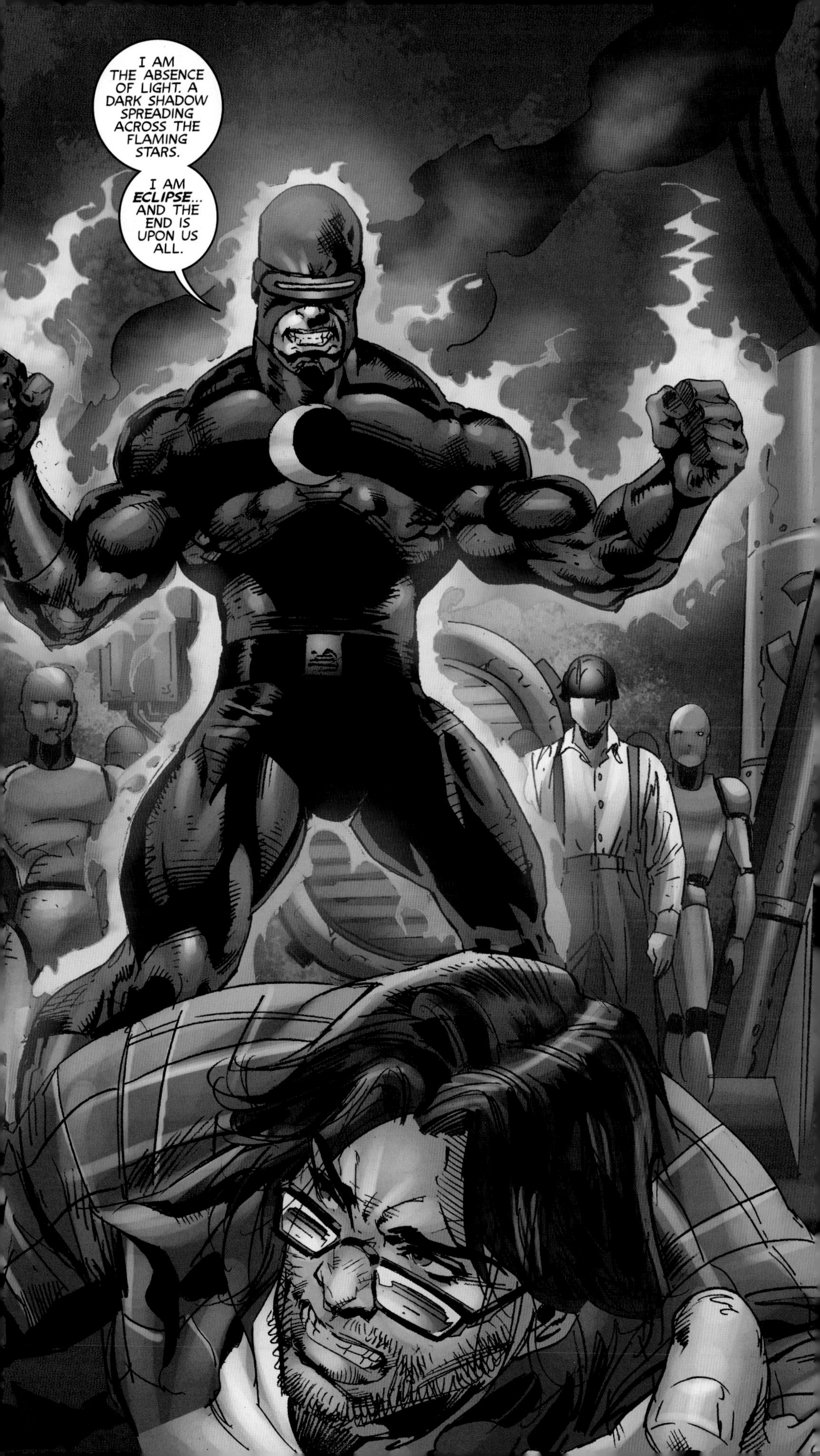
I AM THE ABSENCE OF LIGHT. A DARK SHADOW SPREADING ACROSS THE FLAMING STARS.
I AM *ECLIPSE*... AND THE END IS UPON US ALL.

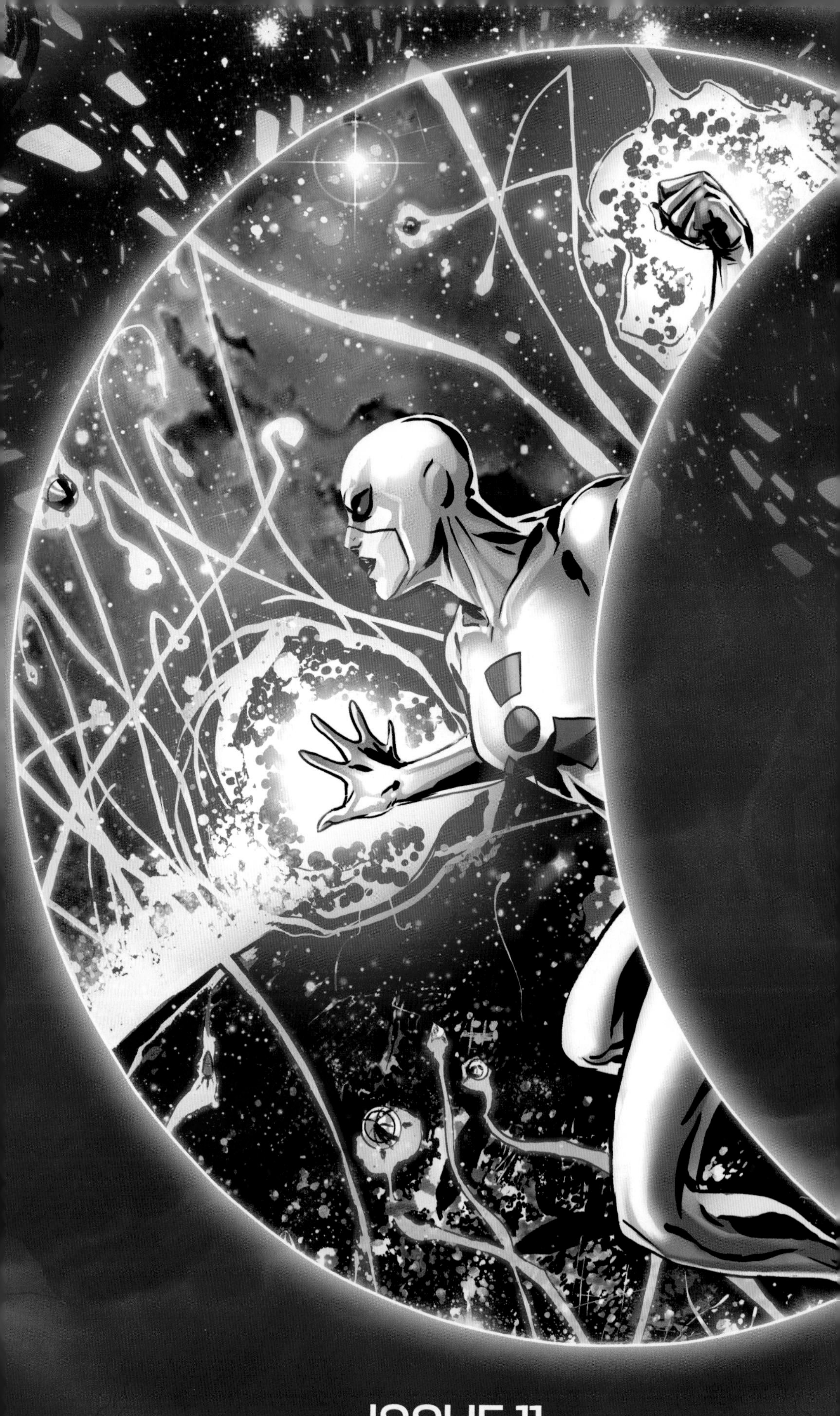

ISSUE 11

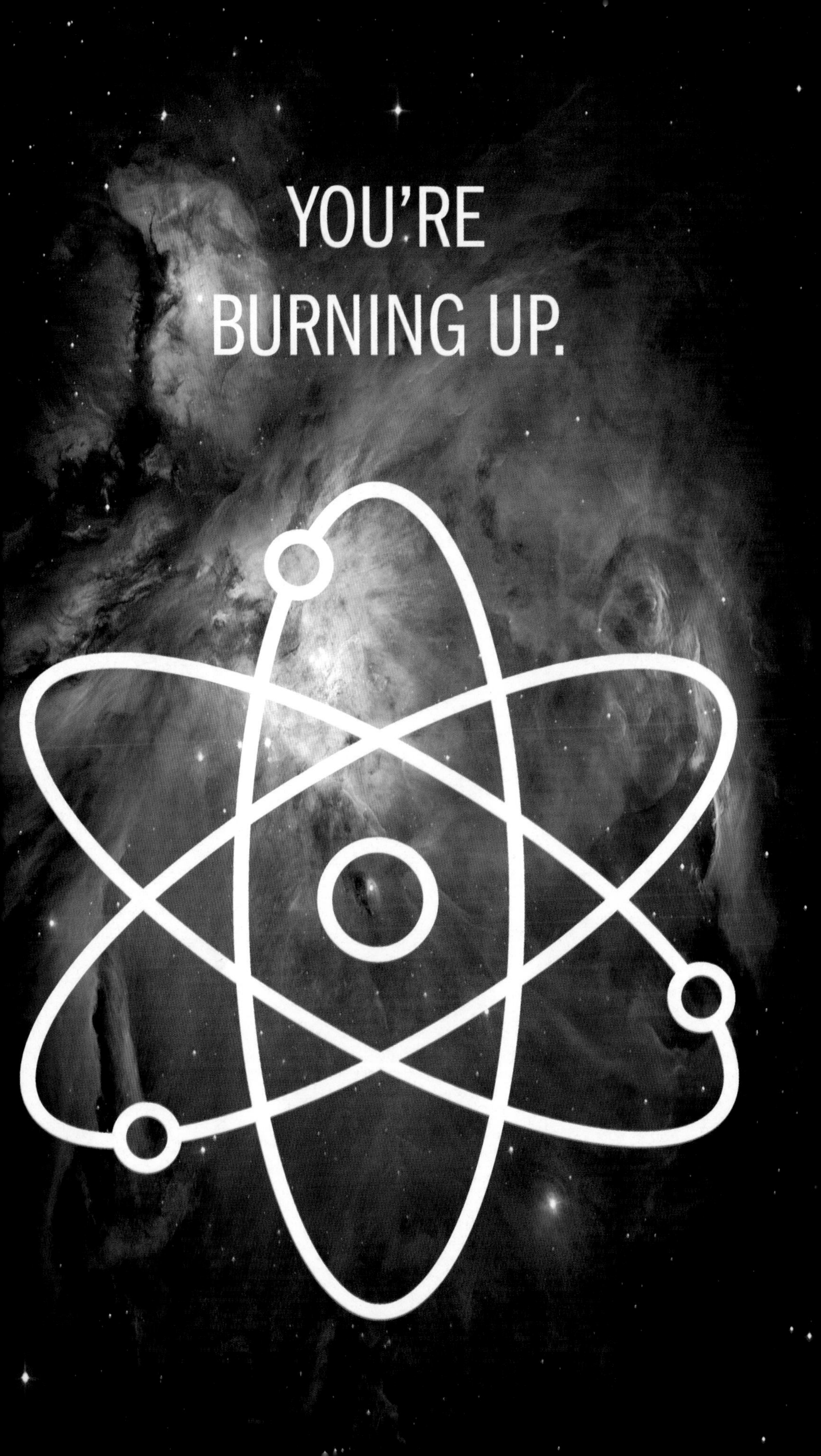
YOU'RE
BURNING UP.

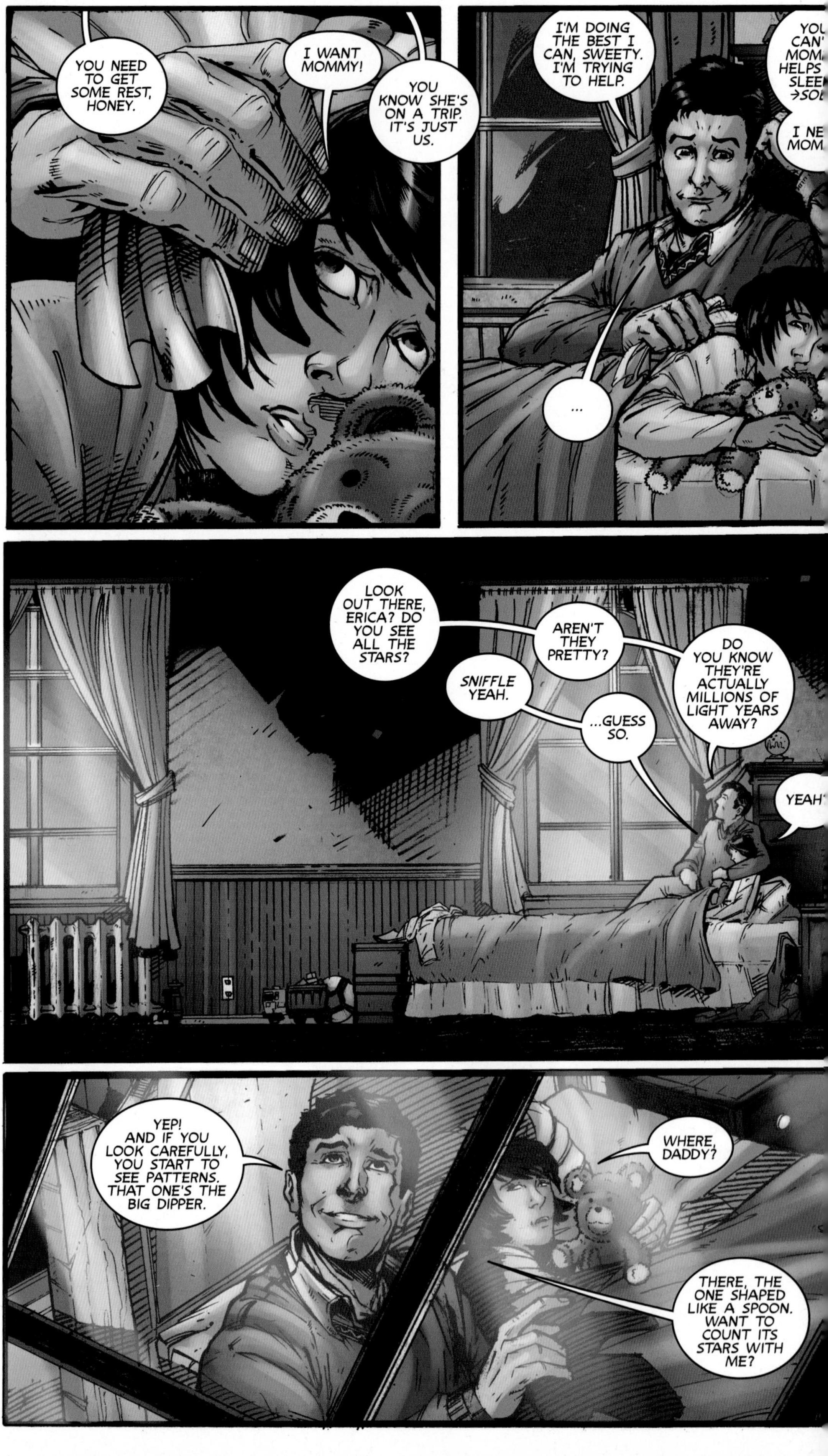
YOU NEED TO GET SOME REST, HONEY.
I WANT MOMMY!
YOU KNOW SHE'S ON A TRIP. IT'S JUST US.
I'M DOING THE BEST I CAN, SWEETY. I'M TRYING TO HELP.
...
LOOK OUT THERE, ERICA? DO YOU SEE ALL THE STARS?
SNIFFLE YEAH.
AREN'T THEY PRETTY?
...GUESS SO.
DO YOU KNOW THEY'RE ACTUALLY MILLIONS OF LIGHT YEARS AWAY?
YEAH
YEP! AND IF YOU LOOK CAREFULLY, YOU START TO SEE PATTERNS. THAT ONE'S THE BIG DIPPER.
WHERE, DADDY?
THERE, THE ONE SHAPED LIKE A SPOON. WANT TO COUNT ITS STARS WITH ME?

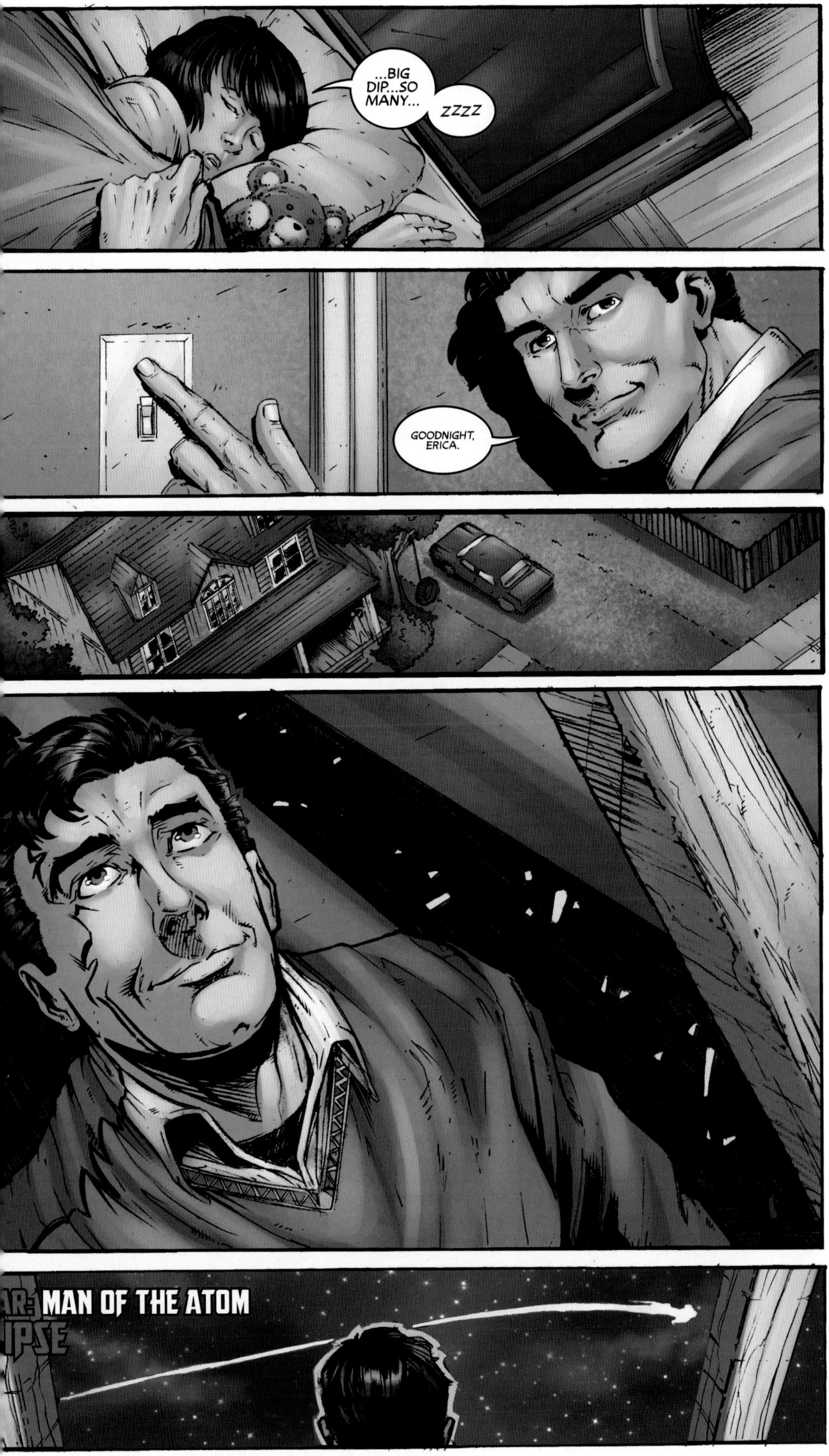
...BIG DIP...SO MANY...
ZZZZ
GOODNIGHT, ERICA.
MAN OF THE ATOM

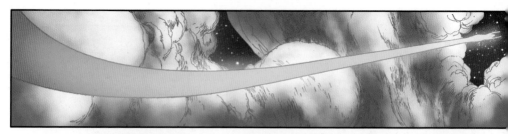

I SENSE WE'RE CLOSING IN...

OH MY GOD, PHIL...

IT'S... THE E OF T WORL

"TYPICAL ERICA..."

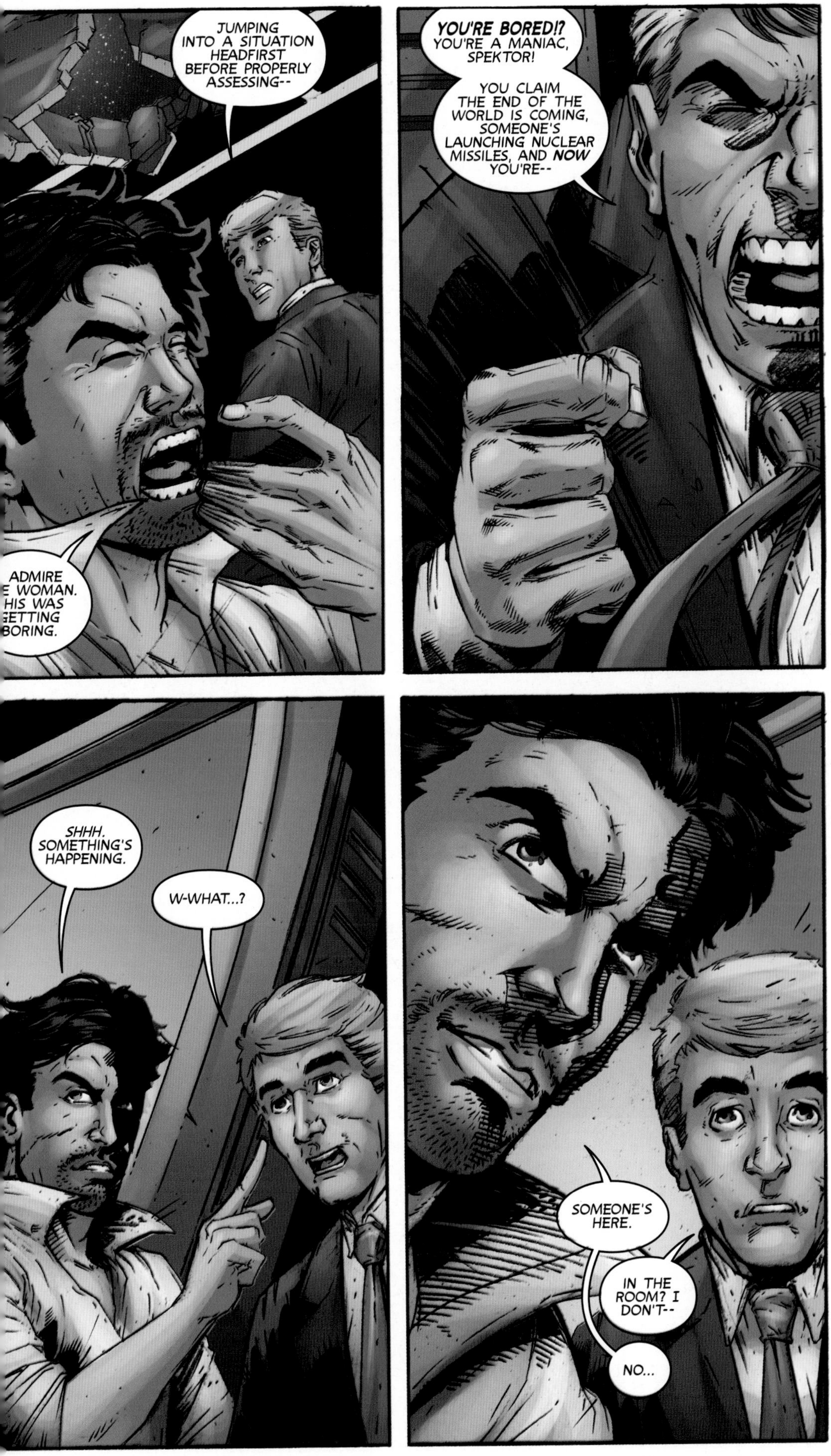

JUMPING INTO A SITUATION HEADFIRST BEFORE PROPERLY ASSESSING--
ADMIRE E WOMAN. HIS WAS GETTING BORING.
YOU'RE BORED!? YOU'RE A MANIAC, SPEKTOR!
YOU CLAIM THE END OF THE WORLD IS COMING, SOMEONE'S LAUNCHING NUCLEAR MISSILES, AND NOW YOU'RE--
SHHH. SOMETHING'S HAPPENING.
W-WHAT...?
SOMEONE'S HERE.
IN THE ROOM? I DON'T--
NO...

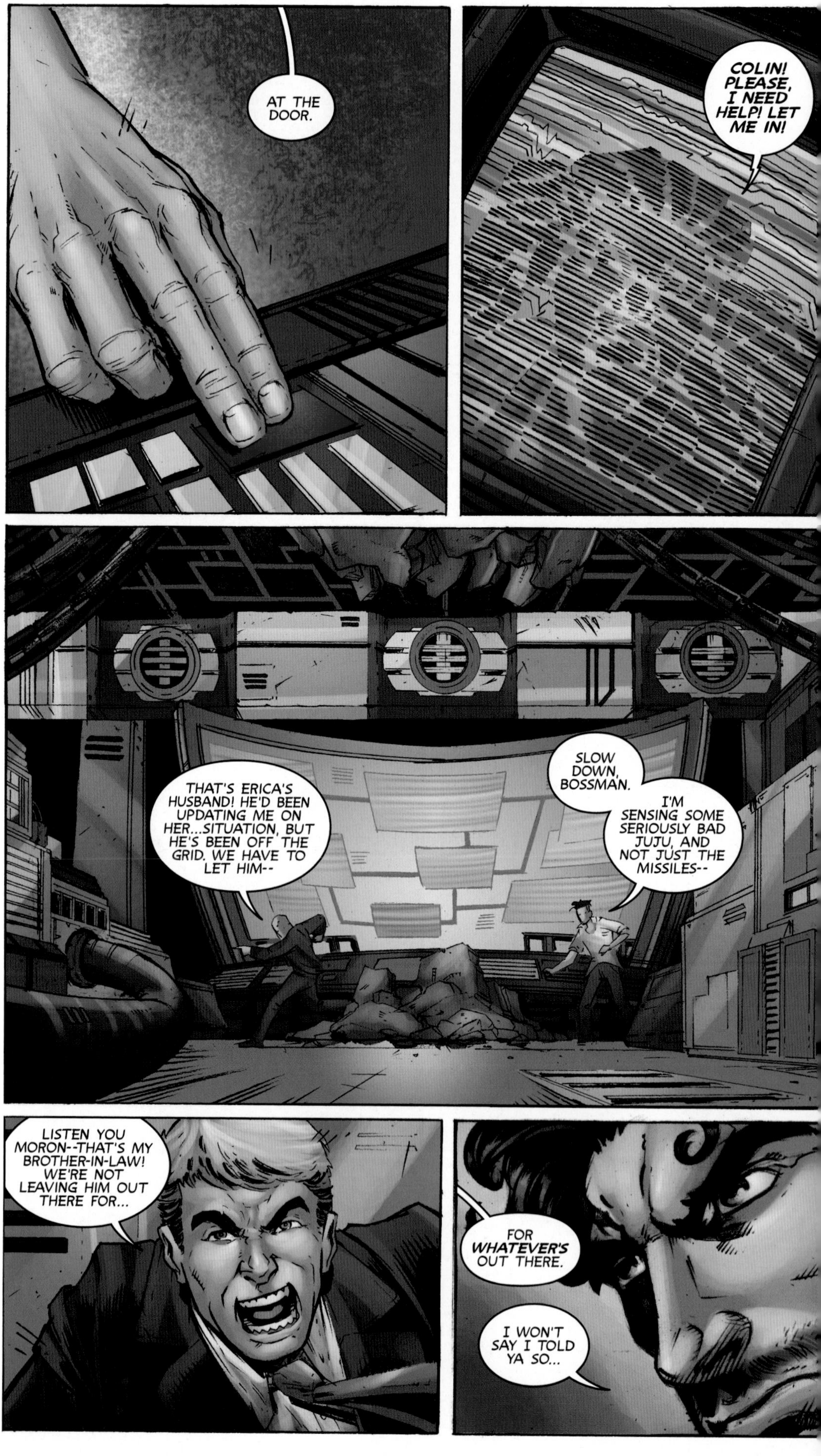
AT THE DOOR.
COLIN! PLEASE, I NEED HELP! LET ME IN!
THAT'S ERICA'S HUSBAND! HE'D BEEN UPDATING ME ON HER...SITUATION, BUT HE'S BEEN OFF THE GRID. WE HAVE TO LET HIM--
SLOW DOWN, BOSSMAN.
I'M SENSING SOME SERIOUSLY BAD JUJU, AND NOT JUST THE MISSILES--
LISTEN YOU MORON--THAT'S MY BROTHER-IN-LAW! WE'RE NOT LEAVING HIM OUT THERE FOR...
FOR *WHATEVER'S* OUT THERE.
I WON'T SAY I TOLD YA SO...

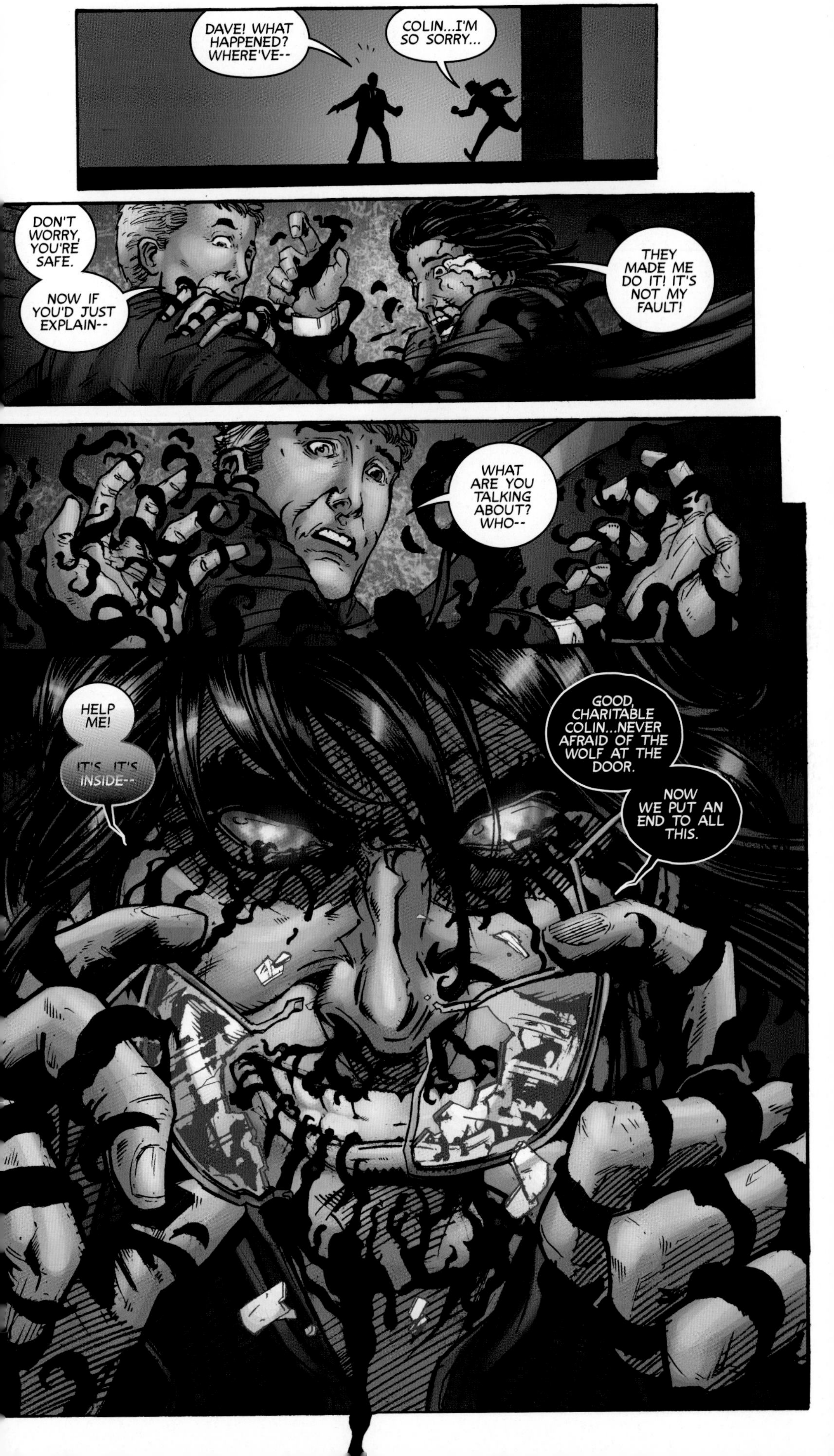
DAVE! WHAT HAPPENED? WHERE'VE--
COLIN...I'M SO SORRY...
DON'T WORRY, YOU'RE SAFE.
NOW IF YOU'D JUST EXPLAIN--
THEY MADE ME DO IT! IT'S NOT MY FAULT!
WHAT ARE YOU TALKING ABOUT? WHO--
HELP ME!
IT'S, IT'S INSIDE--
GOOD, CHARITABLE COLIN...NEVER AFRAID OF THE WOLF AT THE DOOR.
NOW WE PUT AN END TO ALL THIS.

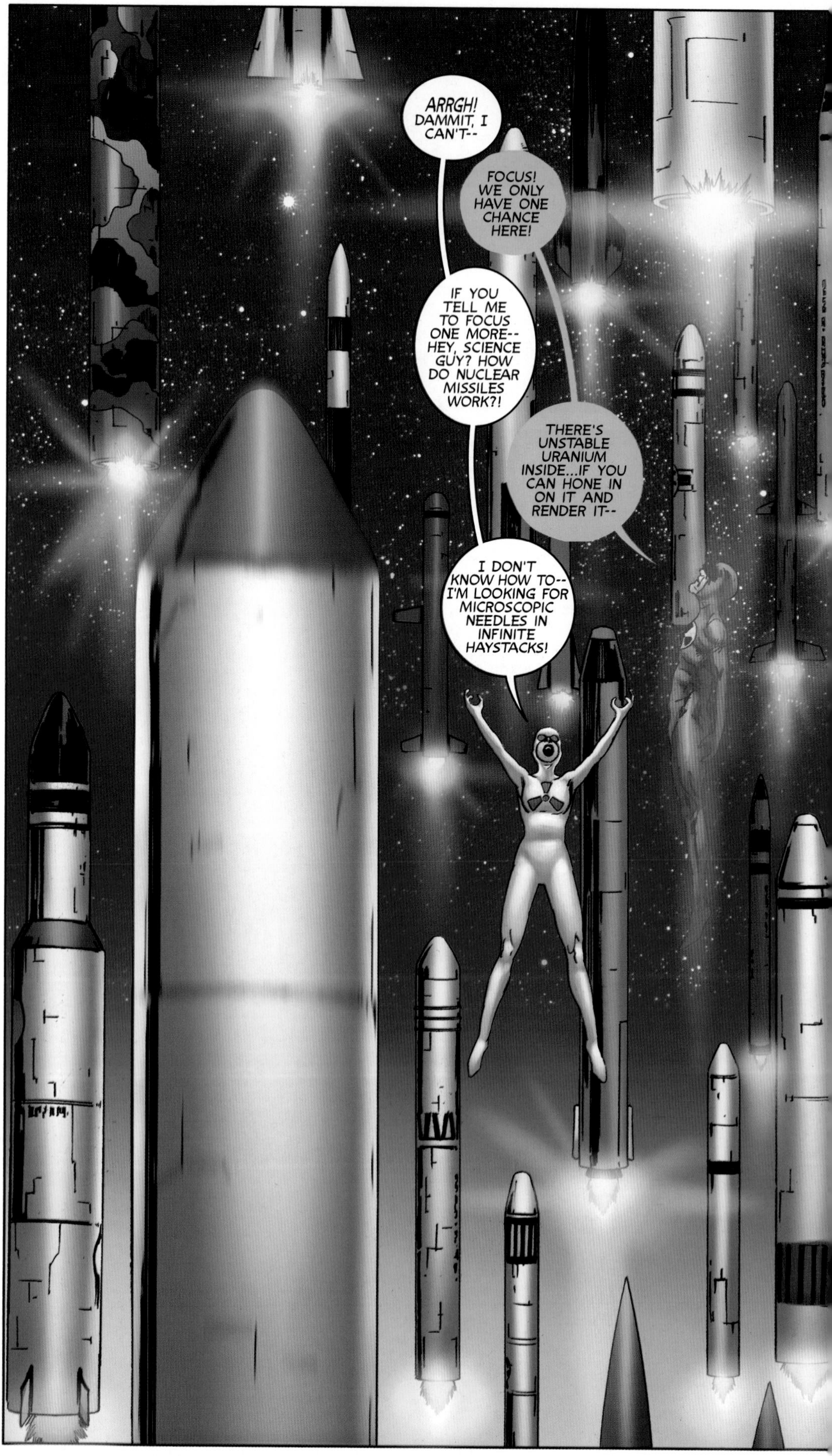

ARRGH! DAMMIT, I CAN'T--
FOCUS! WE ONLY HAVE ONE CHANCE HERE!
IF YOU TELL ME TO FOCUS ONE MORE-- HEY, SCIENCE GUY? HOW DO NUCLEAR MISSILES WORK?!
THERE'S UNSTABLE URANIUM INSIDE...IF YOU CAN HONE IN ON IT AND RENDER IT--
I DON'T KNOW HOW TO-- I'M LOOKING FOR MICROSCOPIC NEEDLES IN INFINITE HAYSTACKS!

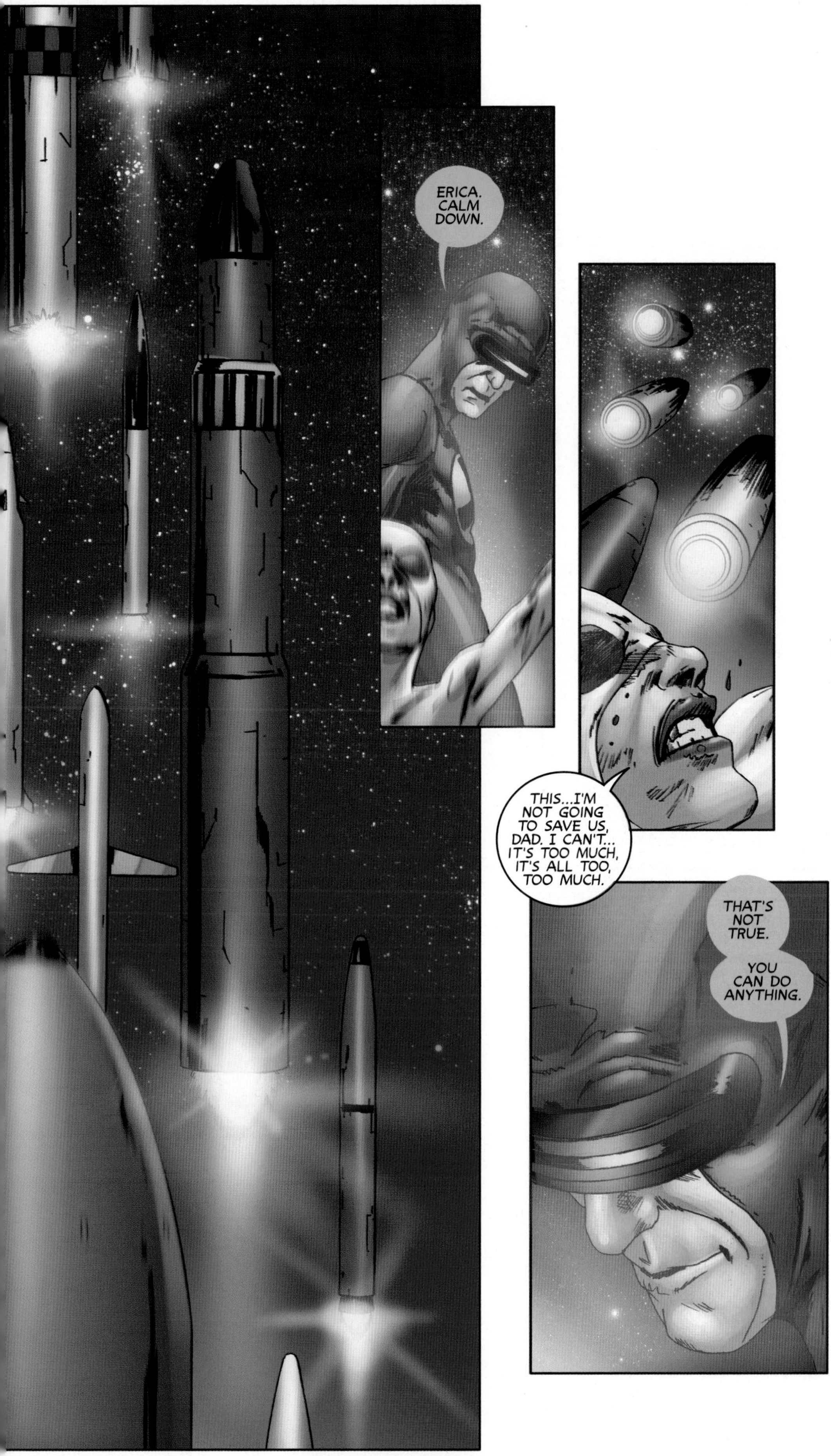
ERICA. CALM DOWN.
THIS...I'M NOT GOING TO SAVE US, DAD. I CAN'T... IT'S TOO MUCH, IT'S ALL TOO, TOO MUCH.
THAT'S NOT TRUE.
YOU CAN DO ANYTHING.

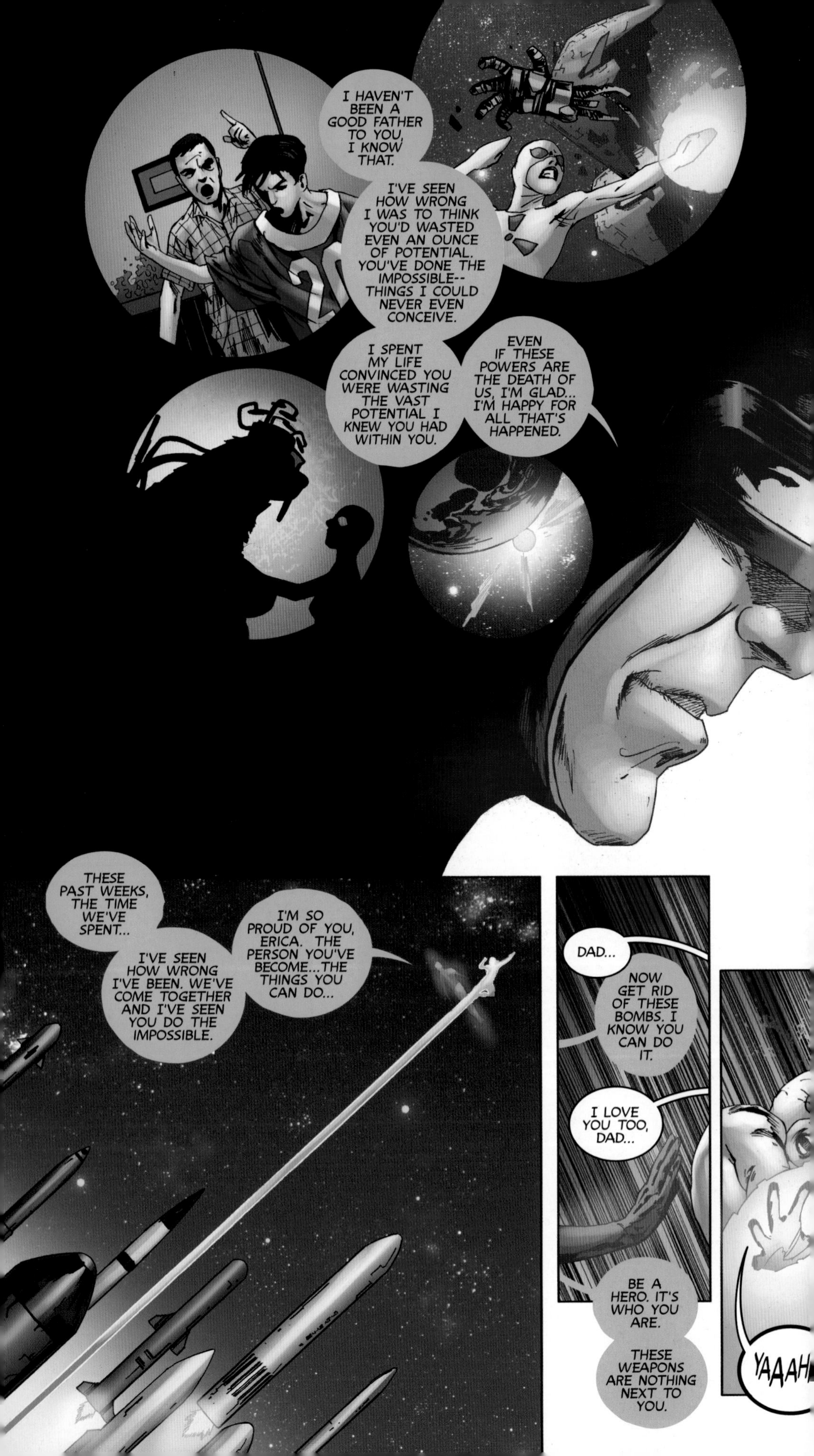
I HAVEN'T BEEN A GOOD FATHER TO YOU, I KNOW THAT.
I'VE SEEN HOW WRONG I WAS TO THINK YOU'D WASTED EVEN AN OUNCE OF POTENTIAL. YOU'VE DONE THE IMPOSSIBLE-- THINGS I COULD NEVER EVEN CONCEIVE.
I SPENT MY LIFE CONVINCED YOU WERE WASTING THE VAST POTENTIAL I KNEW YOU HAD WITHIN YOU.
EVEN IF THESE POWERS ARE THE DEATH OF US, I'M GLAD... I'M HAPPY FOR ALL THAT'S HAPPENED.
THESE PAST WEEKS, THE TIME WE'VE SPENT...
I'VE SEEN HOW WRONG I'VE BEEN. WE'VE COME TOGETHER AND I'VE SEEN YOU DO THE IMPOSSIBLE.
I'M SO PROUD OF YOU, ERICA. THE PERSON YOU'VE BECOME...THE THINGS YOU CAN DO...
DAD...
NOW GET RID OF THESE BOMBS. I KNOW YOU CAN DO IT.
I LOVE YOU TOO, DAD...
BE A HERO. IT'S WHO YOU ARE.
THESE WEAPONS ARE NOTHING NEXT TO YOU.
YAAAH

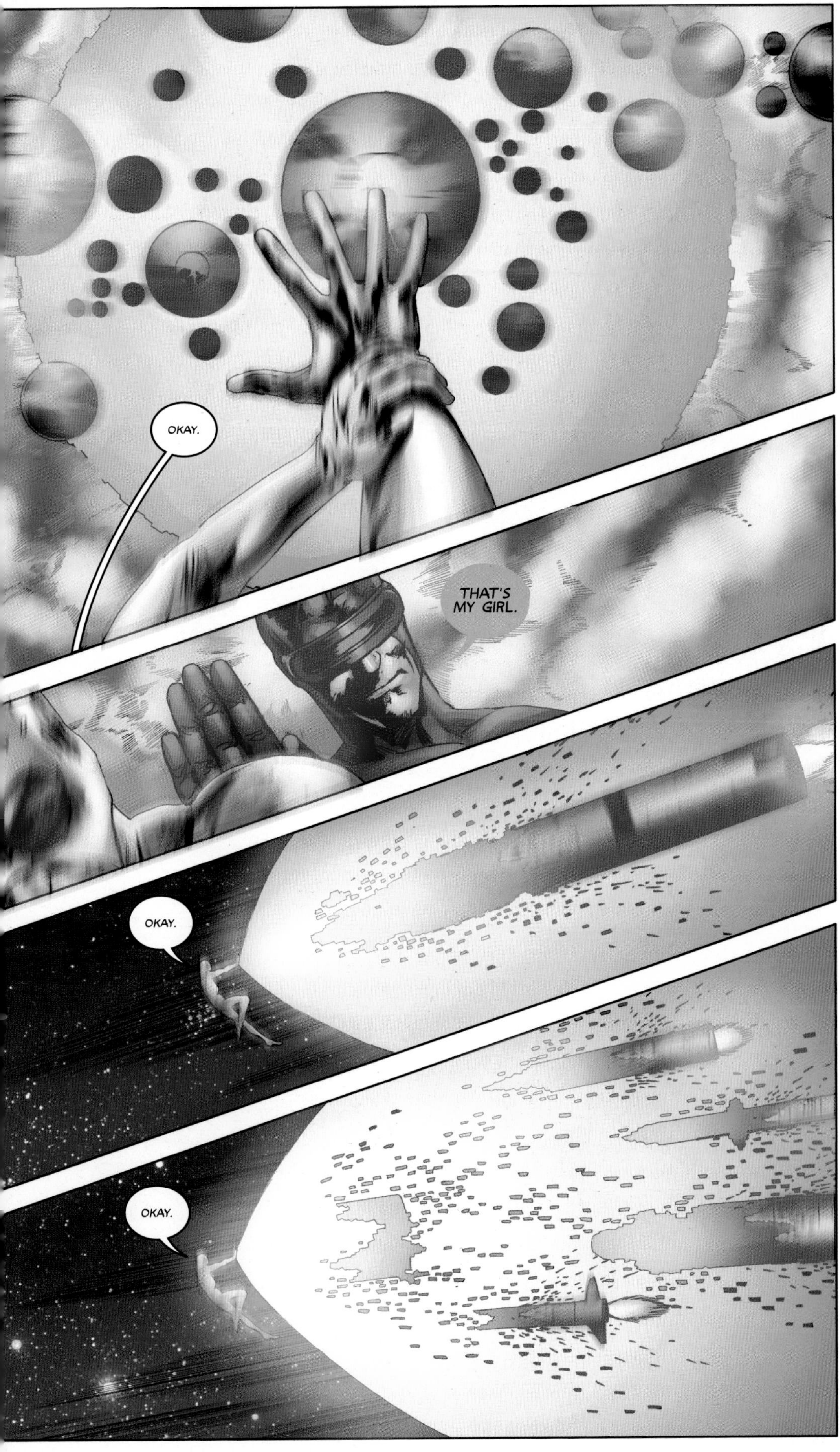
OKAY.
THAT'S MY GIRL.
OKAY.
OKAY.

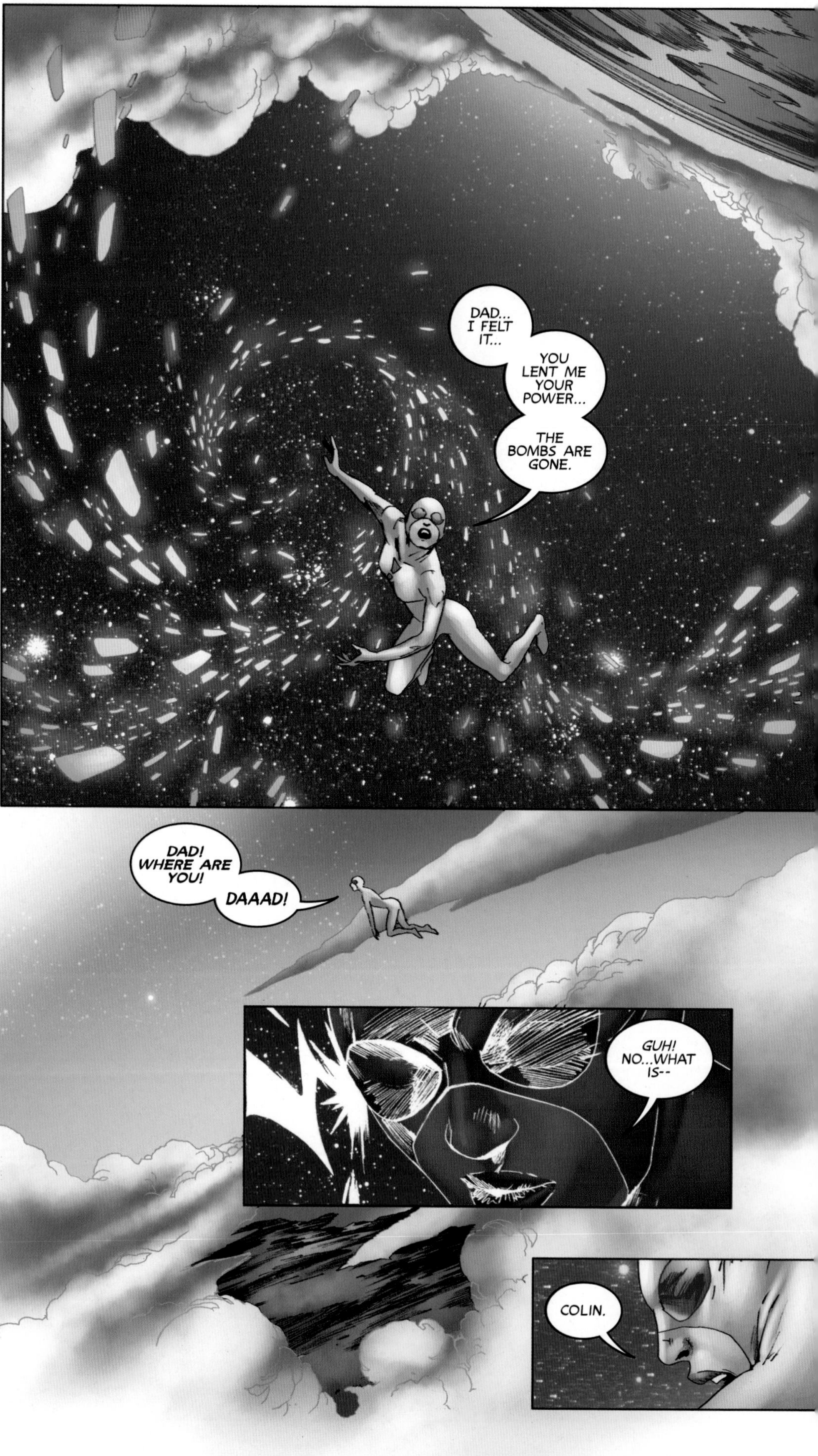
DAD... I FELT IT...
YOU LENT ME YOUR POWER...
THE BOMBS ARE GONE.
DAD! WHERE ARE YOU!
DAAAD!
GUH! NO...WHAT IS--
COLIN.

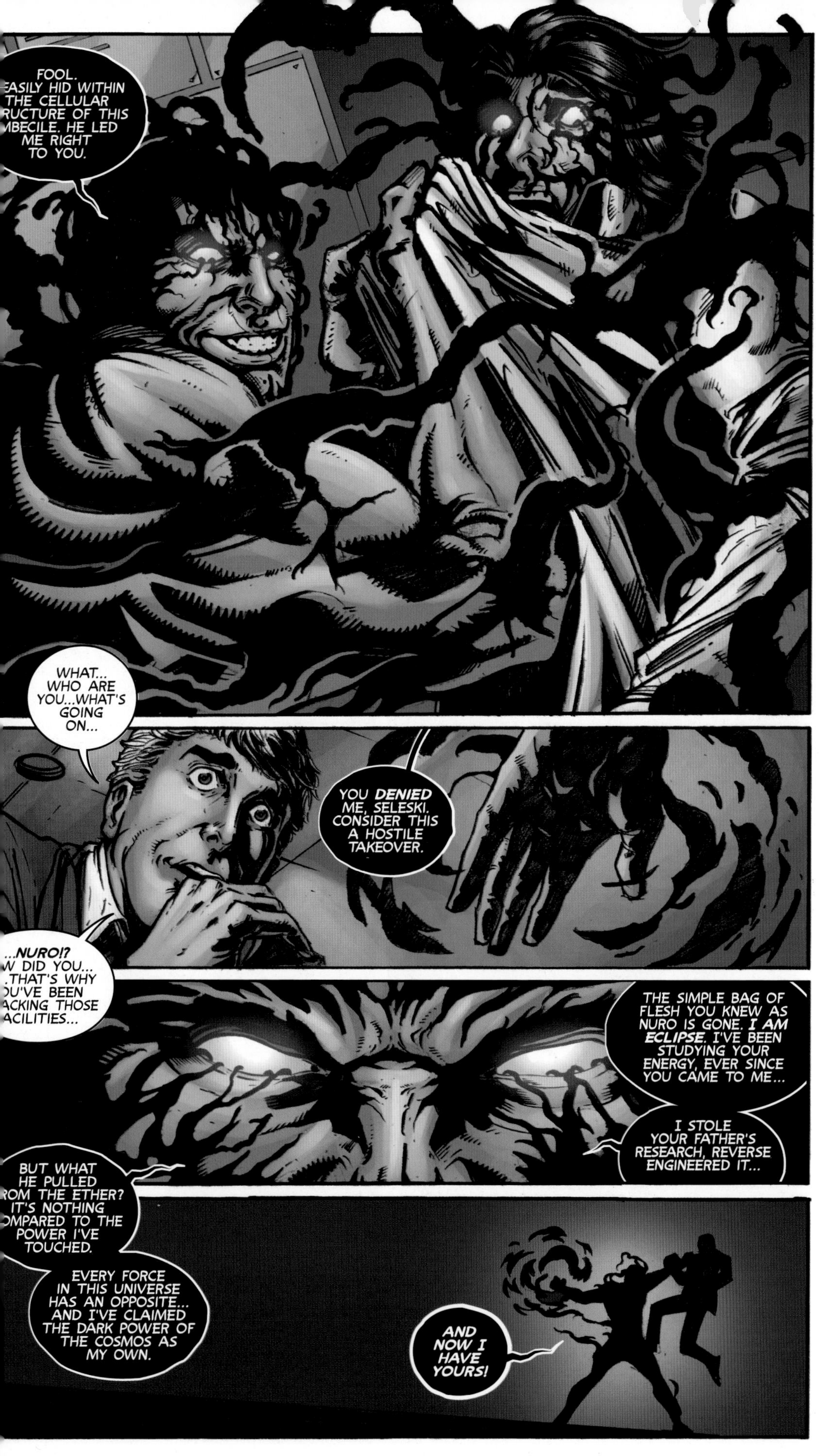
FOOL. EASILY HID WITHIN THE CELLULAR RUCTURE OF THIS MBECILE. HE LED ME RIGHT TO YOU.
WHAT... WHO ARE YOU...WHAT'S GOING ON...
YOU **DENIED** ME, SELESKI. CONSIDER THIS A HOSTILE TAKEOVER.
...**NURO!?** W DID YOU... .THAT'S WHY OU'VE BEEN ACKING THOSE ACILITIES...
THE SIMPLE BAG OF FLESH YOU KNEW AS NURO IS GONE. ***I AM ECLIPSE***. I'VE BEEN STUDYING YOUR ENERGY, EVER SINCE YOU CAME TO ME...
I STOLE YOUR FATHER'S RESEARCH, REVERSE ENGINEERED IT...
BUT WHAT HE PULLED ROM THE ETHER? IT'S NOTHING OMPARED TO THE POWER I'VE TOUCHED.
EVERY FORCE IN THIS UNIVERSE HAS AN OPPOSITE... AND I'VE CLAIMED THE DARK POWER OF THE COSMOS AS MY OWN.
AND NOW I HAVE YOURS!

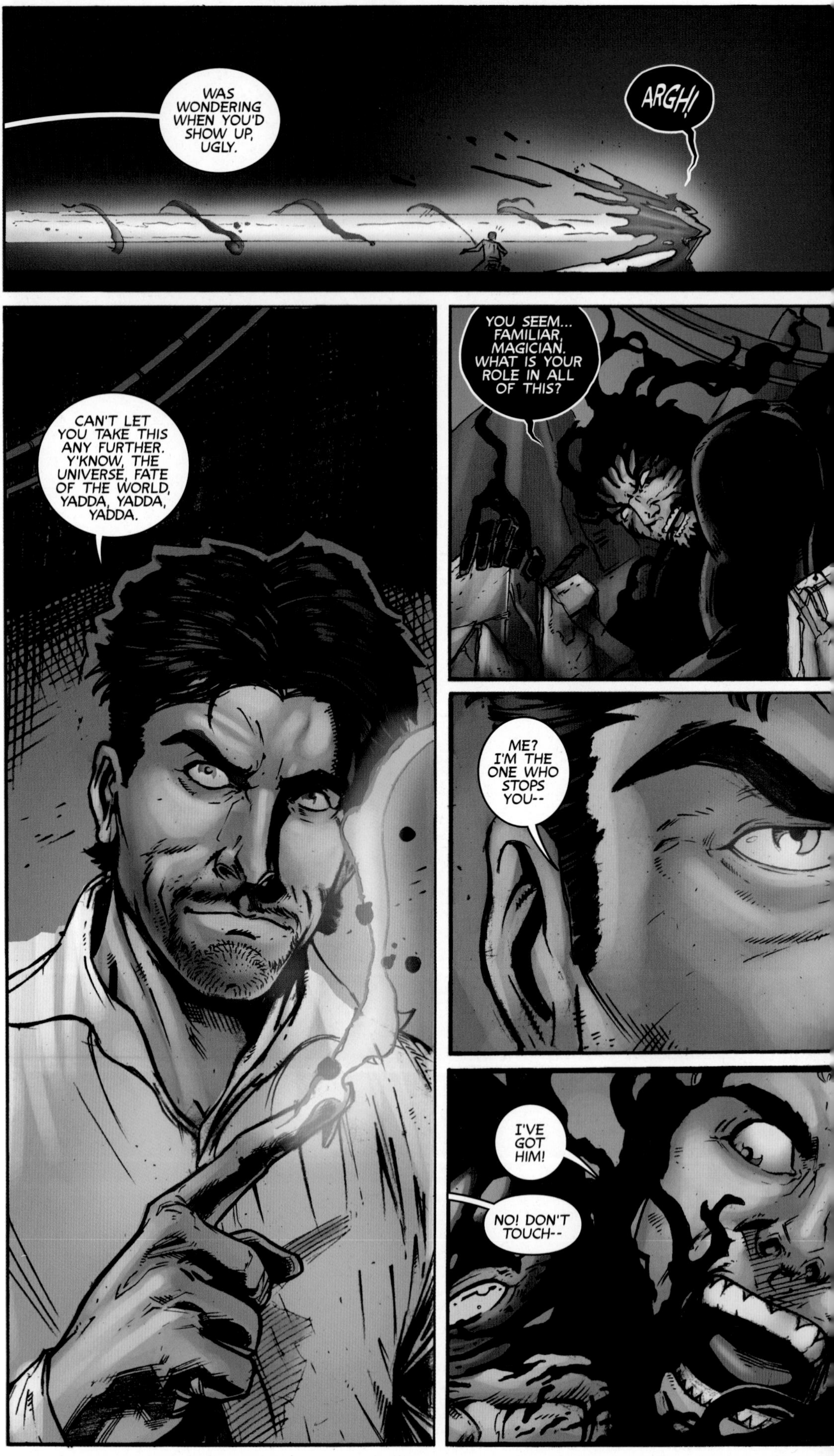
WAS WONDERING WHEN YOU'D SHOW UP, UGLY.
ARGH!
CAN'T LET YOU TAKE THIS ANY FURTHER. Y'KNOW, THE UNIVERSE, FATE OF THE WORLD, YADDA, YADDA, YADDA.
YOU SEEM... FAMILIAR, MAGICIAN. WHAT IS YOUR ROLE IN ALL OF THIS?
ME? I'M THE ONE WHO STOPS YOU--
I'VE GOT HIM!
NO! DON'T TOUCH--

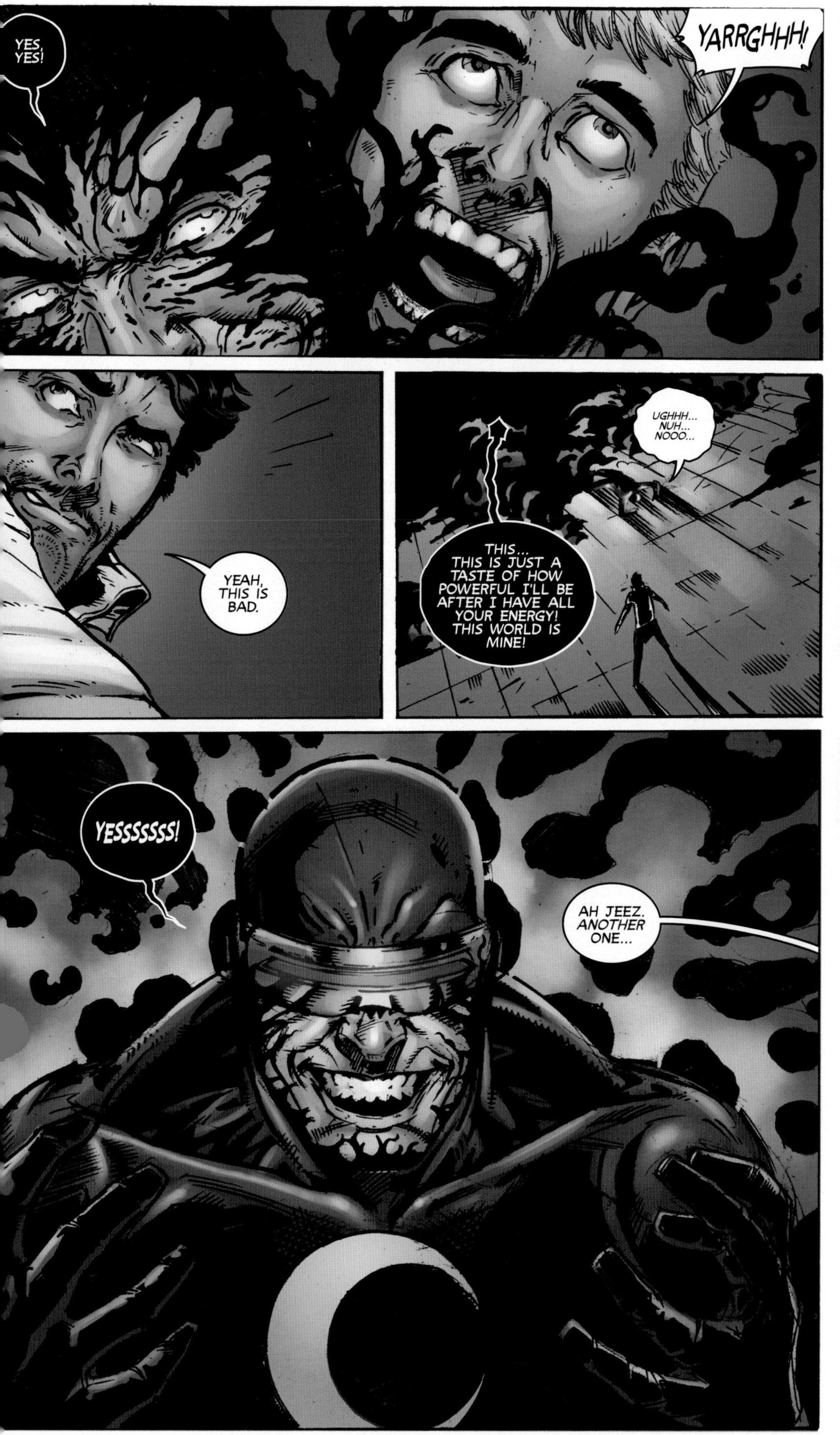
YES, YES!
YARRGHHH!
YEAH, THIS IS BAD.
UGHHH... NUH... NOOO...
THIS... THIS IS JUST A TASTE OF HOW POWERFUL I'LL BE AFTER I HAVE ALL YOUR ENERGY! THIS WORLD IS MINE!
YESSSSSSS!
AH JEEZ. ANOTHER ONE...

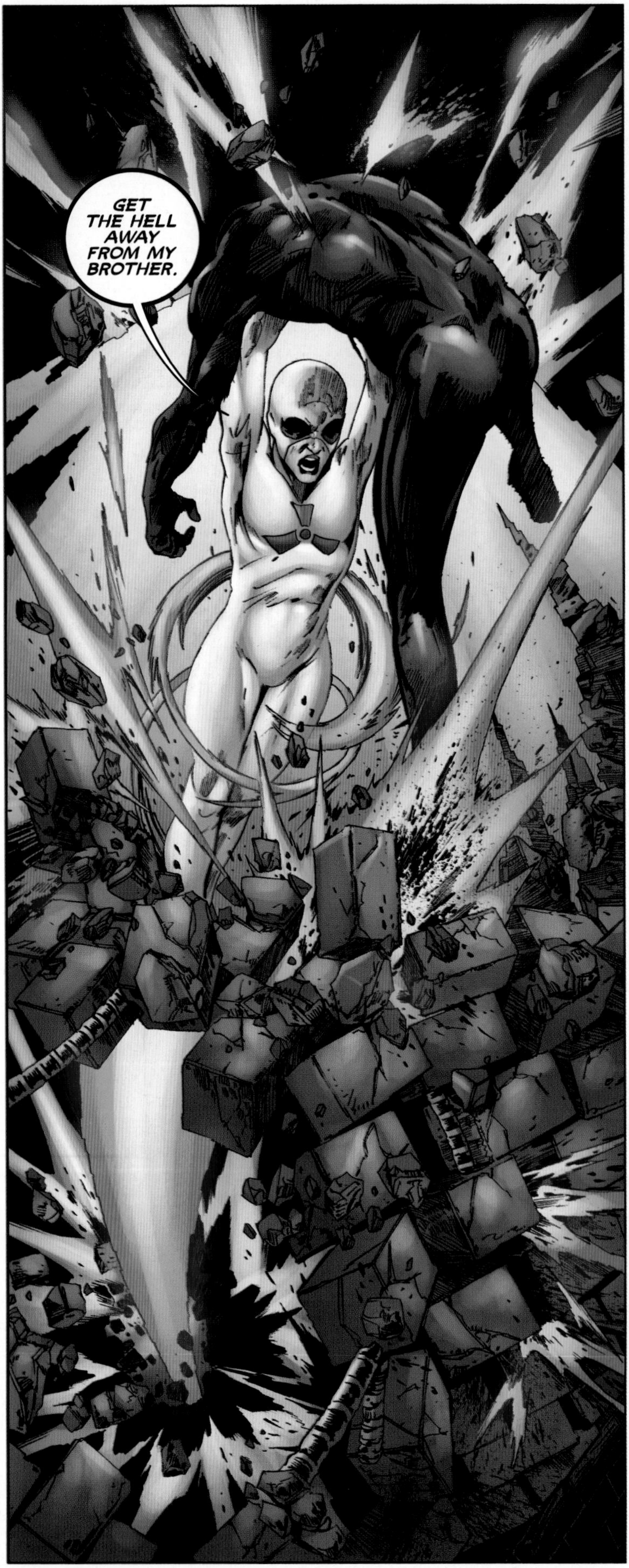
GET THE HELL AWAY FROM MY BROTHER.

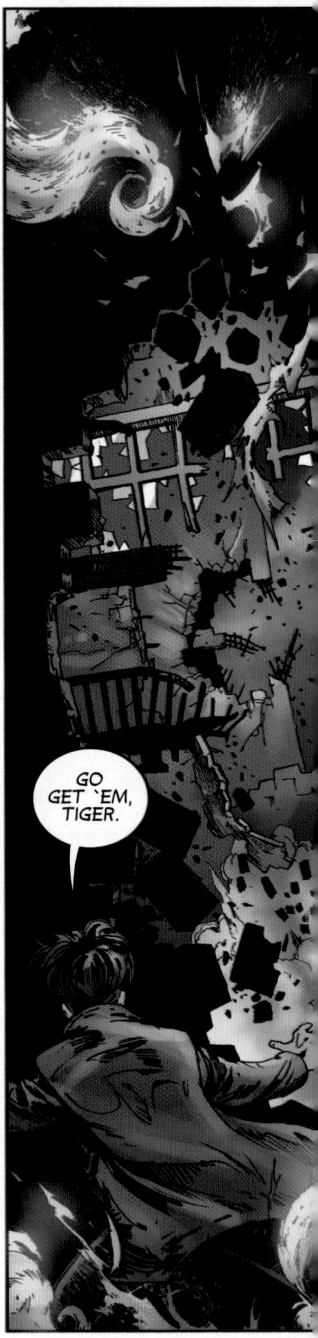
GO GET `EM, TIGER.

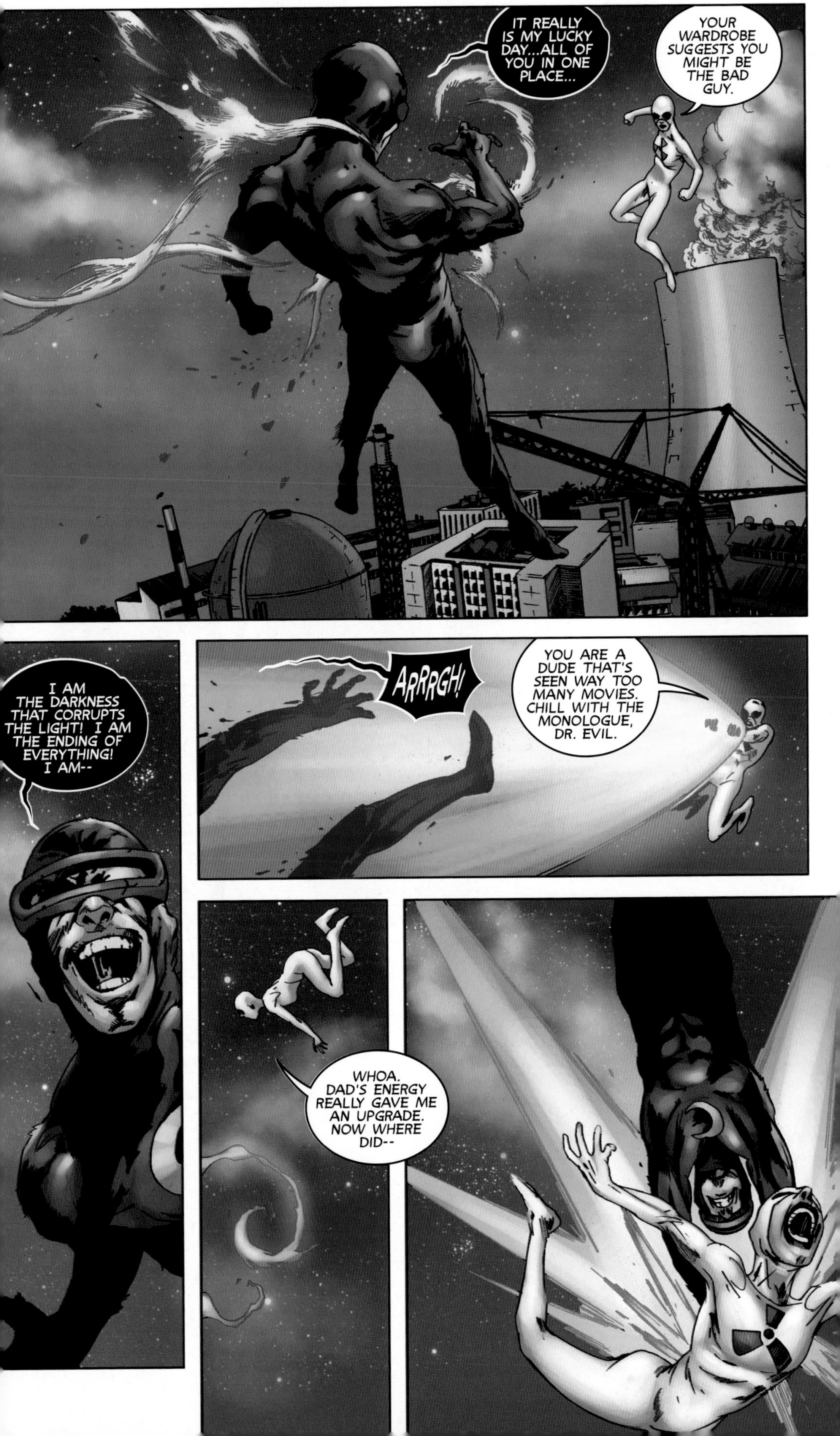
IT REALLY IS MY LUCKY DAY...ALL OF YOU IN ONE PLACE...
YOUR WARDROBE SUGGESTS YOU MIGHT BE THE BAD GUY.
I AM THE DARKNESS THAT CORRUPTS THE LIGHT! I AM THE ENDING OF EVERYTHING! I AM--
ARRRGH!
YOU ARE A DUDE THAT'S SEEN WAY TOO MANY MOVIES. CHILL WITH THE MONOLOGUE, DR. EVIL.
WHOA. DAD'S ENERGY REALLY GAVE ME AN UPGRADE. NOW WHERE DID--

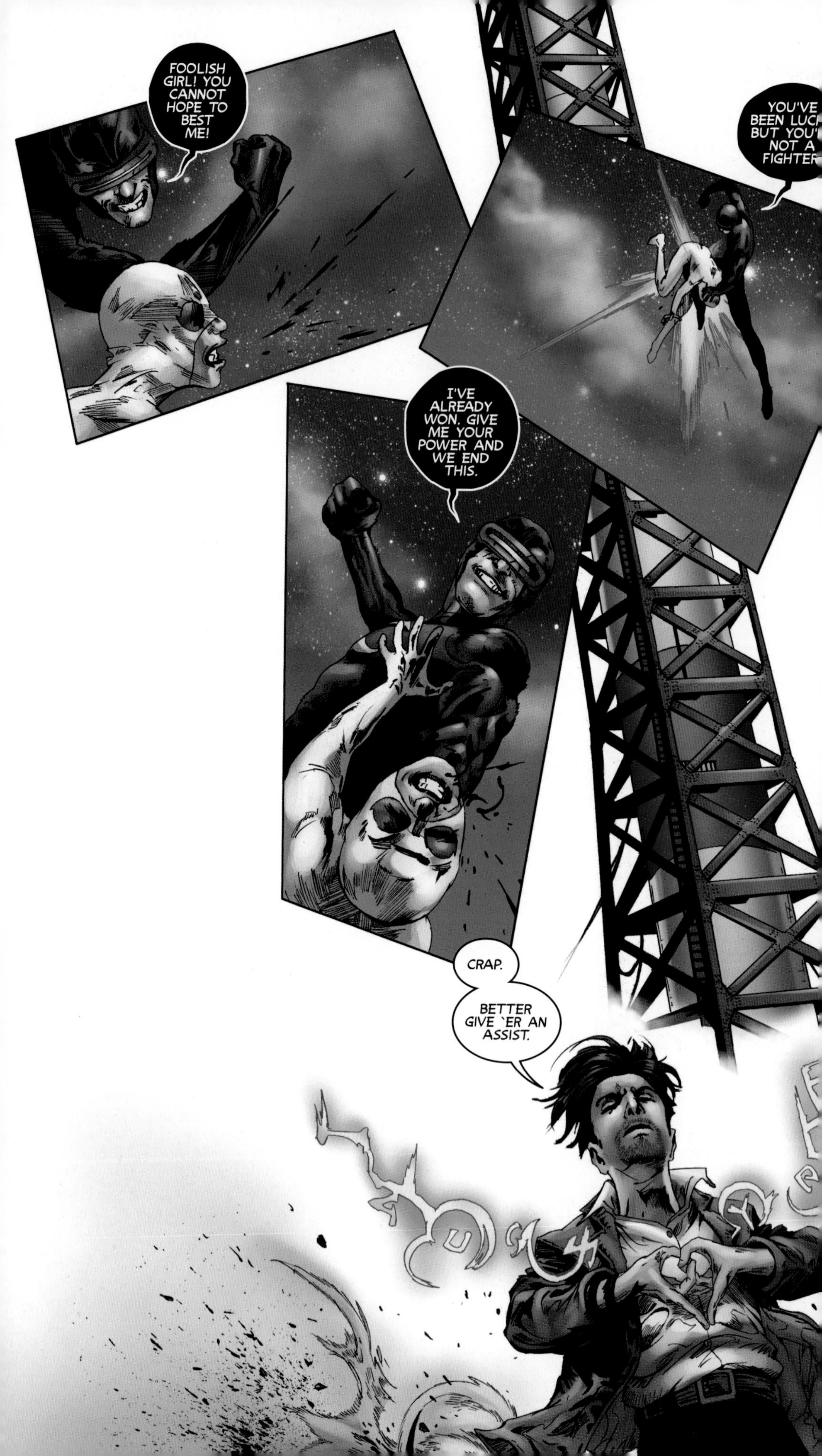
FOOLISH GIRL! YOU CANNOT HOPE TO BEST ME!
YOU'VE BEEN LUC BUT YOU' NOT A FIGHTER
I'VE ALREADY WON. GIVE ME YOUR POWER AND WE END THIS.
CRAP.
BETTER GIVE `ER AN ASSIST.

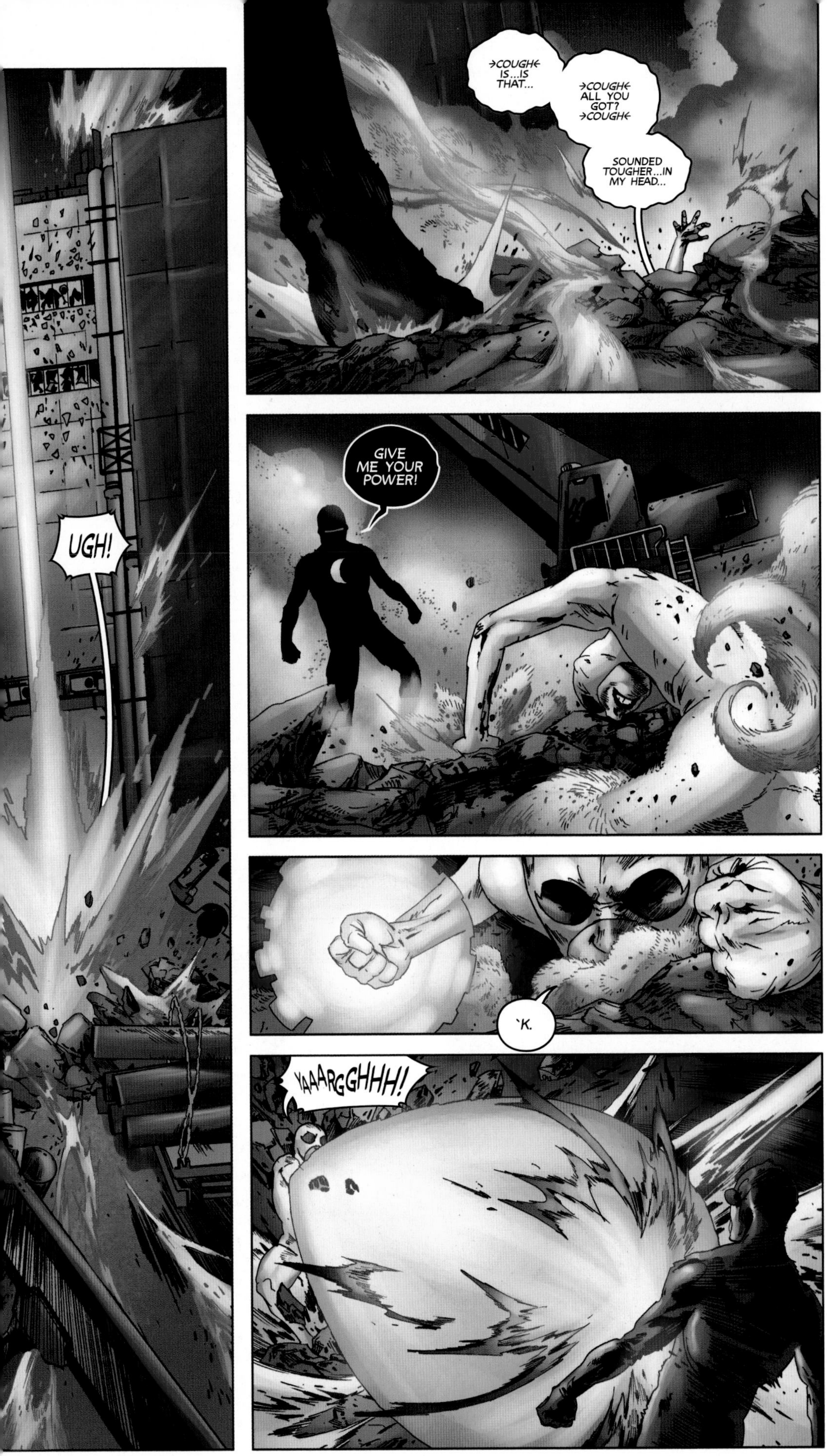
UGH!
→COUGH← IS...IS THAT...
→COUGH← ALL YOU GOT? →COUGH←
SOUNDED TOUGHER...IN MY HEAD...
GIVE ME YOUR POWER!
`K.
YAAARGGHHH!

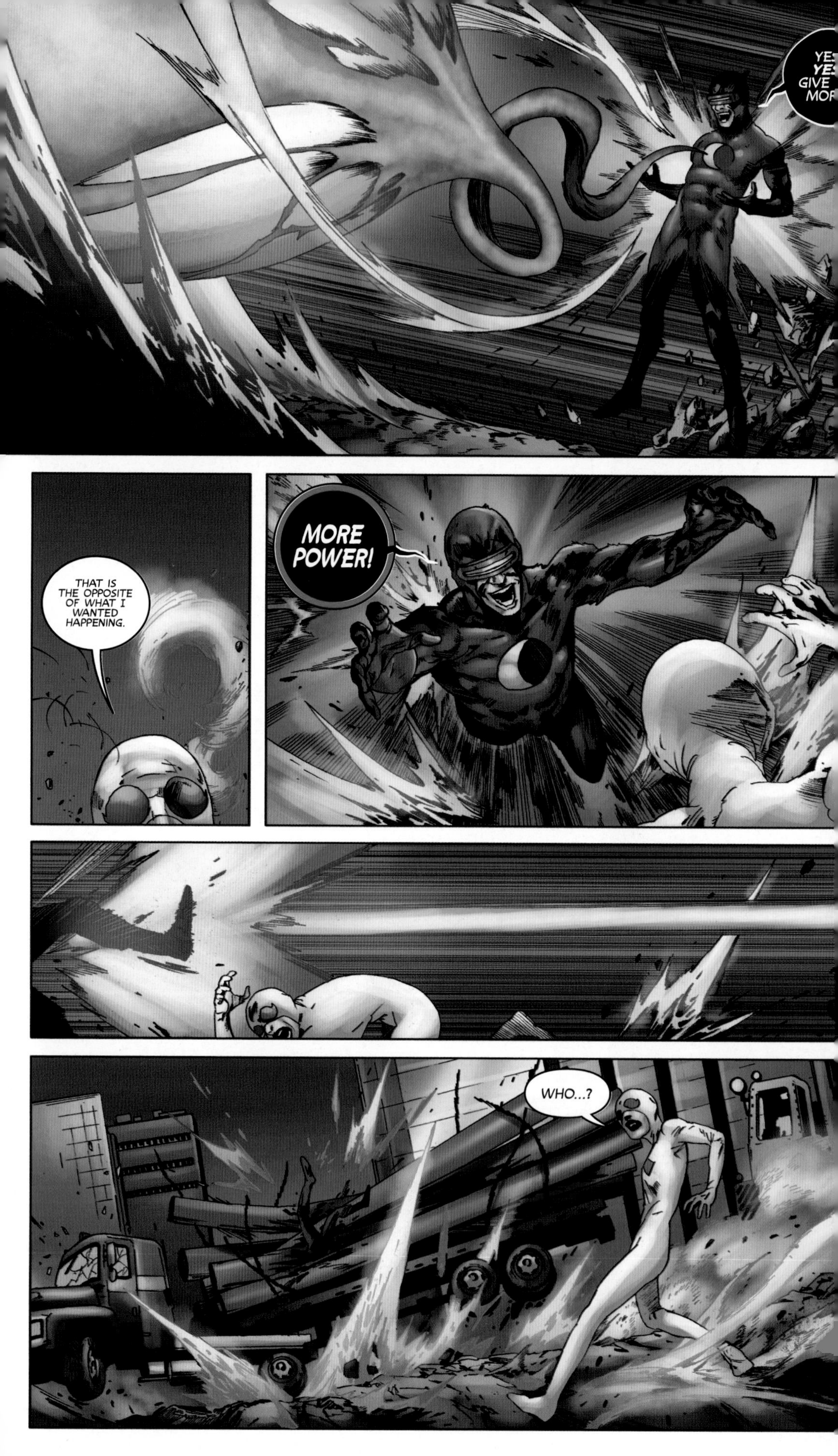
THAT IS THE OPPOSITE OF WHAT I WANTED HAPPENING.
MORE POWER!
WHO...?

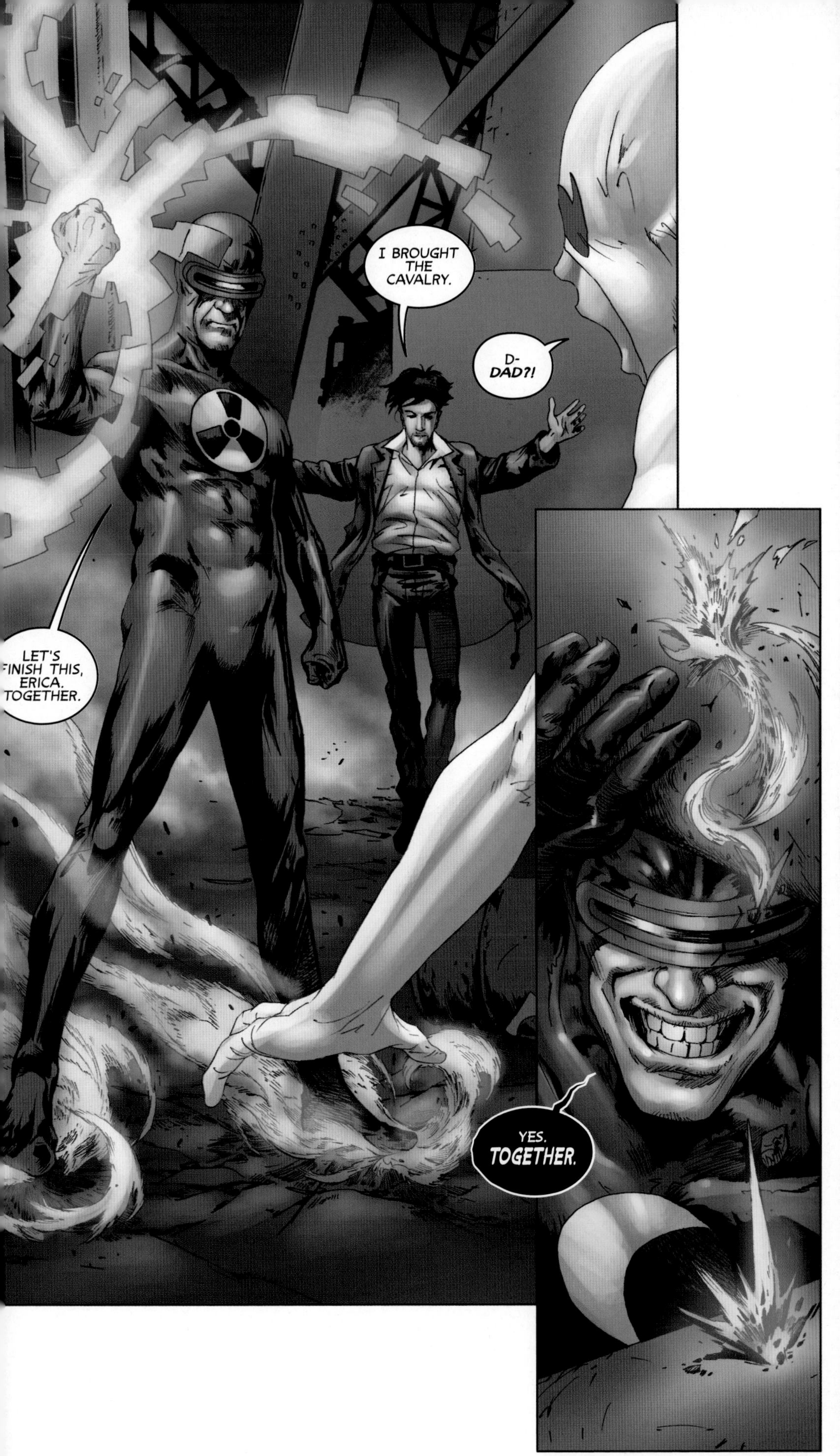
I BROUGHT THE CAVALRY.
D-DAD?!
LET'S FINISH THIS, ERICA. TOGETHER.
YES. TOGETHER.

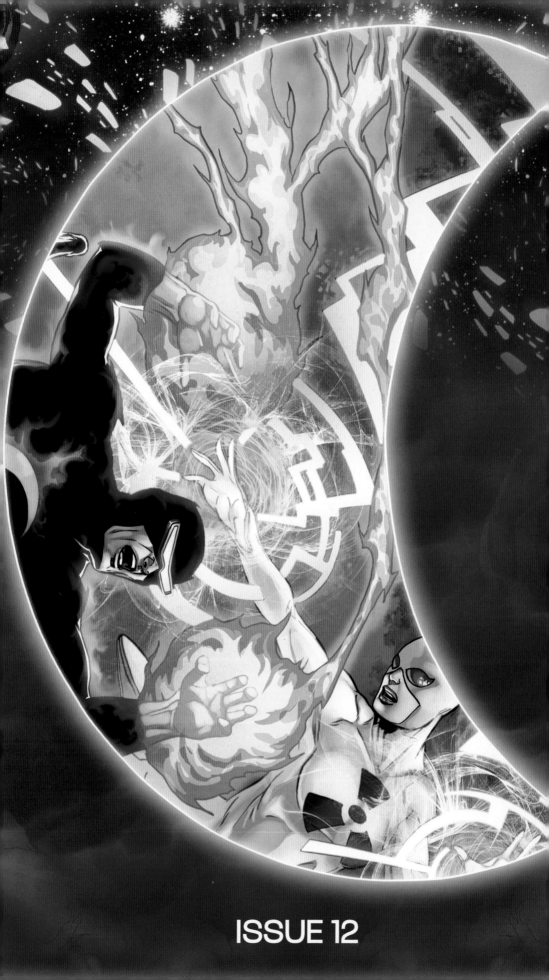

ISSUE 12

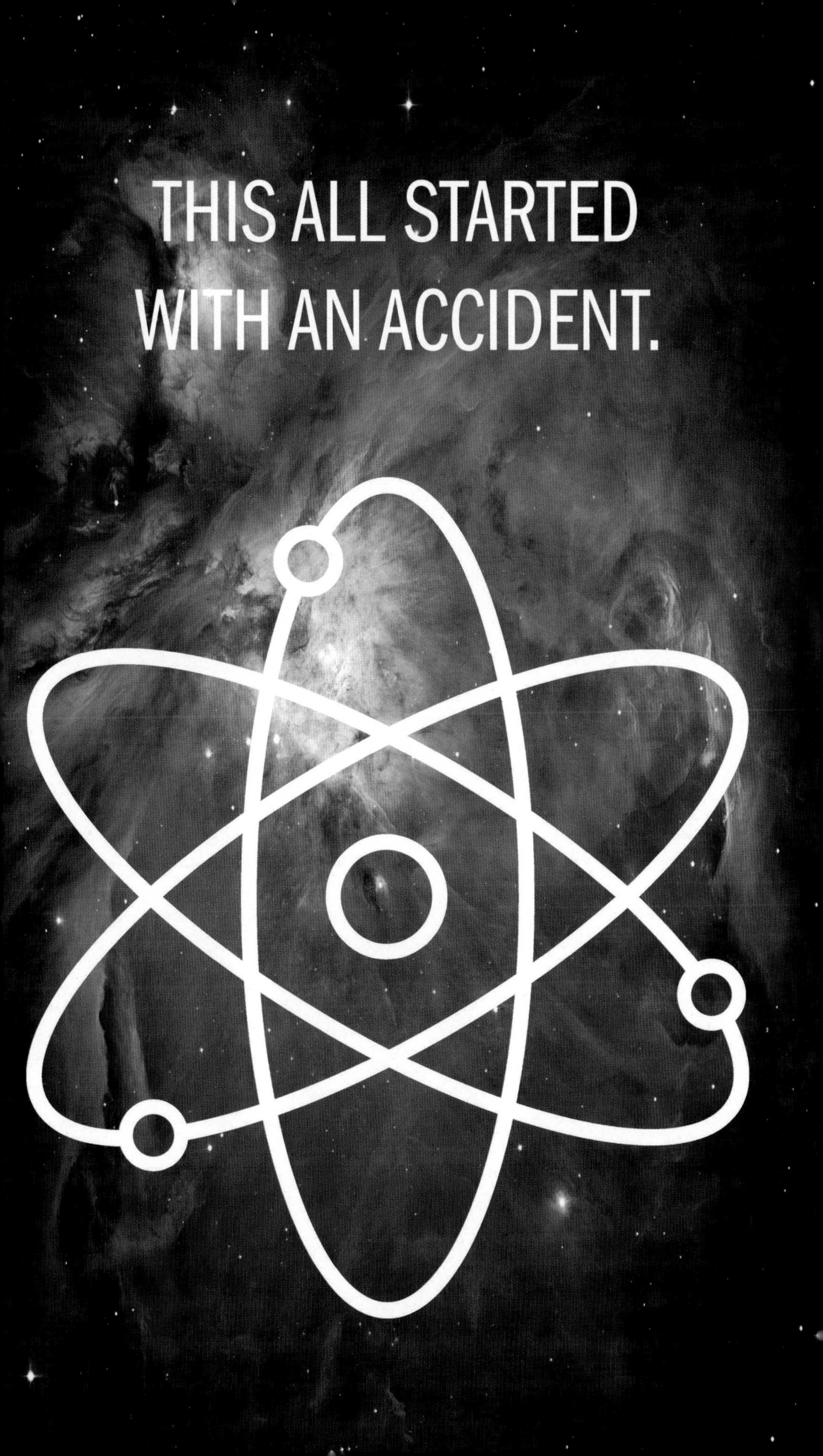
THIS ALL STARTED
WITH AN ACCIDENT.

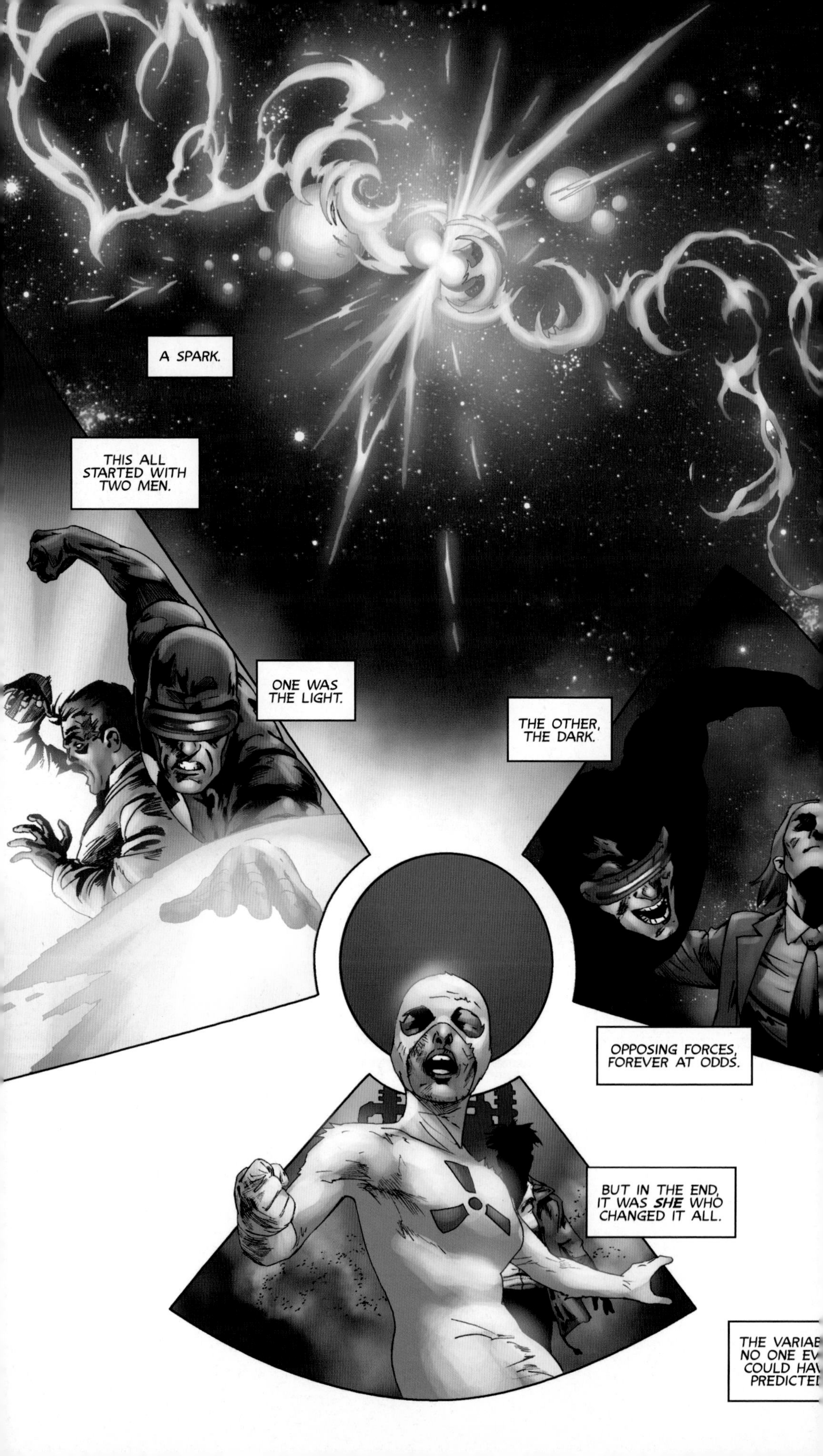
A SPARK.
THIS ALL STARTED WITH TWO MEN.
ONE WAS THE LIGHT.
THE OTHER, THE DARK.
OPPOSING FORCES, FOREVER AT ODDS.
BUT IN THE END, IT WAS *SHE* WHO CHANGED IT ALL.
THE VARIAB NO ONE EV COULD HAV PREDICTE

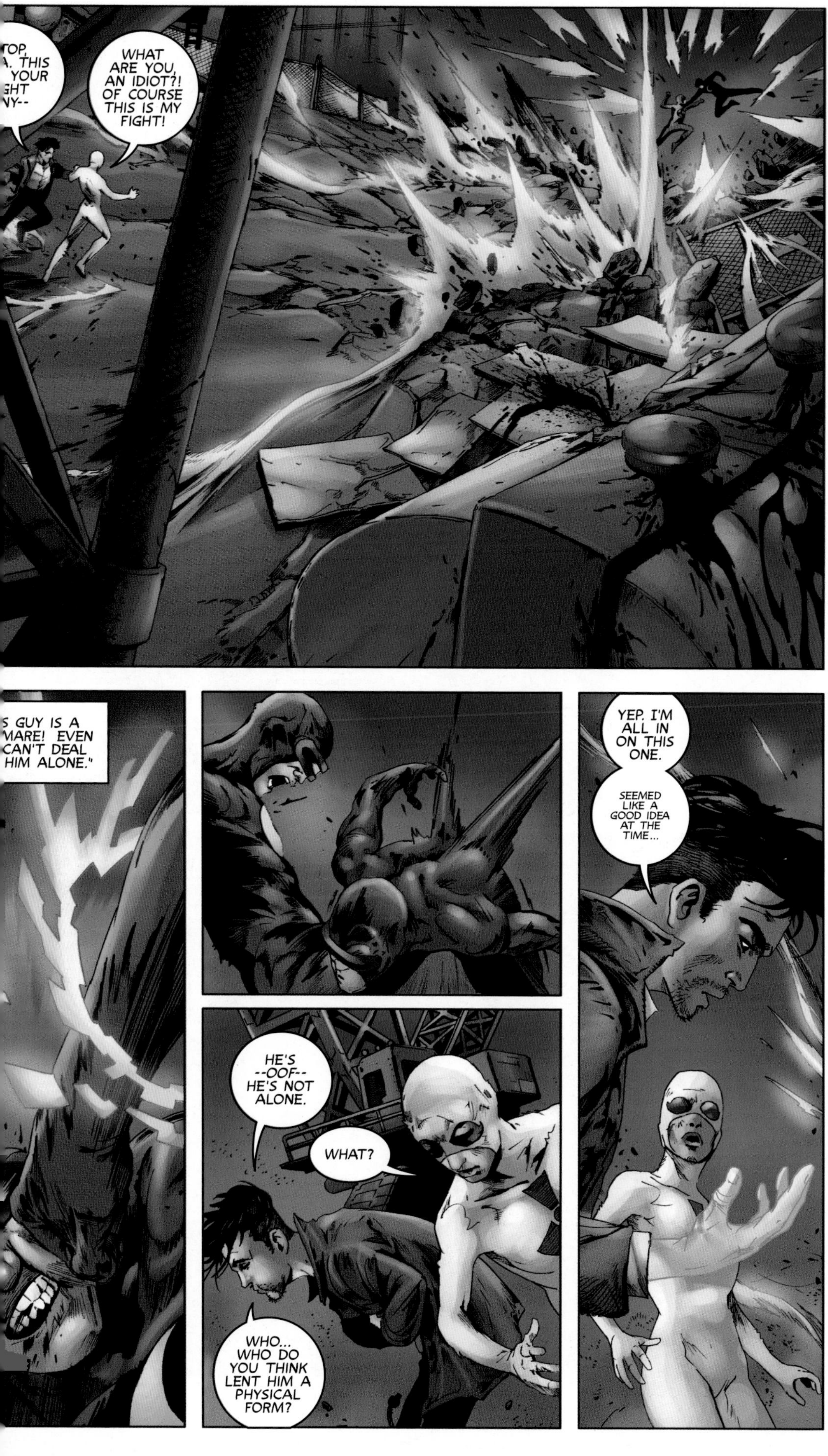
TOP, A. THIS YOUR GHT NY--
WHAT ARE YOU, AN IDIOT?! OF COURSE THIS IS MY FIGHT!
S GUY IS A MARE! EVEN CAN'T DEAL HIM ALONE."
HE'S --OOF-- HE'S NOT ALONE.
WHAT?
WHO... WHO DO YOU THINK LENT HIM A PHYSICAL FORM?
YEP. I'M ALL IN ON THIS ONE.
SEEMED LIKE A GOOD IDEA AT THE TIME...

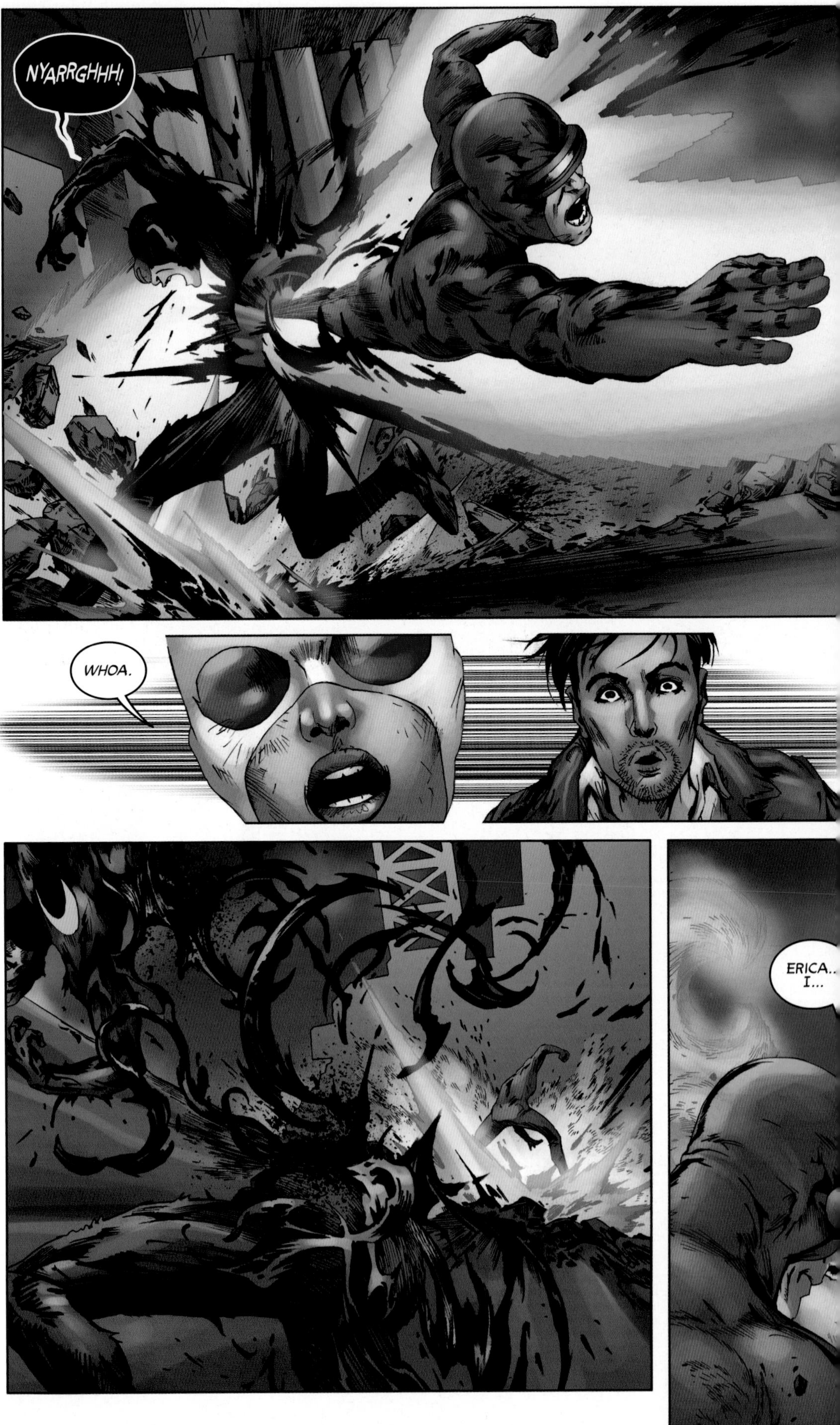
NYARRGHHH!
WHOA.
ERICA...
I...

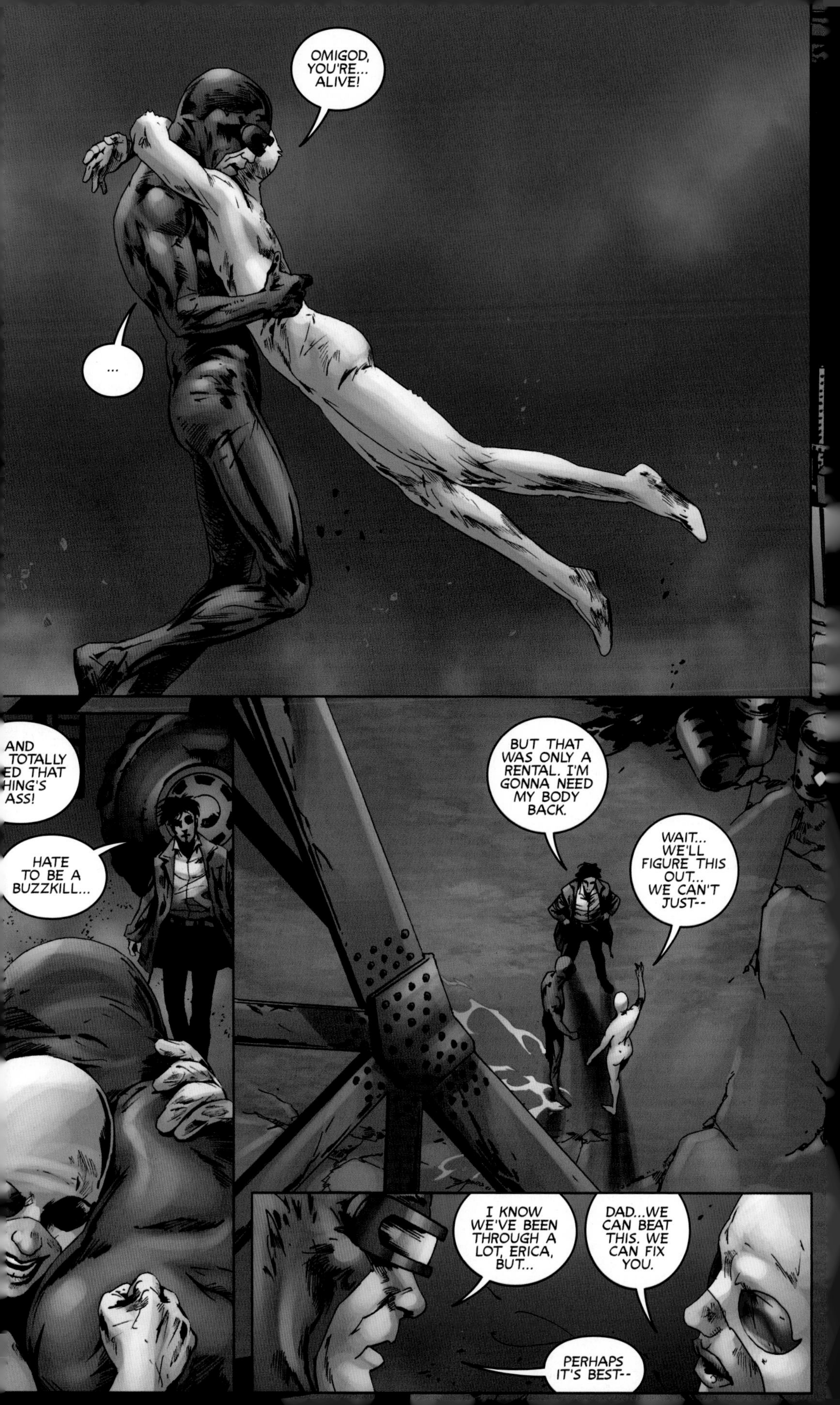
OMIGOD, YOU'RE... ALIVE!
...
AND TOTALLY ED THAT HING'S ASS!
HATE TO BE A BUZZKILL...
BUT THAT WAS ONLY A RENTAL. I'M GONNA NEED MY BODY BACK.
WAIT... WE'LL FIGURE THIS OUT... WE CAN'T JUST--
I KNOW WE'VE BEEN THROUGH A LOT, ERICA, BUT...
DAD...WE CAN BEAT THIS. WE CAN FIX YOU.
PERHAPS IT'S BEST--

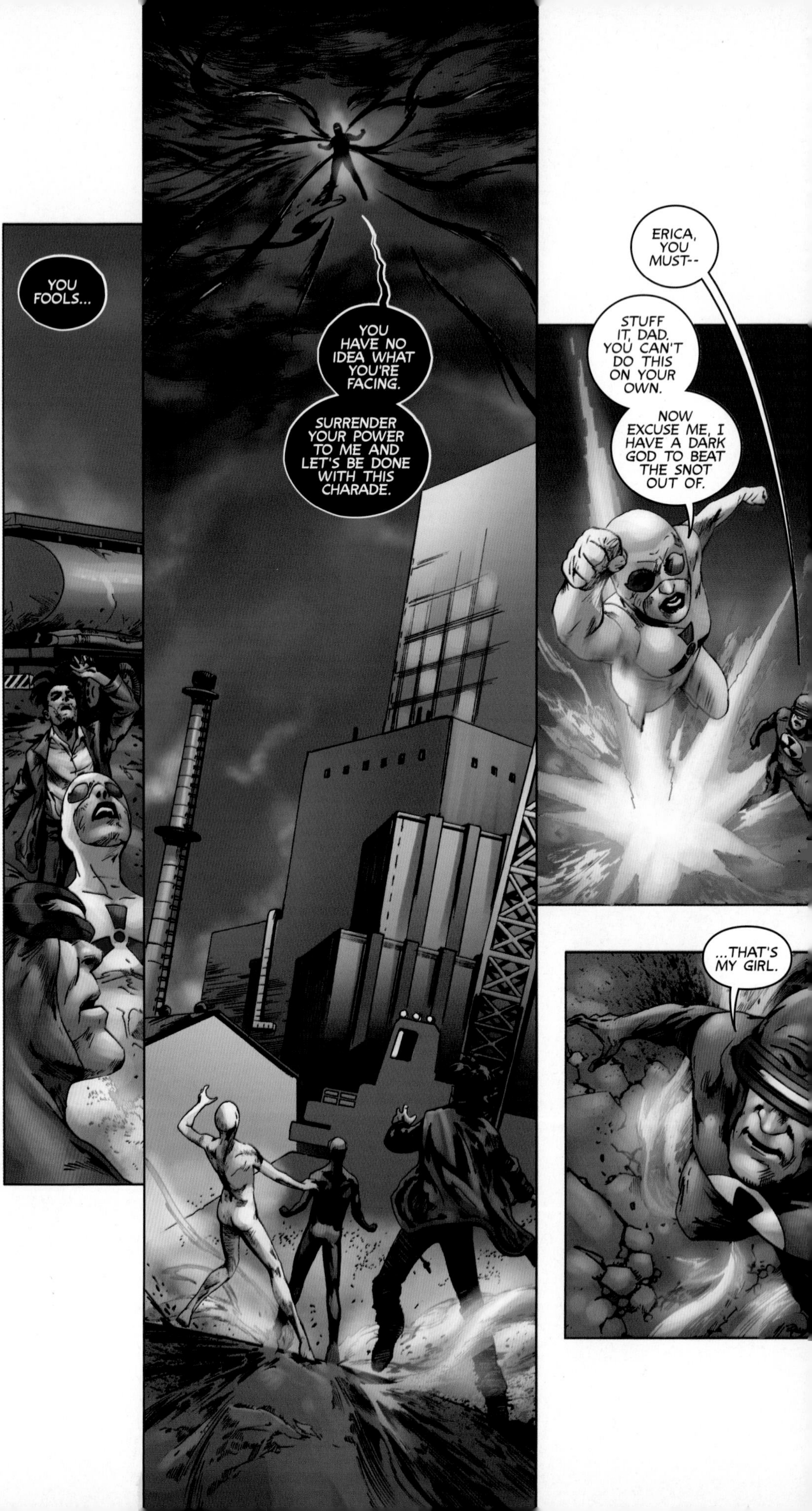
YOU FOOLS...
YOU HAVE NO IDEA WHAT YOU'RE FACING.
SURRENDER YOUR POWER TO ME AND LET'S BE DONE WITH THIS CHARADE.
ERICA, YOU MUST--
STUFF IT, DAD. YOU CAN'T DO THIS ON YOUR OWN.
NOW EXCUSE ME, I HAVE A DARK GOD TO BEAT THE SNOT OUT OF.
...THAT'S MY GIRL.

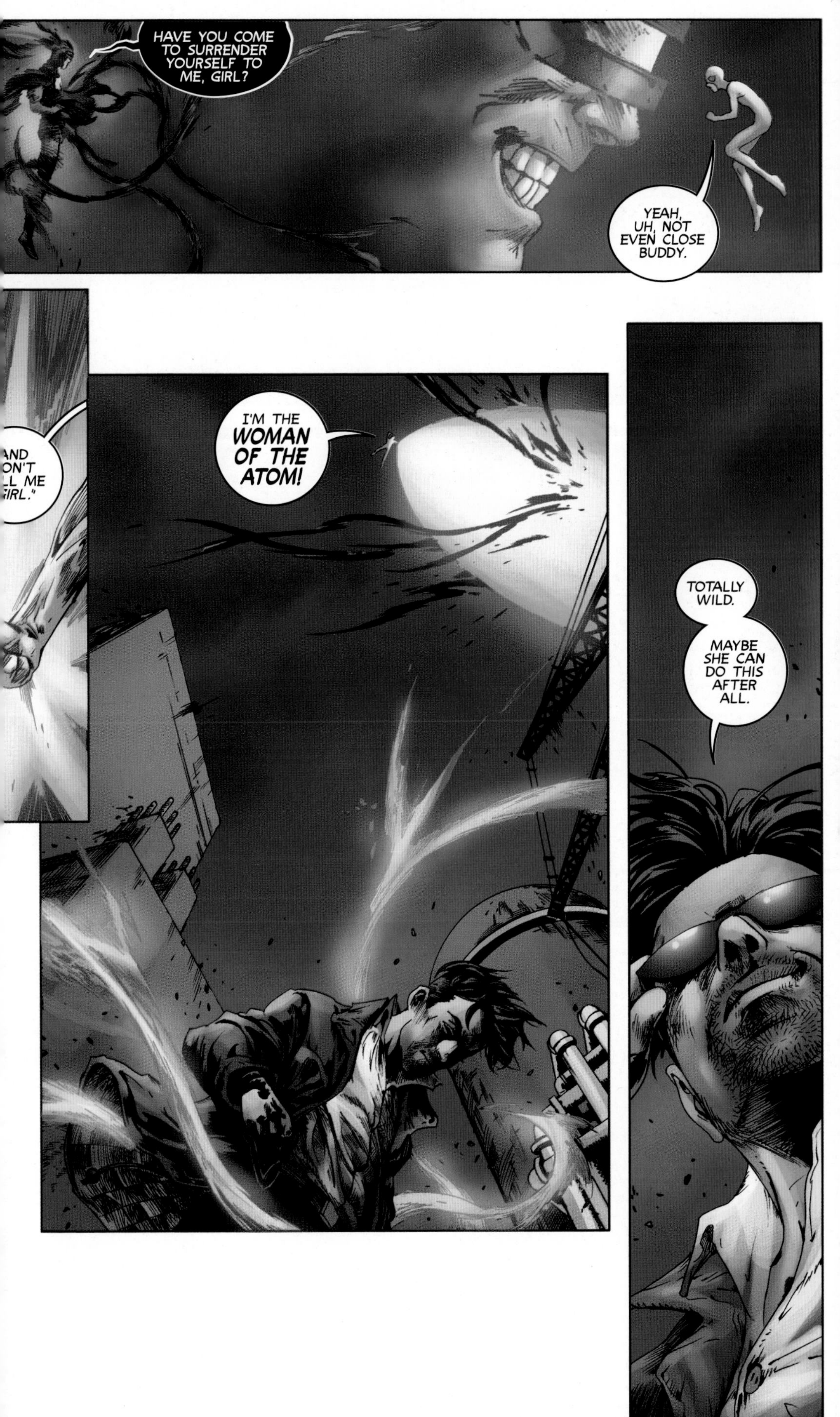
HAVE YOU COME TO SURRENDER YOURSELF TO ME, GIRL?
YEAH, UH, NOT EVEN CLOSE BUDDY.
AND ...ON'T ...LL ME ...GIRL."
I'M THE WOMAN OF THE ATOM!
TOTALLY WILD.
MAYBE SHE CAN DO THIS AFTER ALL.

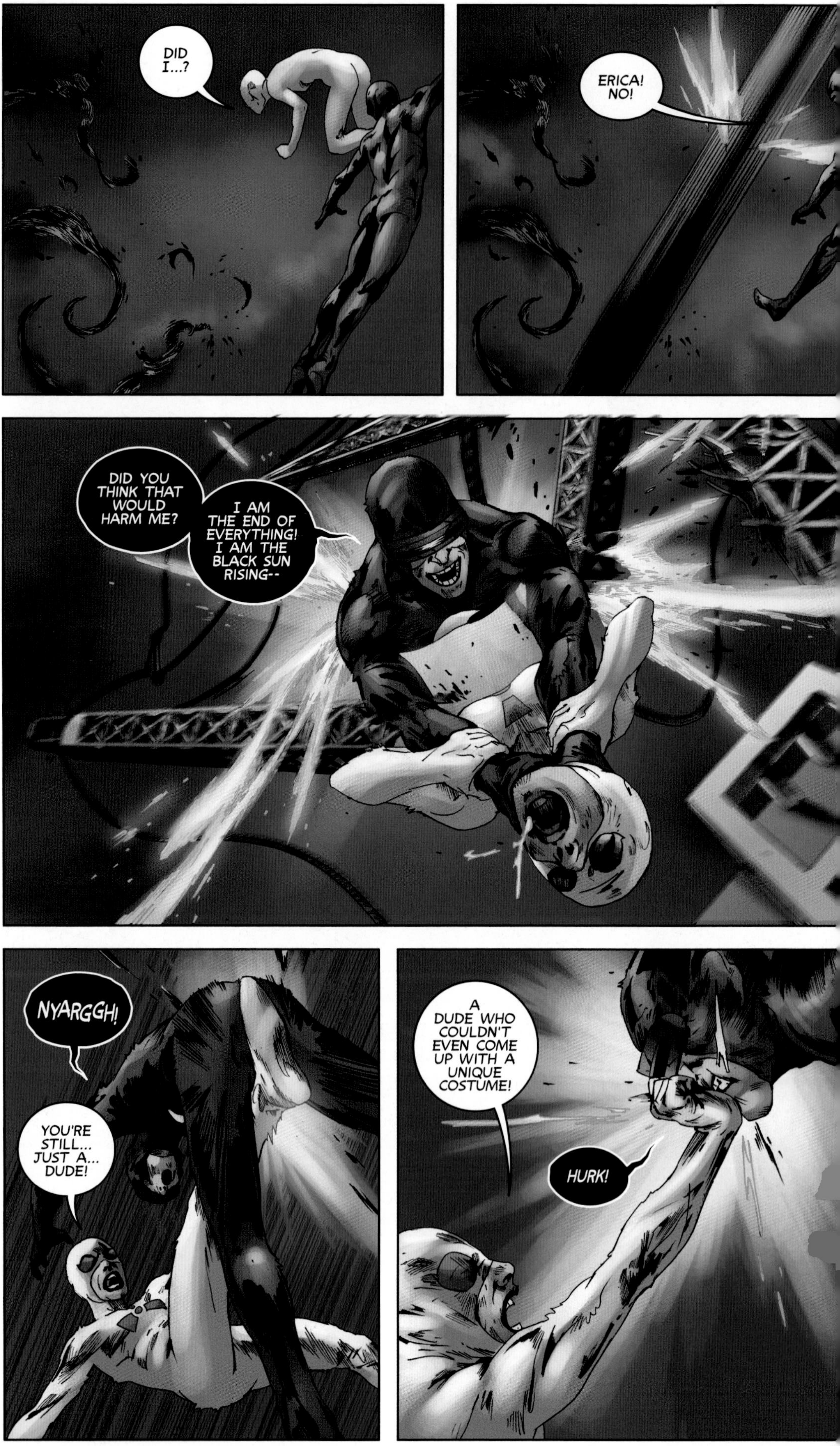
DID I...?
ERICA! NO!
DID YOU THINK THAT WOULD HARM ME?
I AM THE END OF EVERYTHING! I AM THE BLACK SUN RISING--
NYARGGH!
YOU'RE STILL... JUST A... DUDE!
A DUDE WHO COULDN'T EVEN COME UP WITH A UNIQUE COSTUME!
HURK!

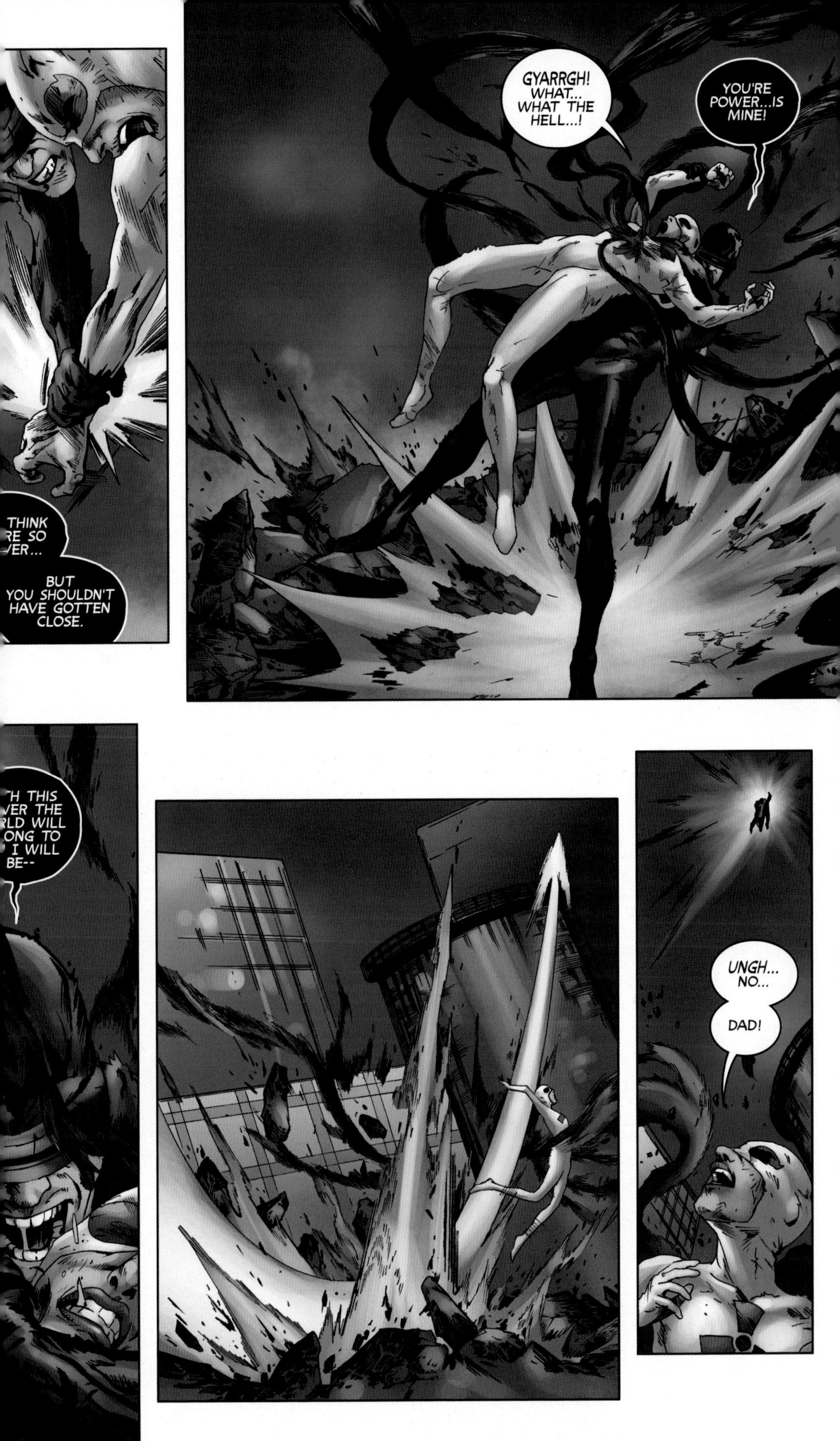
THINK
RE SO
VER...
BUT YOU SHOULDN'T HAVE GOTTEN CLOSE.
GYARRGH! WHAT... WHAT THE HELL...!
YOU'RE POWER...IS MINE!
TH THIS VER THE RLD WILL ONG TO I WILL BE--
UNGH... NO...
DAD!

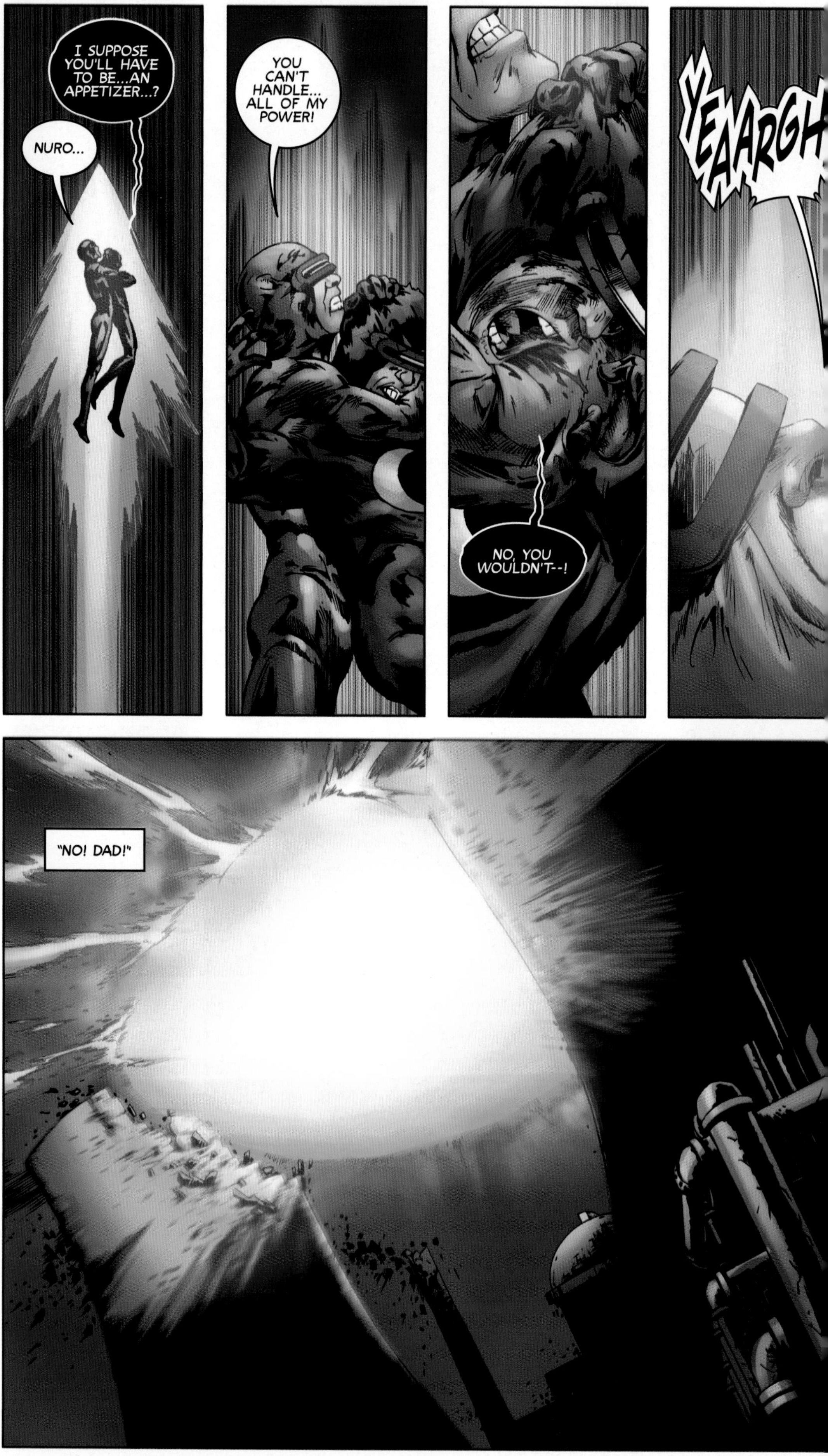
I SUPPOSE YOU'LL HAVE TO BE...AN APPETIZER...?
NURO...
YOU CAN'T HANDLE... ALL OF MY POWER!
NO, YOU WOULDN'T--!
YEAARGH
"NO! DAD!"

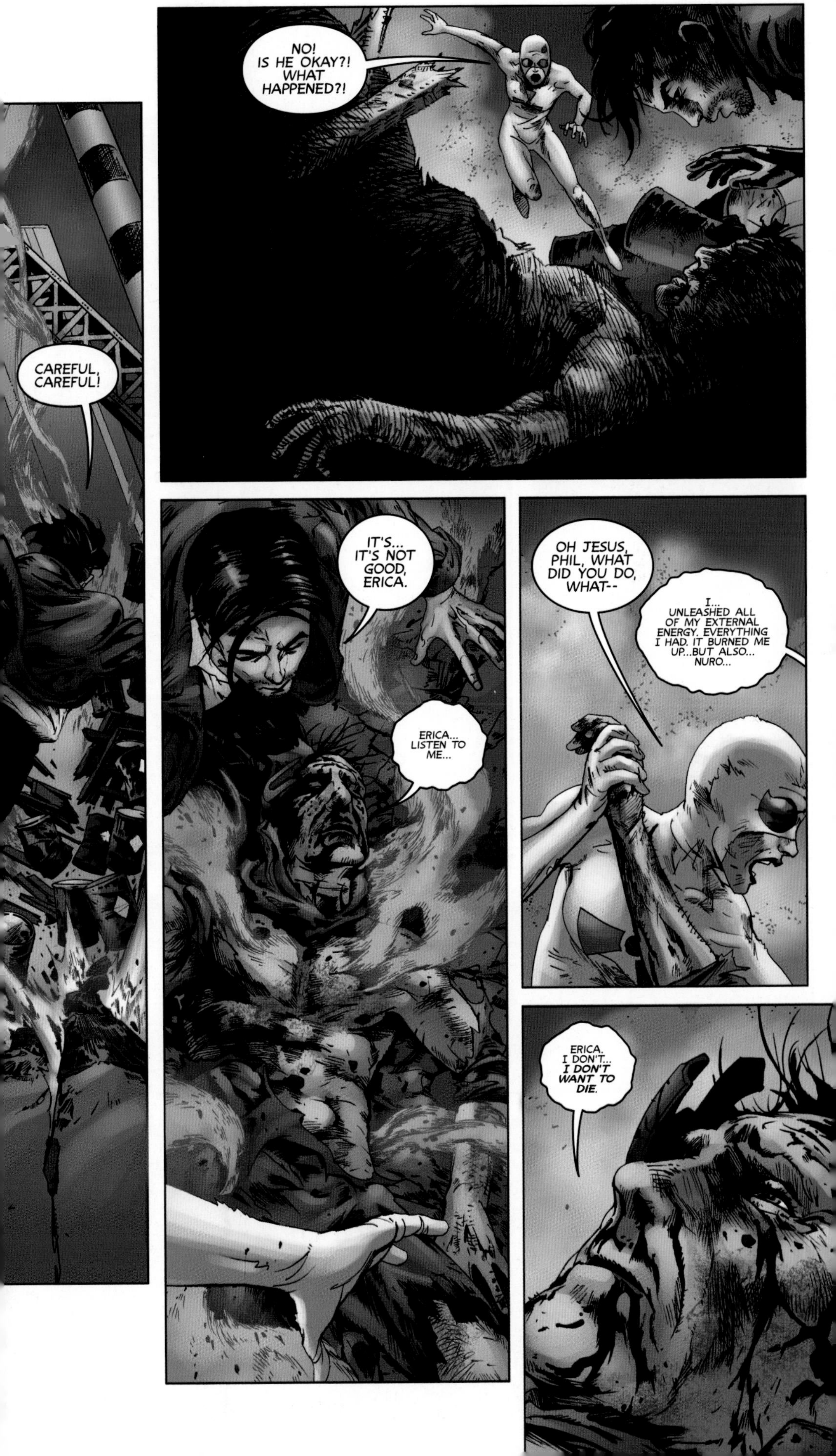
CAREFUL, CAREFUL!
NO! IS HE OKAY?! WHAT HAPPENED?!
IT'S... IT'S NOT GOOD, ERICA.
ERICA... LISTEN TO ME...
OH JESUS, PHIL, WHAT DID YOU DO, WHAT--
I... UNLEASHED ALL OF MY EXTERNAL ENERGY. EVERYTHING I HAD. IT BURNED ME UP...BUT ALSO... NURO...
ERICA. I DON'T... ***I DON'T WANT TO DIE***.

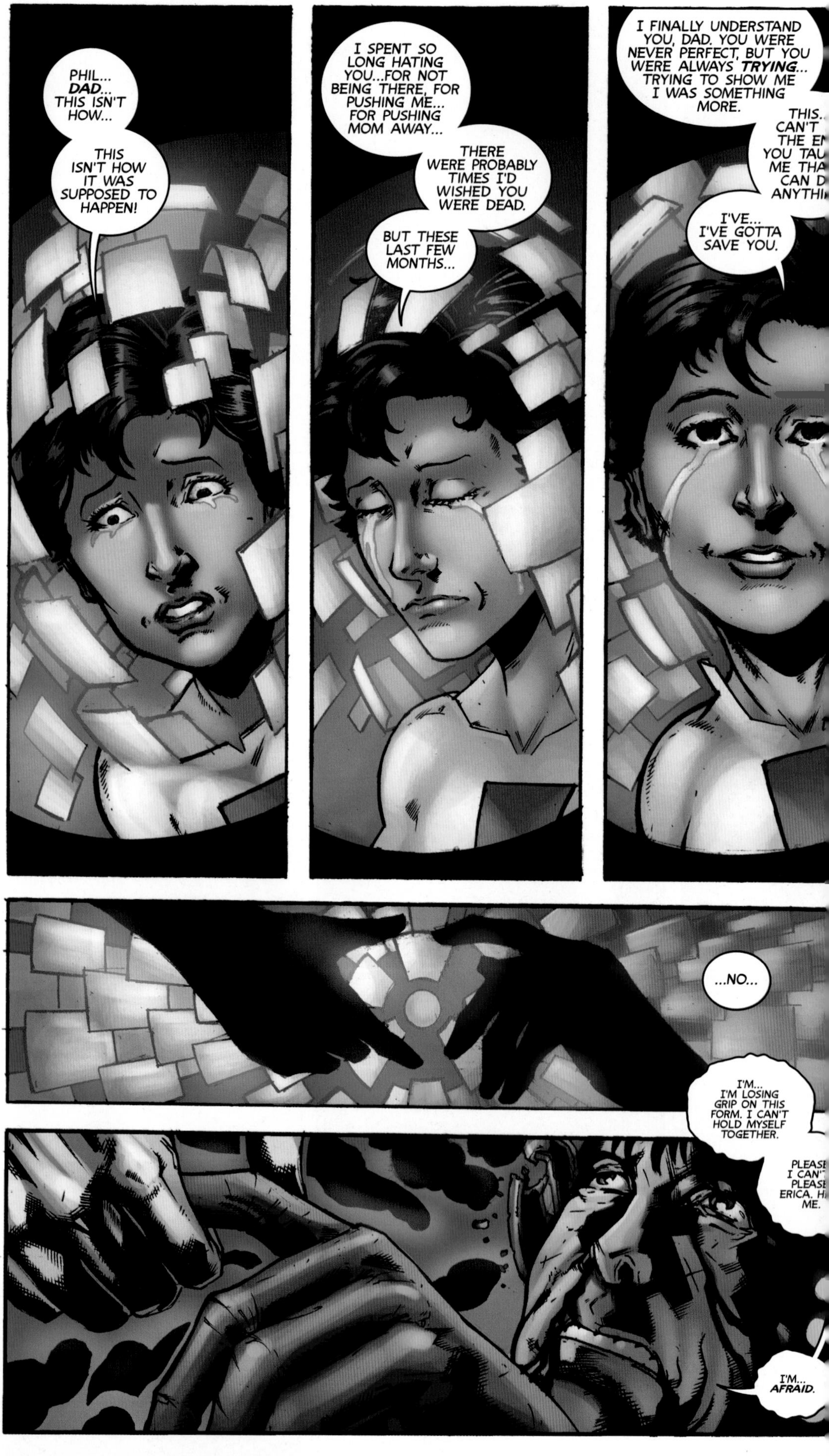
PHIL... DAD... THIS ISN'T HOW...
THIS ISN'T HOW IT WAS SUPPOSED TO HAPPEN!
I SPENT SO LONG HATING YOU...FOR NOT BEING THERE, FOR PUSHING ME... FOR PUSHING MOM AWAY...
THERE WERE PROBABLY TIMES I'D WISHED YOU WERE DEAD.
BUT THESE LAST FEW MONTHS...
I FINALLY UNDERSTAND YOU, DAD. YOU WERE NEVER PERFECT, BUT YOU WERE ALWAYS TRYING... TRYING TO SHOW ME I WAS SOMETHING MORE.
THIS... CAN'T THE EN YOU TAU ME THA CAN D ANYTHI
I'VE... I'VE GOTTA SAVE YOU.
...NO...
I'M... I'M LOSING GRIP ON THIS FORM. I CAN'T HOLD MYSELF TOGETHER.
PLEASE I CAN'T PLEASE ERICA. H ME.
I'M... AFRAID.

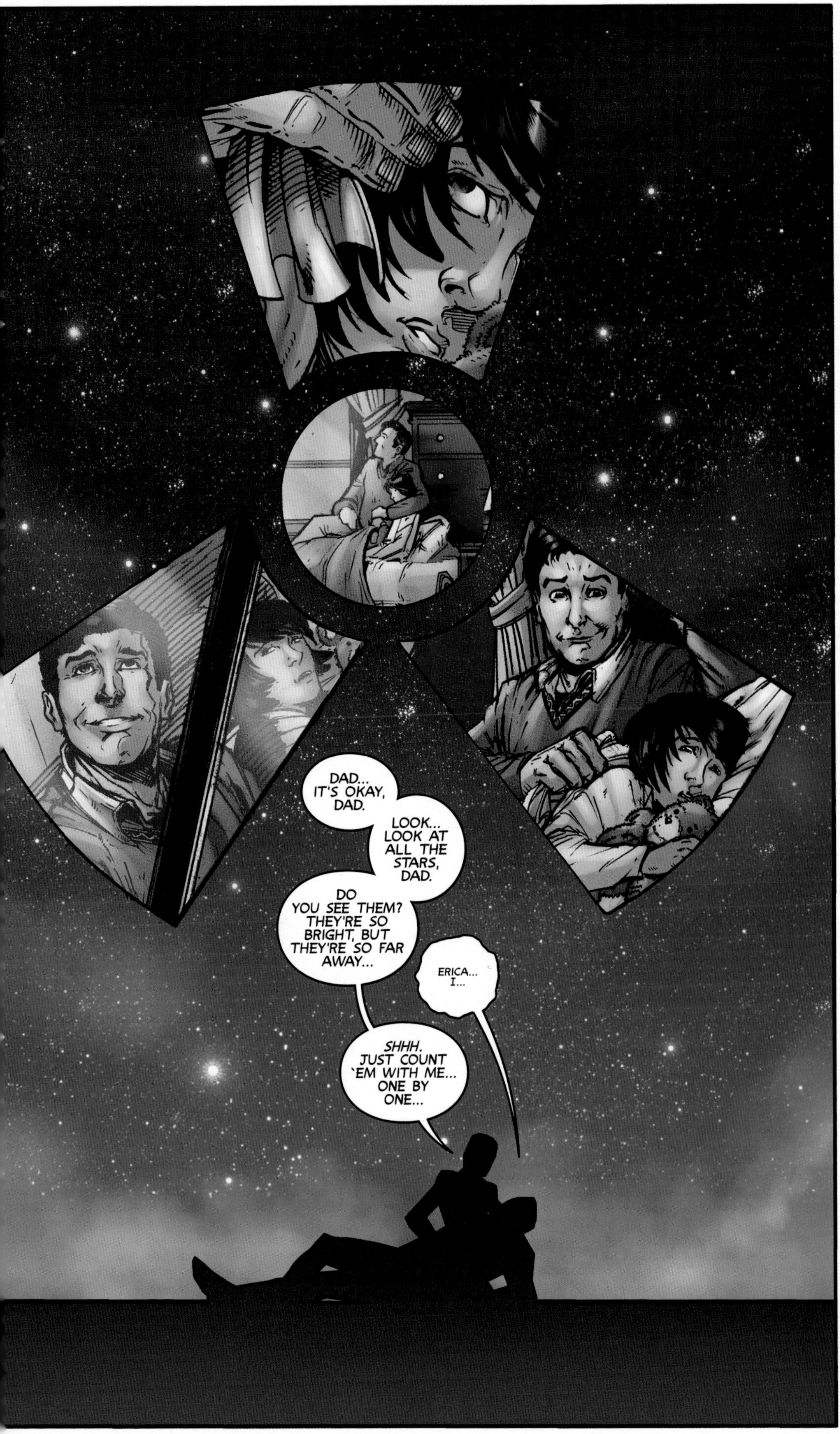
DAD... IT'S OKAY, DAD.
LOOK... LOOK AT ALL THE STARS, DAD.
DO YOU SEE THEM? THEY'RE SO BRIGHT, BUT THEY'RE SO FAR AWAY...
ERICA... I...
SHHH. JUST COUNT `EM WITH ME... ONE BY ONE...

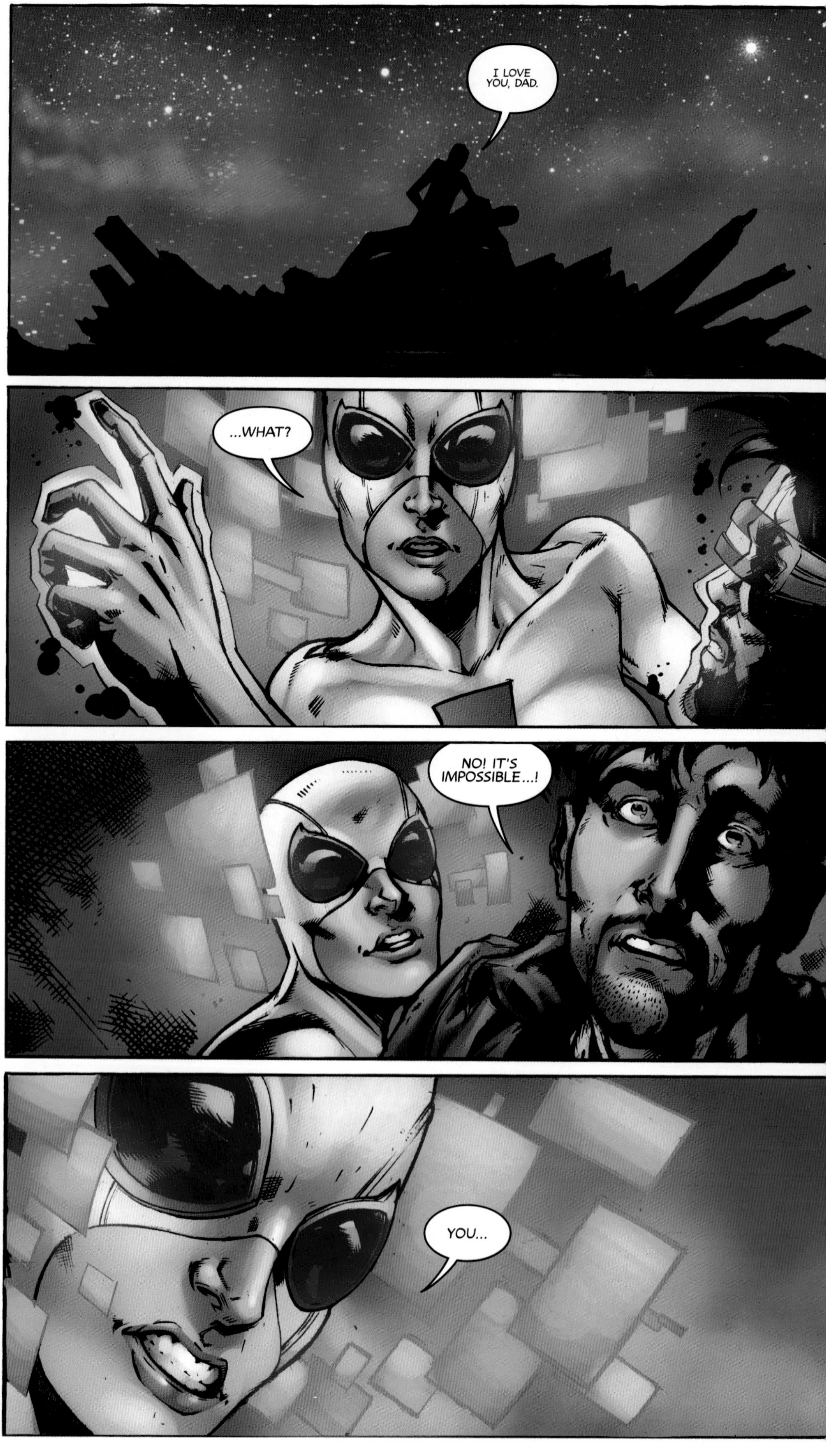
I LOVE YOU, DAD.
...WHAT?
NO! IT'S IMPOSSIBLE...!
YOU...

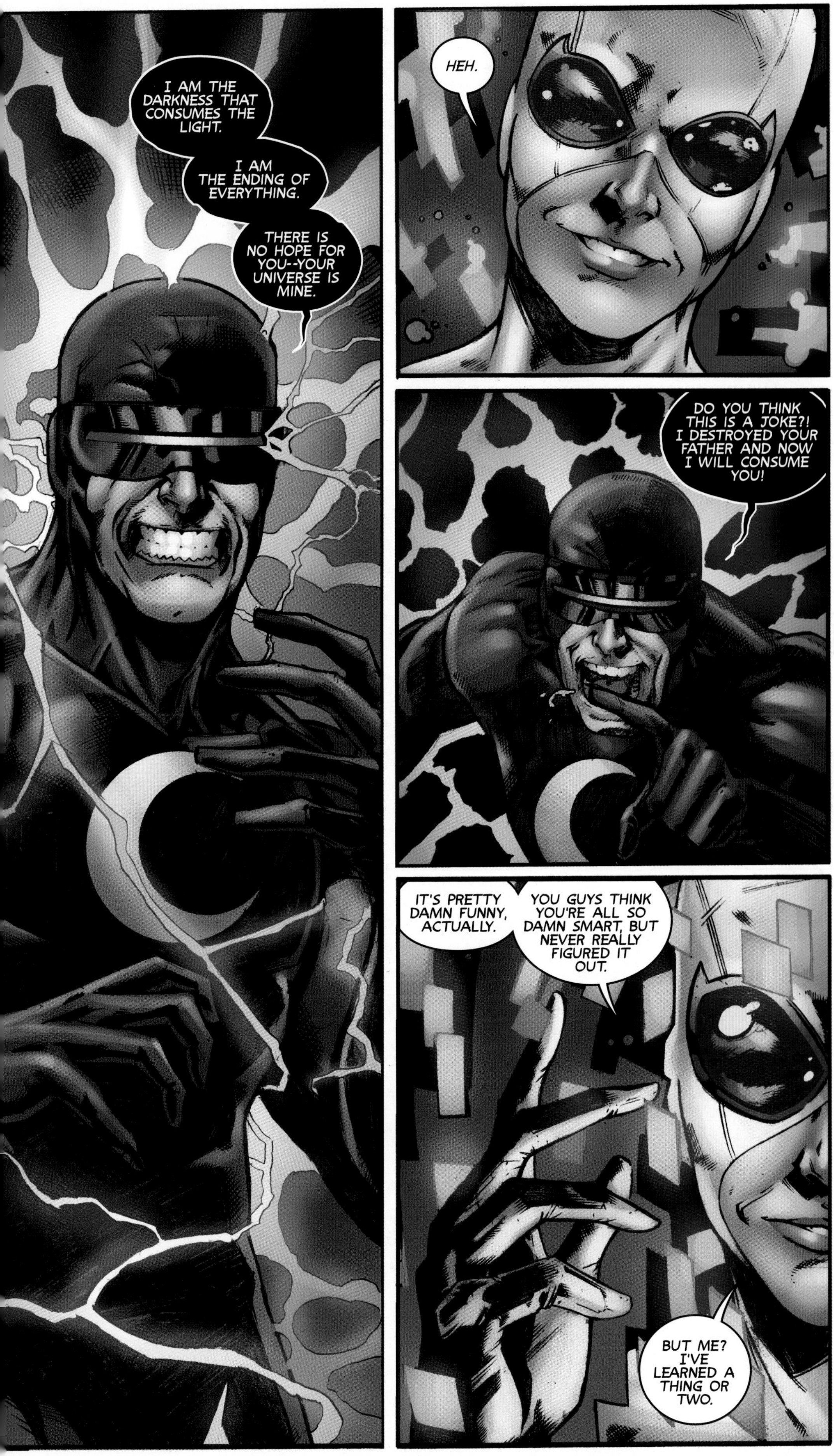
I AM THE DARKNESS THAT CONSUMES THE LIGHT.
I AM THE ENDING OF EVERYTHING.
THERE IS NO HOPE FOR YOU--YOUR UNIVERSE IS MINE.
HEH.
DO YOU THINK THIS IS A JOKE?! I DESTROYED YOUR FATHER AND NOW I WILL CONSUME YOU!
IT'S PRETTY DAMN FUNNY, ACTUALLY.
YOU GUYS THINK YOU'RE ALL SO DAMN SMART, BUT NEVER REALLY FIGURED IT OUT.
BUT ME? I'VE LEARNED A THING OR TWO.

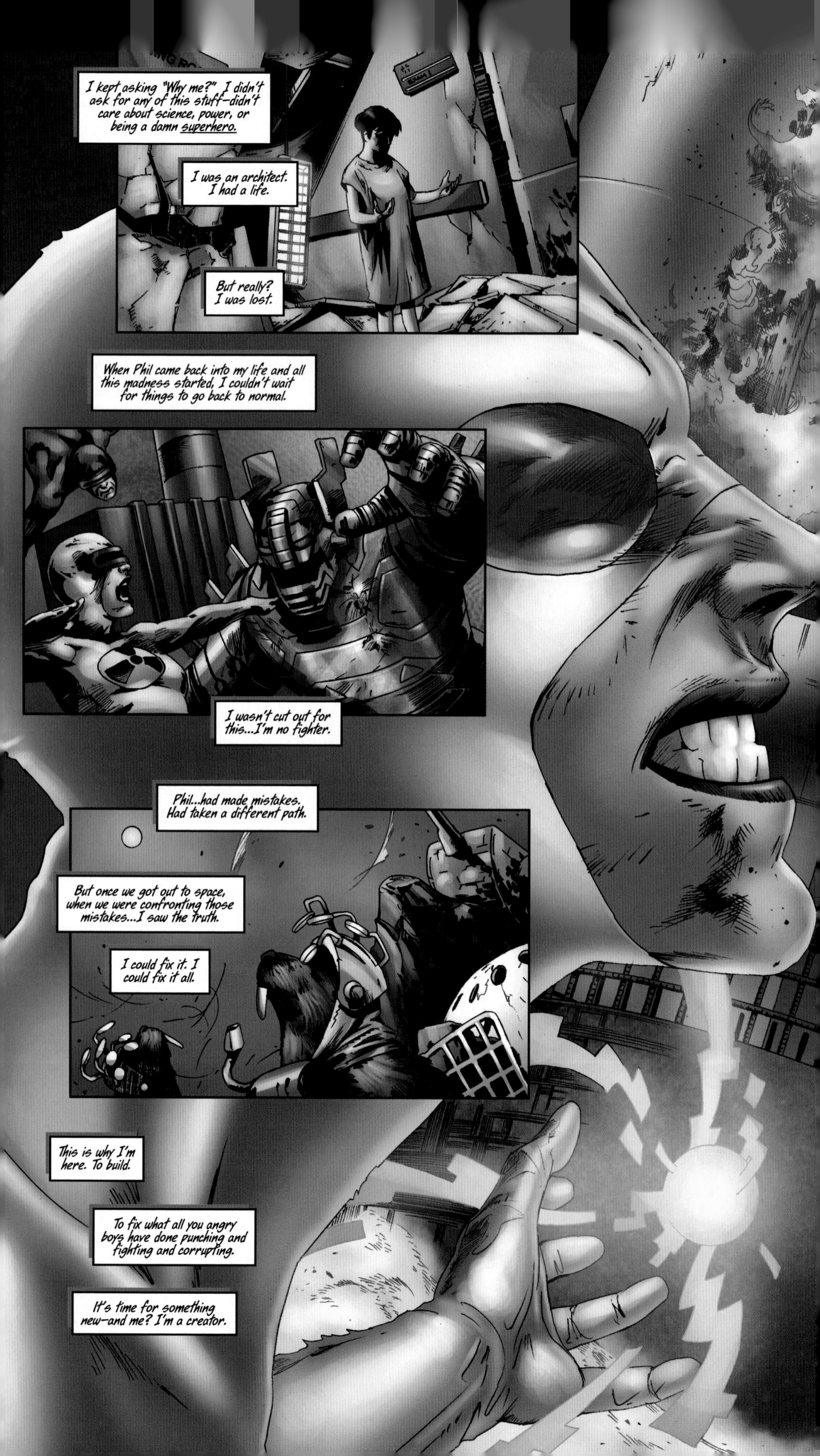
I kept asking "Why me?" I didn't ask for any of this stuff—didn't care about science, power, or being a damn superhero.
I was an architect. I had a life.
But really? I was lost.
When Phil came back into my life and all this madness started, I couldn't wait for things to go back to normal.
I wasn't cut out for this...I'm no fighter.
Phil...had made mistakes. Had taken a different path.
But once we got out to space, when we were confronting those mistakes...I saw the truth.
I could fix it. I could fix it all.
This is why I'm here. To build.
To fix what all you angry boys have done punching and fighting and corrupting.
It's time for something new—and me? I'm a creator.

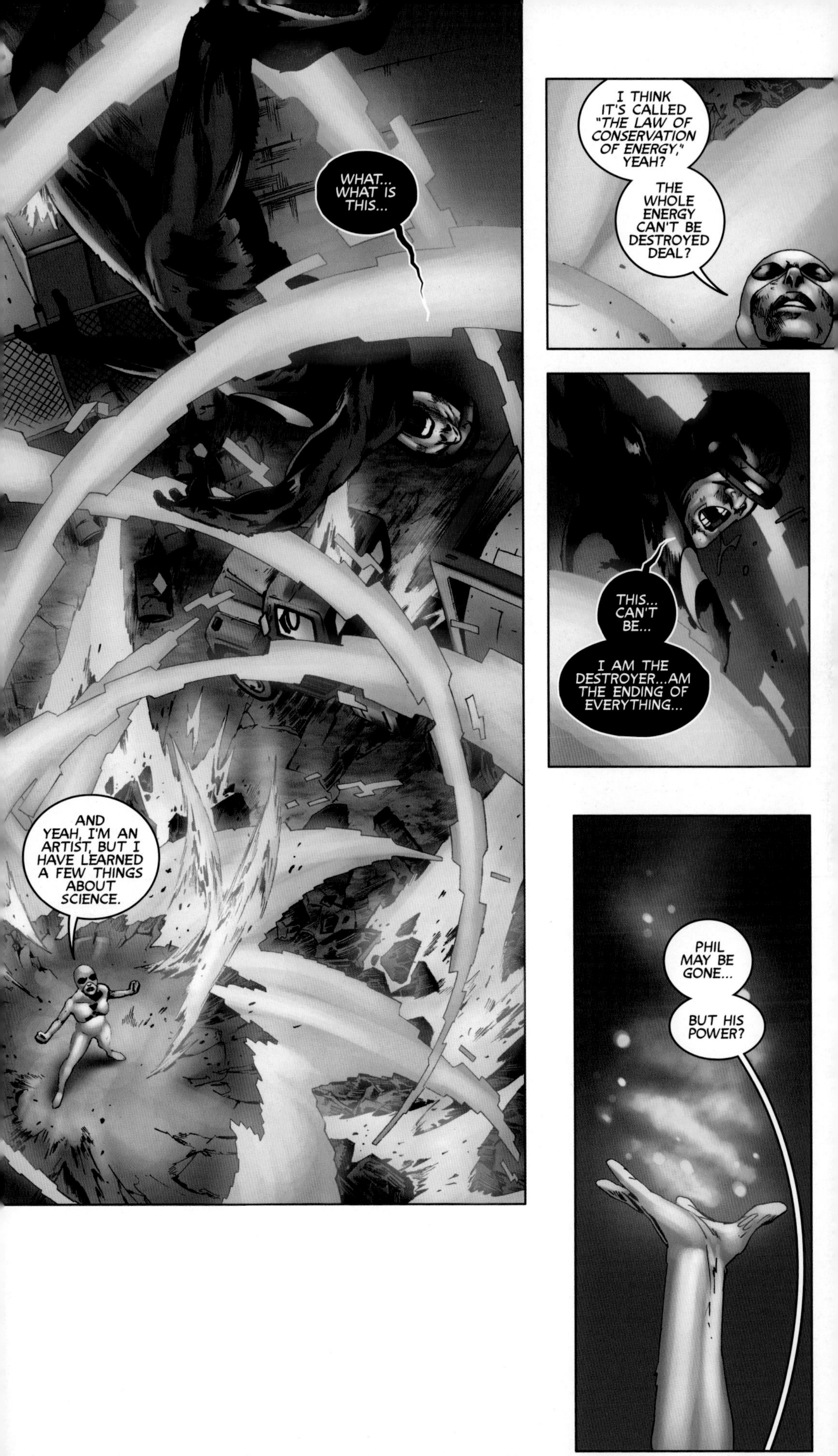
WHAT... WHAT IS THIS...
AND YEAH, I'M AN ARTIST, BUT I HAVE LEARNED A FEW THINGS ABOUT SCIENCE.
I THINK IT'S CALLED "THE LAW OF CONSERVATION OF ENERGY," YEAH?
THE WHOLE ENERGY CAN'T BE DESTROYED DEAL?
THIS... CAN'T BE...
I AM THE DESTROYER...AM THE ENDING OF EVERYTHING...
PHIL MAY BE GONE...
BUT HIS POWER?

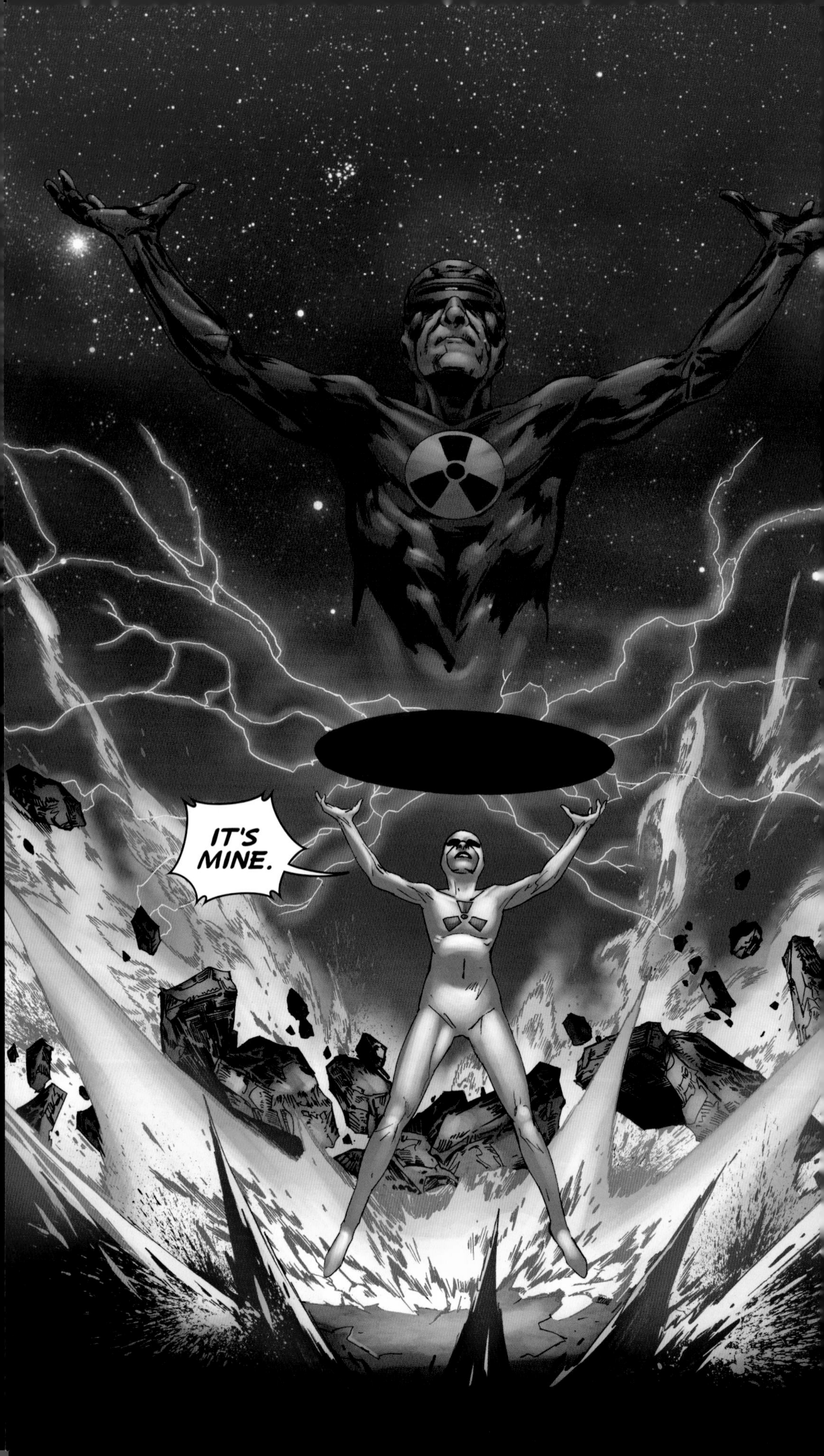
IT'S MINE.

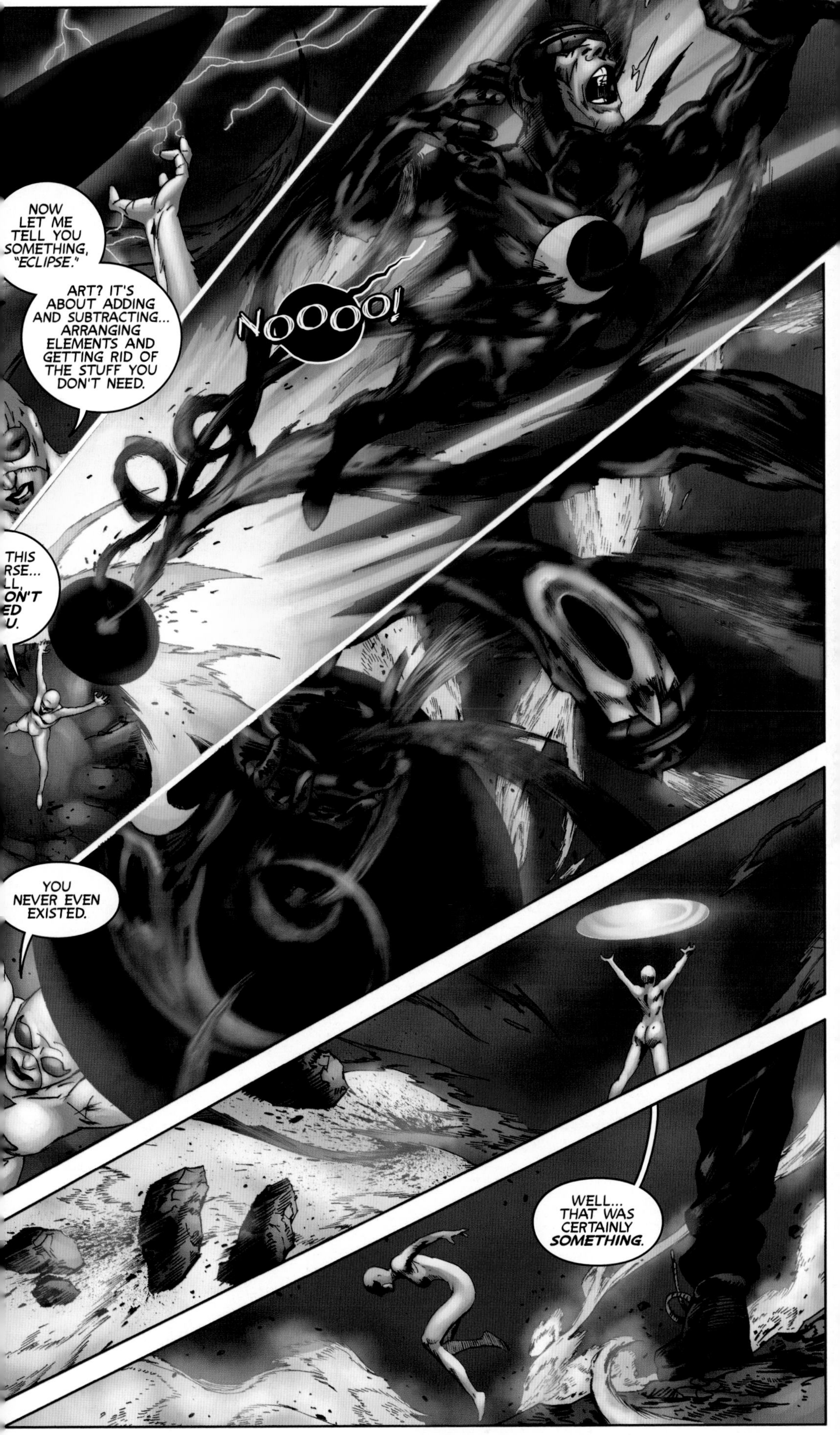
NOW LET ME TELL YOU SOMETHING, "ECLIPSE."
ART? IT'S ABOUT ADDING AND SUBTRACTING... ARRANGING ELEMENTS AND GETTING RID OF THE STUFF YOU DON'T NEED.
NOOOO!
YOU NEVER EVEN EXISTED.
WELL... THAT WAS CERTAINLY *SOMETHING*.

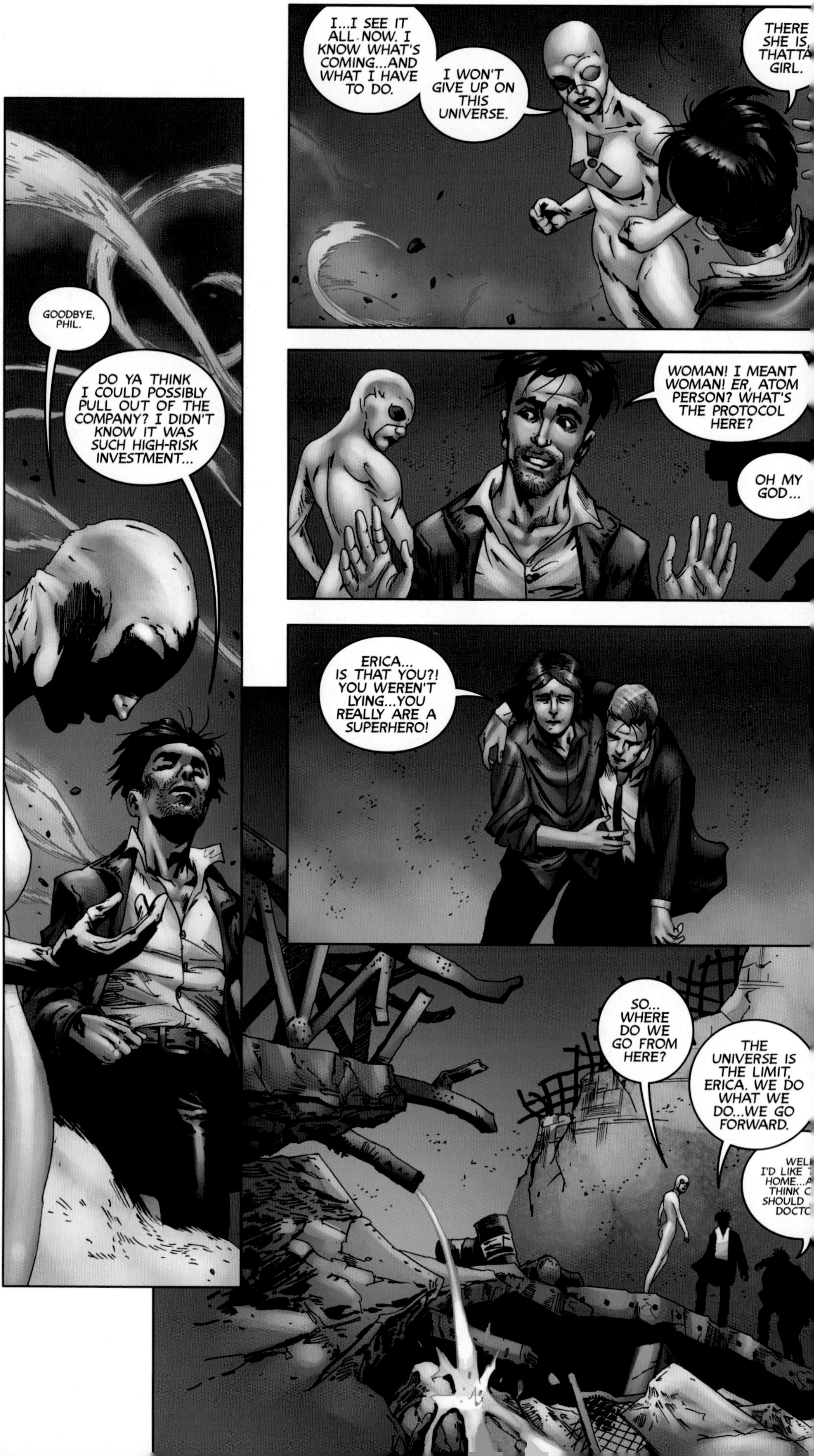

I...I SEE IT ALL NOW. I KNOW WHAT'S COMING...AND WHAT I HAVE TO DO.
I WON'T GIVE UP ON THIS UNIVERSE.
THERE SHE IS, THATTA GIRL.
GOODBYE, PHIL.
DO YA THINK I COULD POSSIBLY PULL OUT OF THE COMPANY? I DIDN'T KNOW IT WAS SUCH HIGH-RISK INVESTMENT...
WOMAN! I MEANT WOMAN! ER, ATOM PERSON? WHAT'S THE PROTOCOL HERE?
OH MY GOD...
ERICA... IS THAT YOU?! YOU WEREN'T LYING...YOU REALLY ARE A SUPERHERO!
SO... WHERE DO WE GO FROM HERE?
THE UNIVERSE IS THE LIMIT, ERICA. WE DO WHAT WE DO...WE GO FORWARD.

This all started with an accident.

But it became something more.

Things change.

It's the nature of the universe.

But light will always outshine the dark.

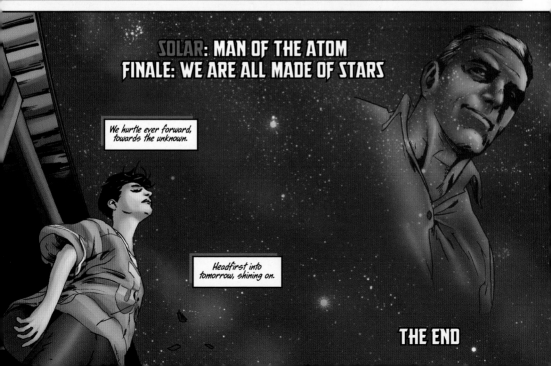

SOLAR: MAN OF THE ATOM
FINALE: WE ARE ALL MADE OF STARS

We hurtle ever forward, towards the unknown.

Headfirst into tomorrow, shining on.

THE END

COVER GALLERY

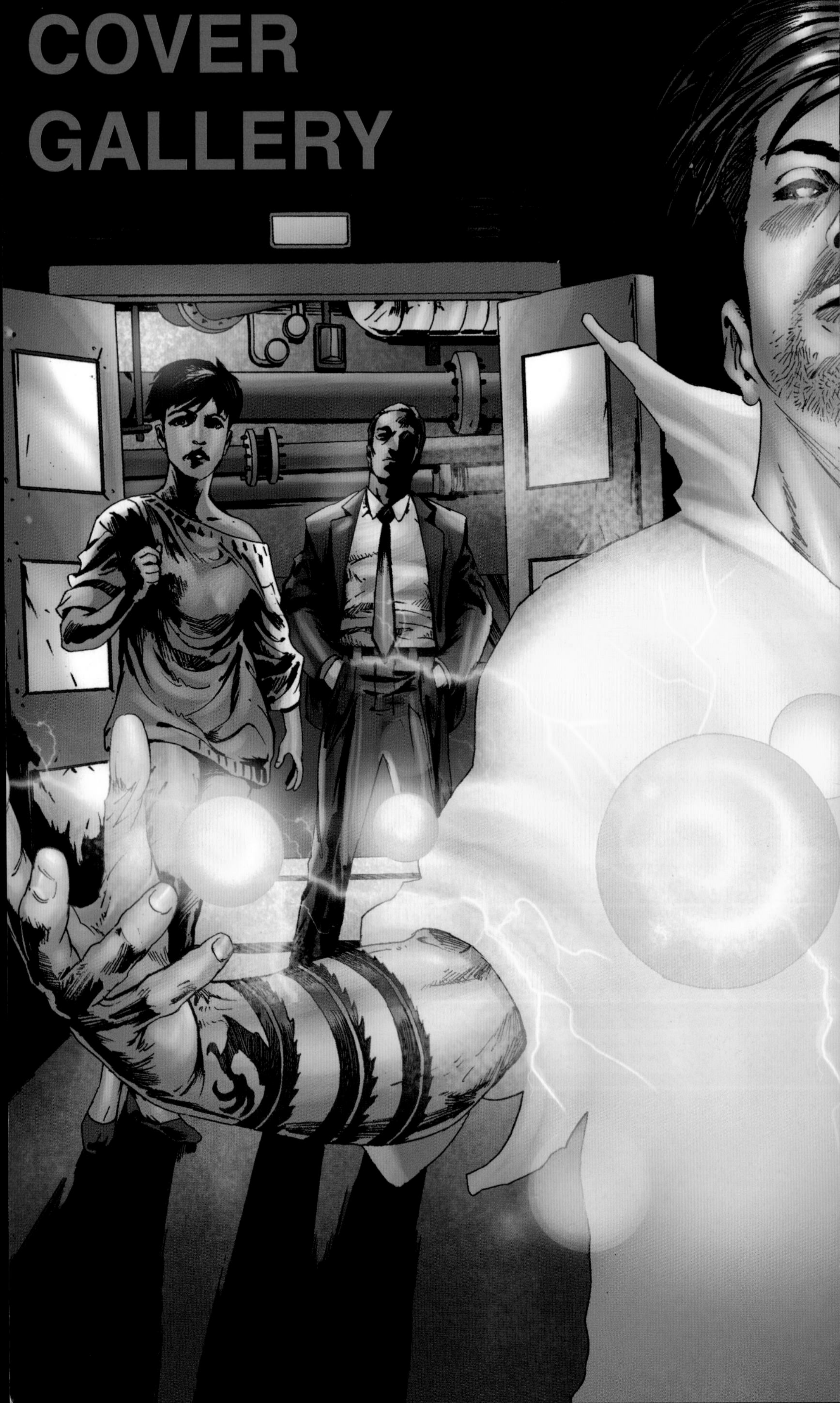

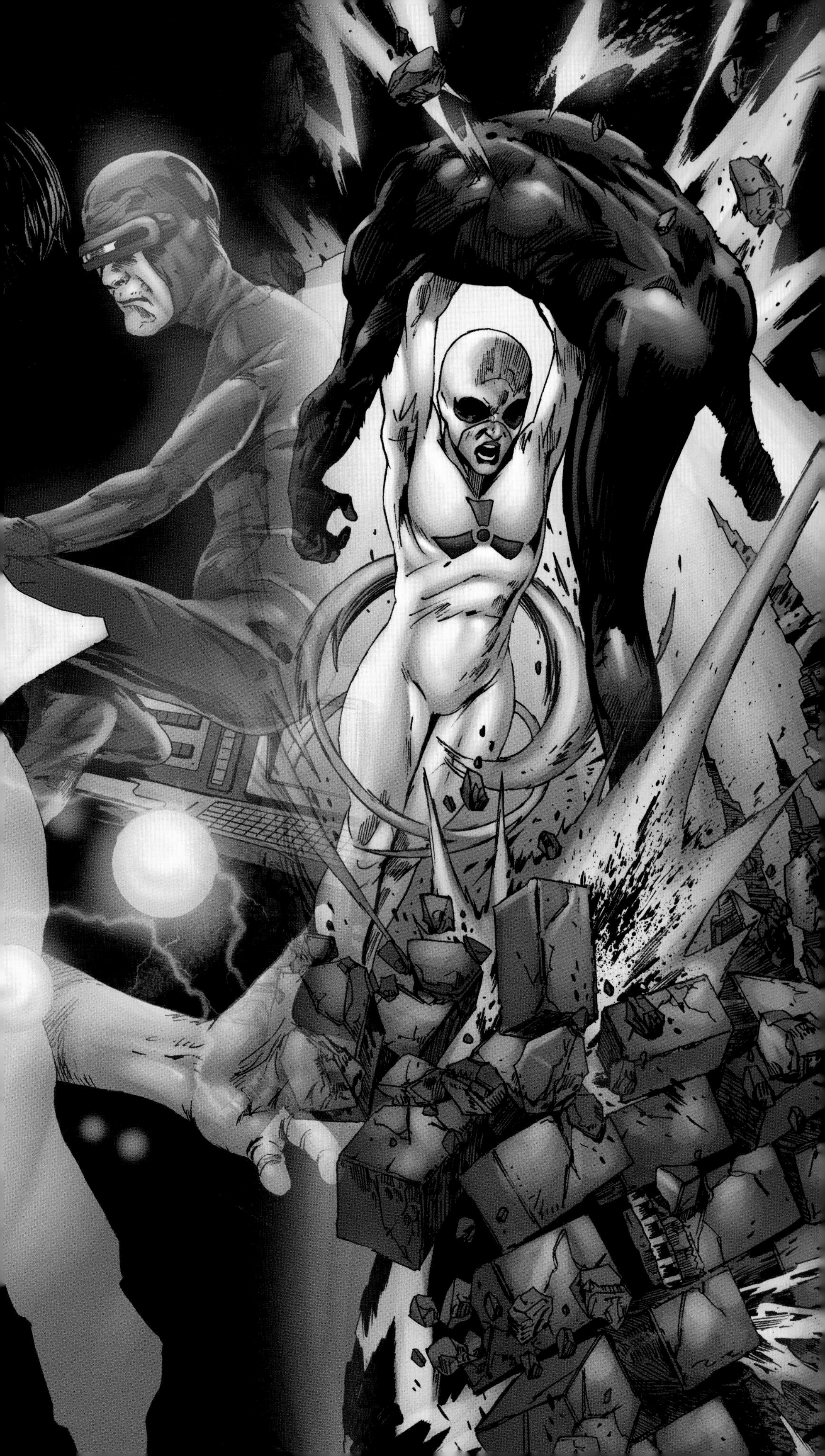

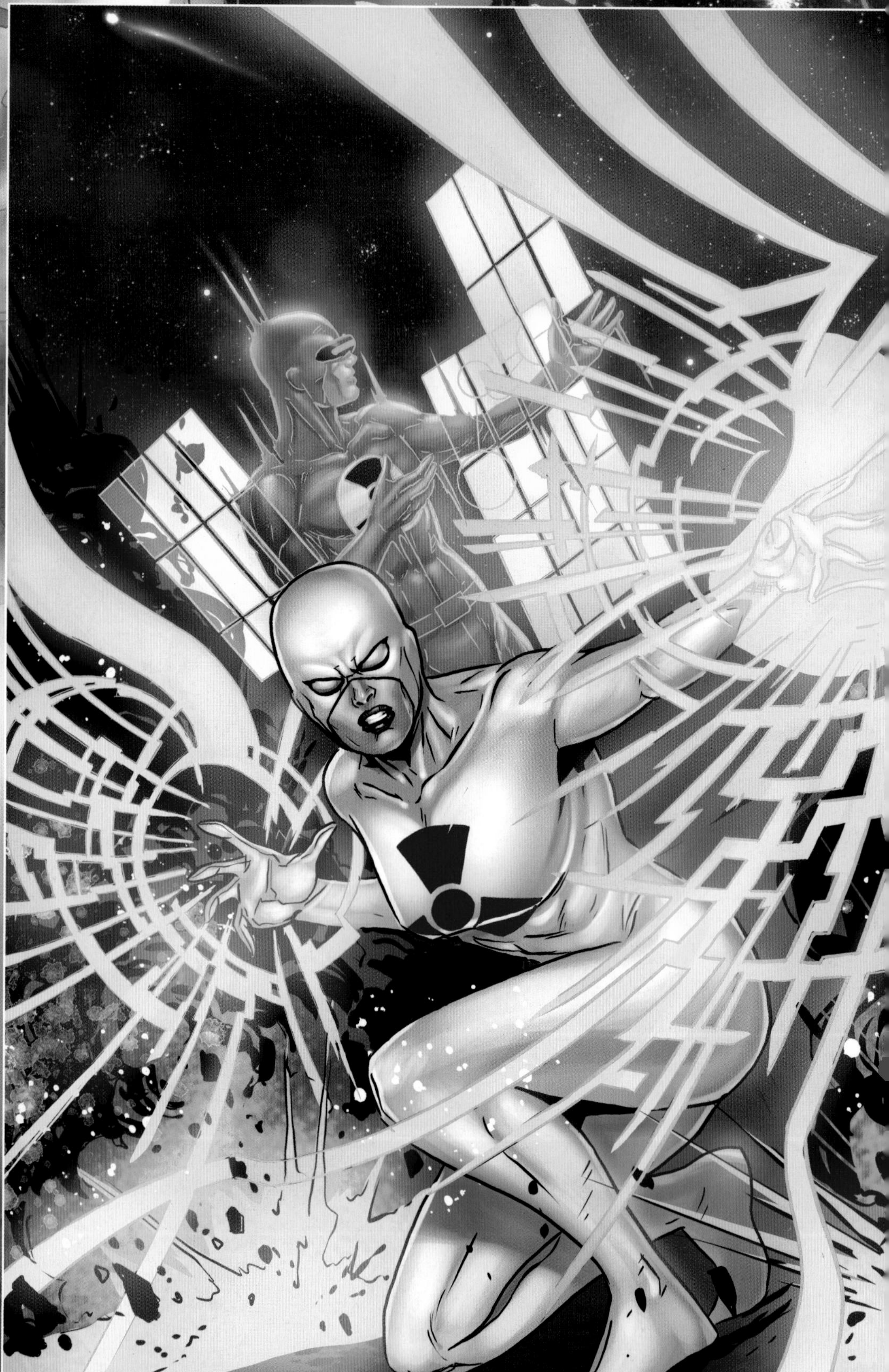

issue #9 cover by MARC LAMING
colors by OMI REMALANTE JR.

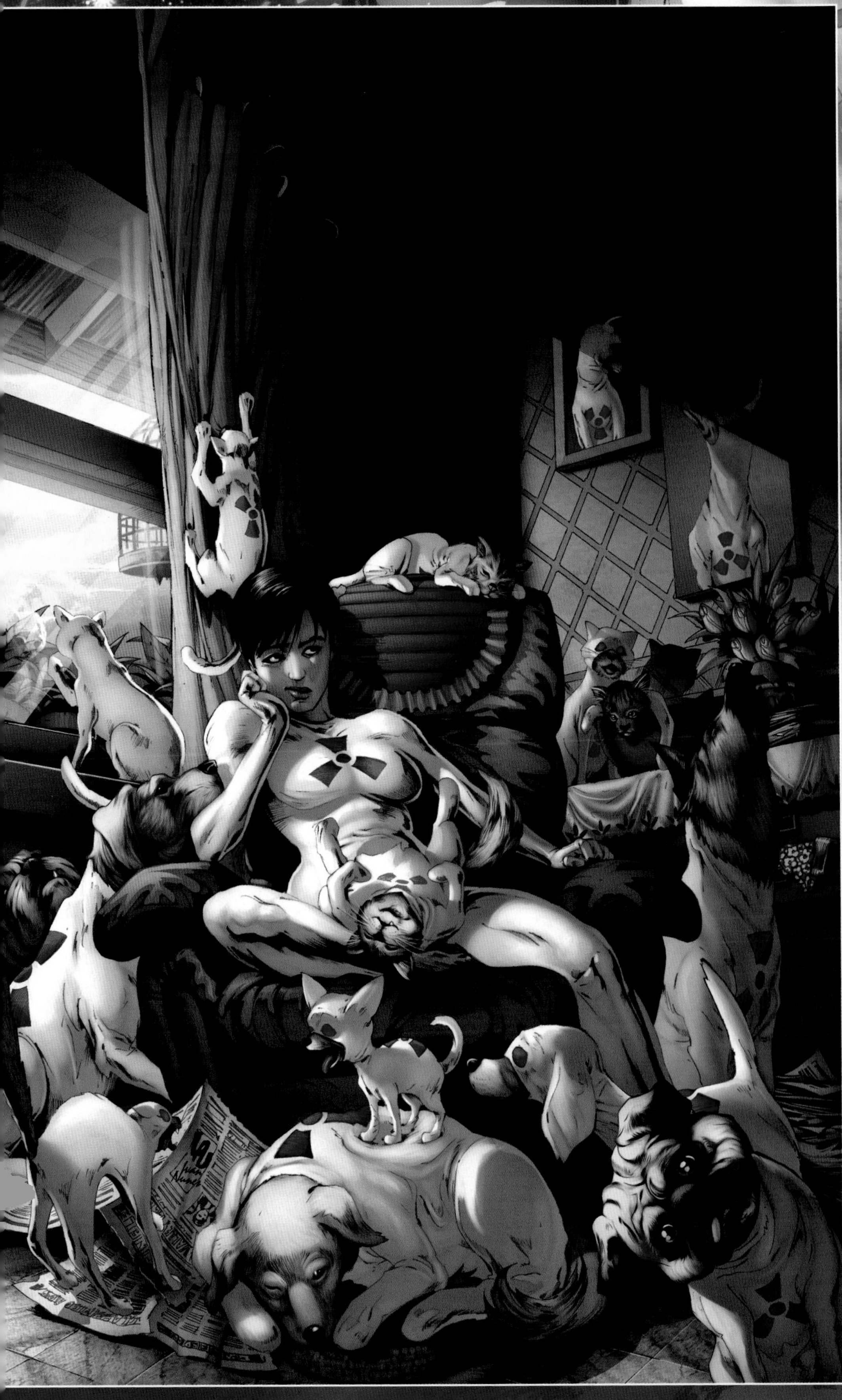

issue #9 cover by JONATHAN LAU
colors by IVAN NUNES

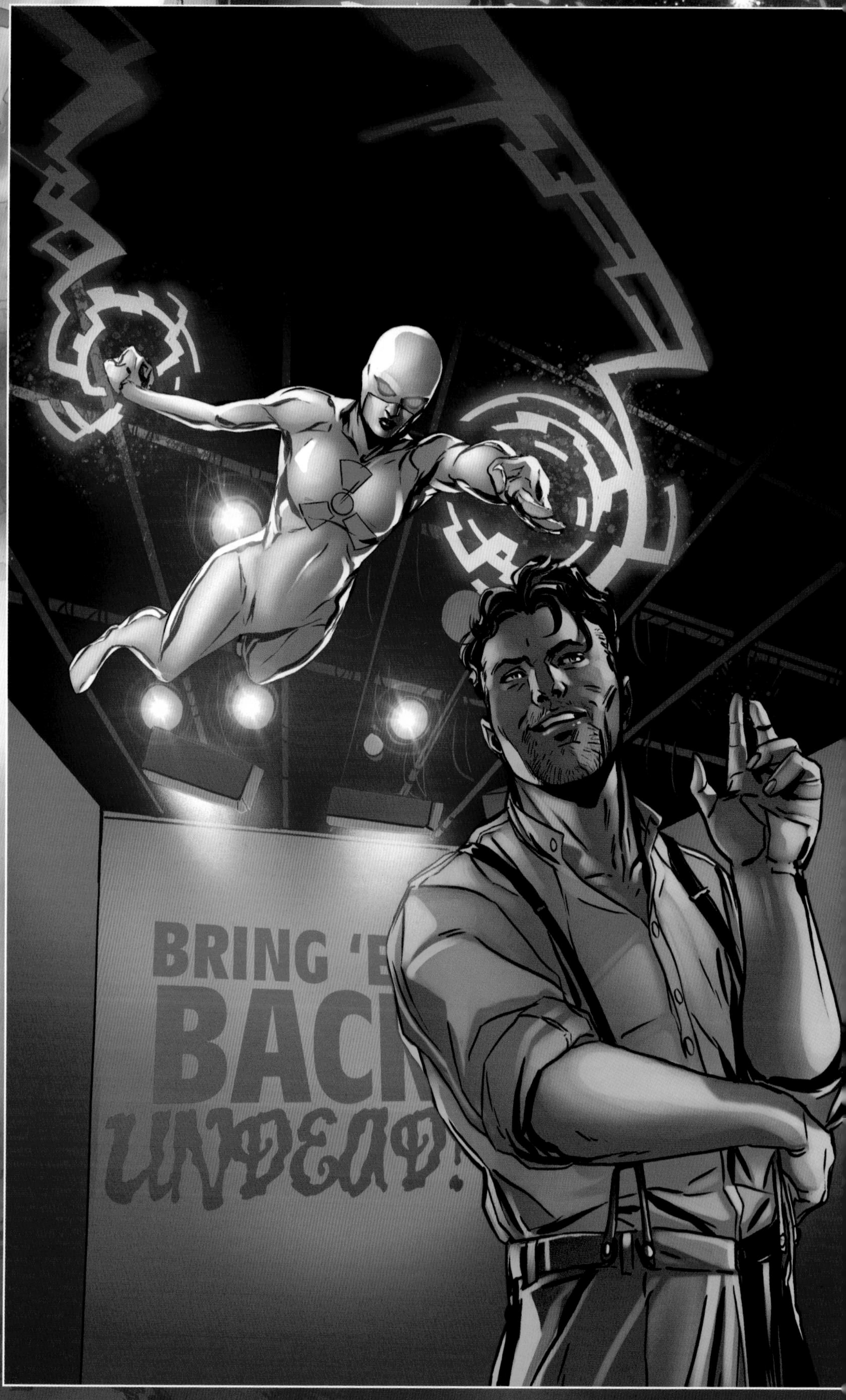
BRING 'E
BACK
UNDEAD!

issue #10 cover by MARC LAMING
colors by IVAN NUNES

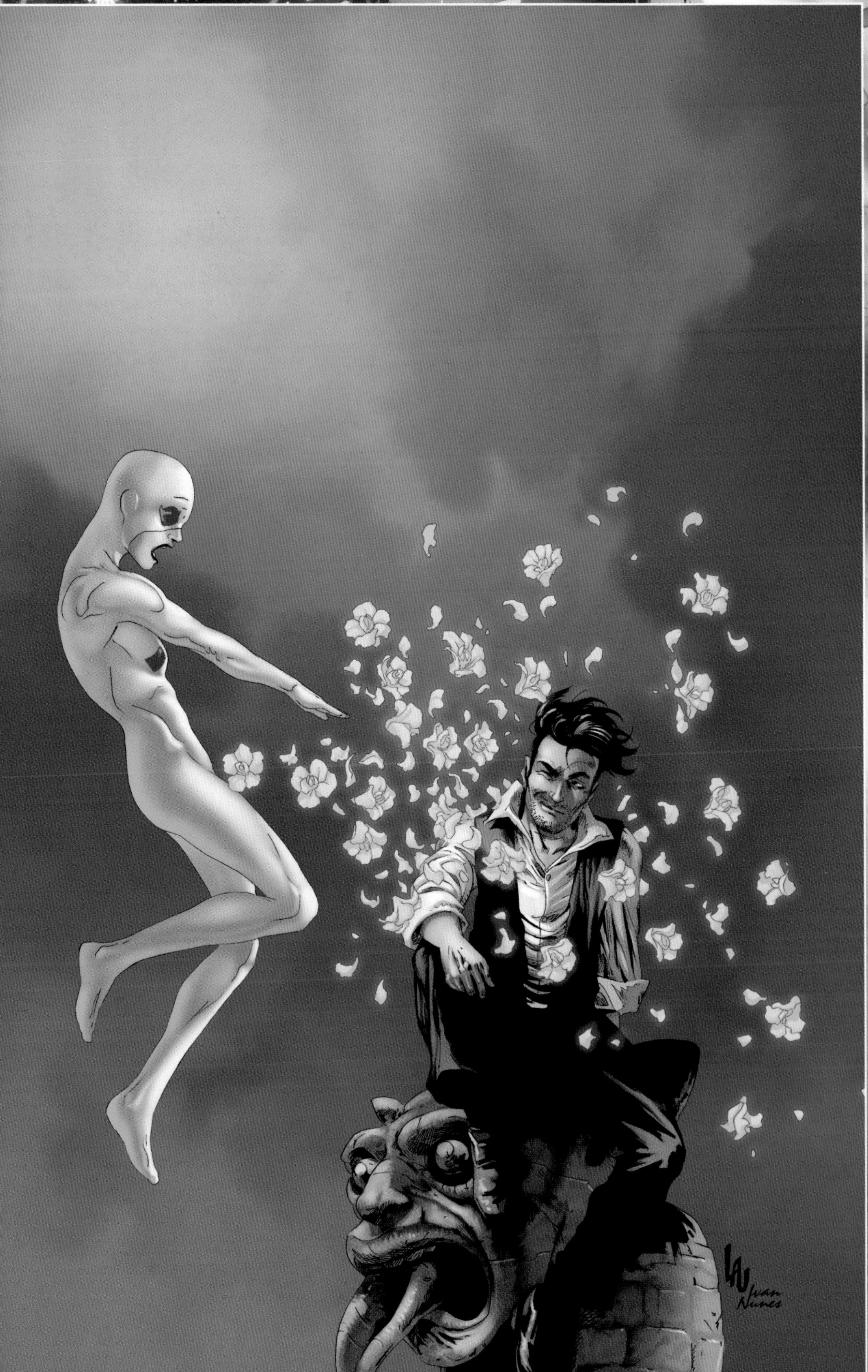
LAU
Ivan Nunes

issue #10 cover by JONATHAN LAU
colors by IVAN NUNES

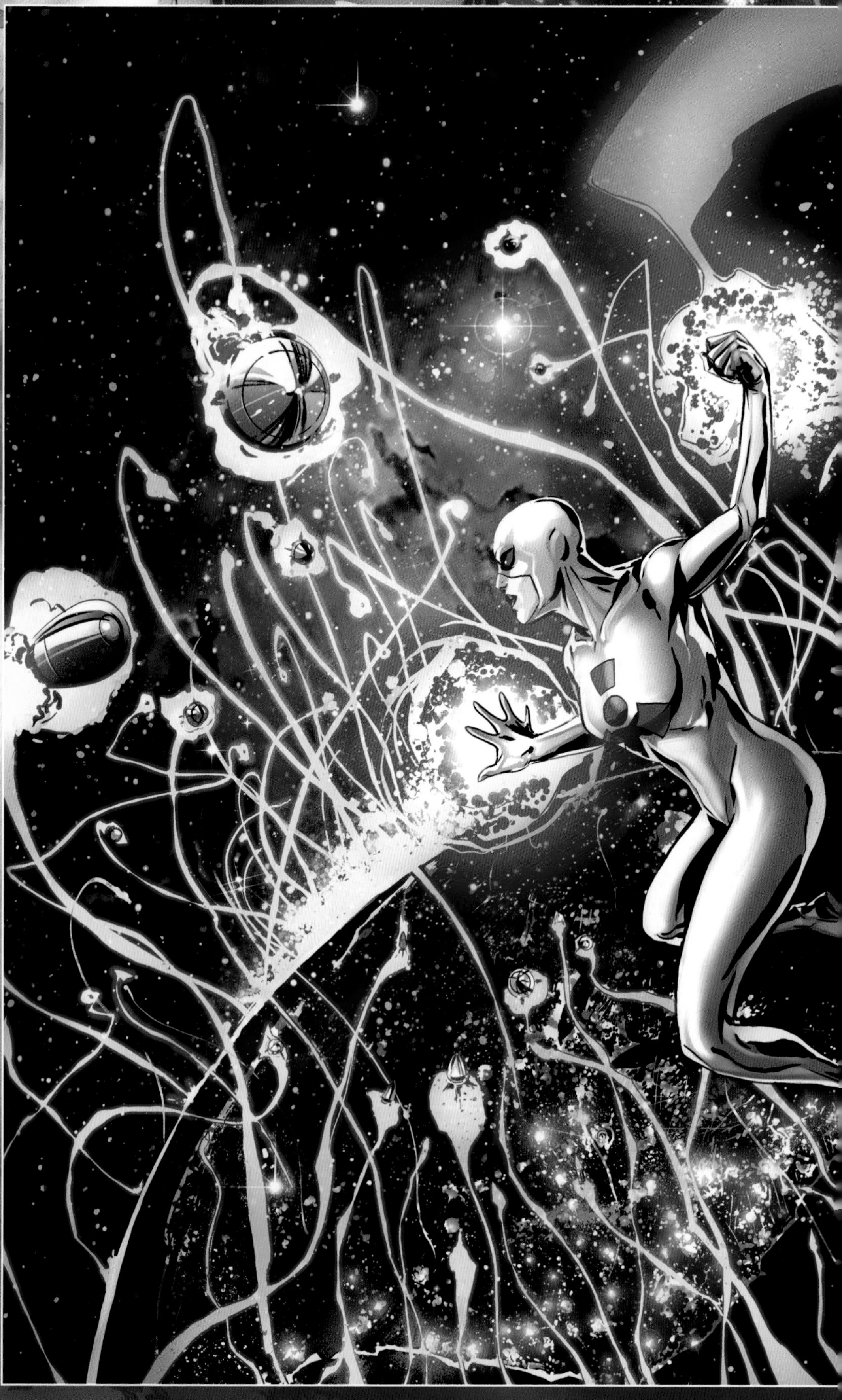

issue #11 cover by MARC LAMING
colors by IVAN NUNES

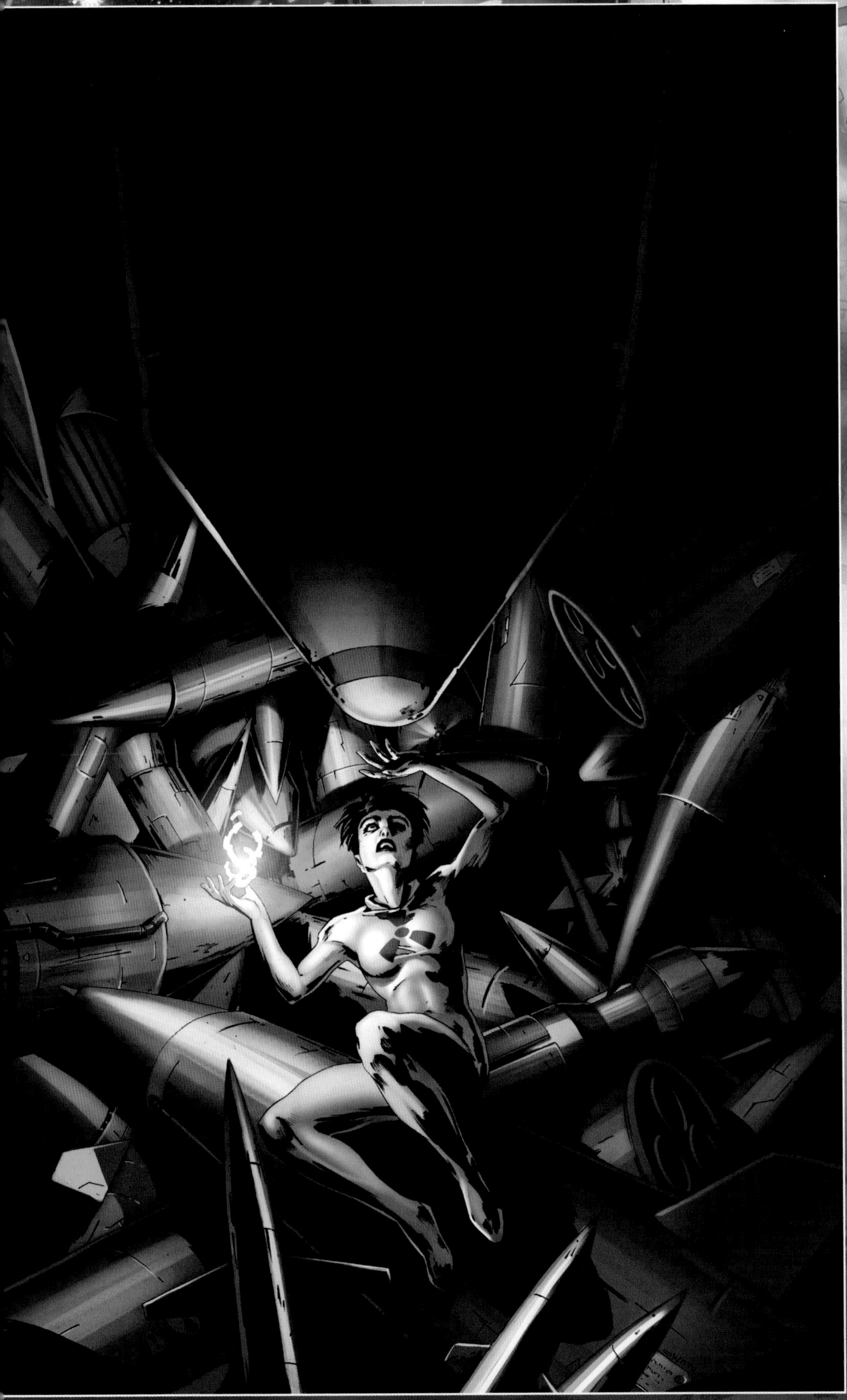

issue #11 cover by JONATHAN LAU
colors by IVAN NUNES

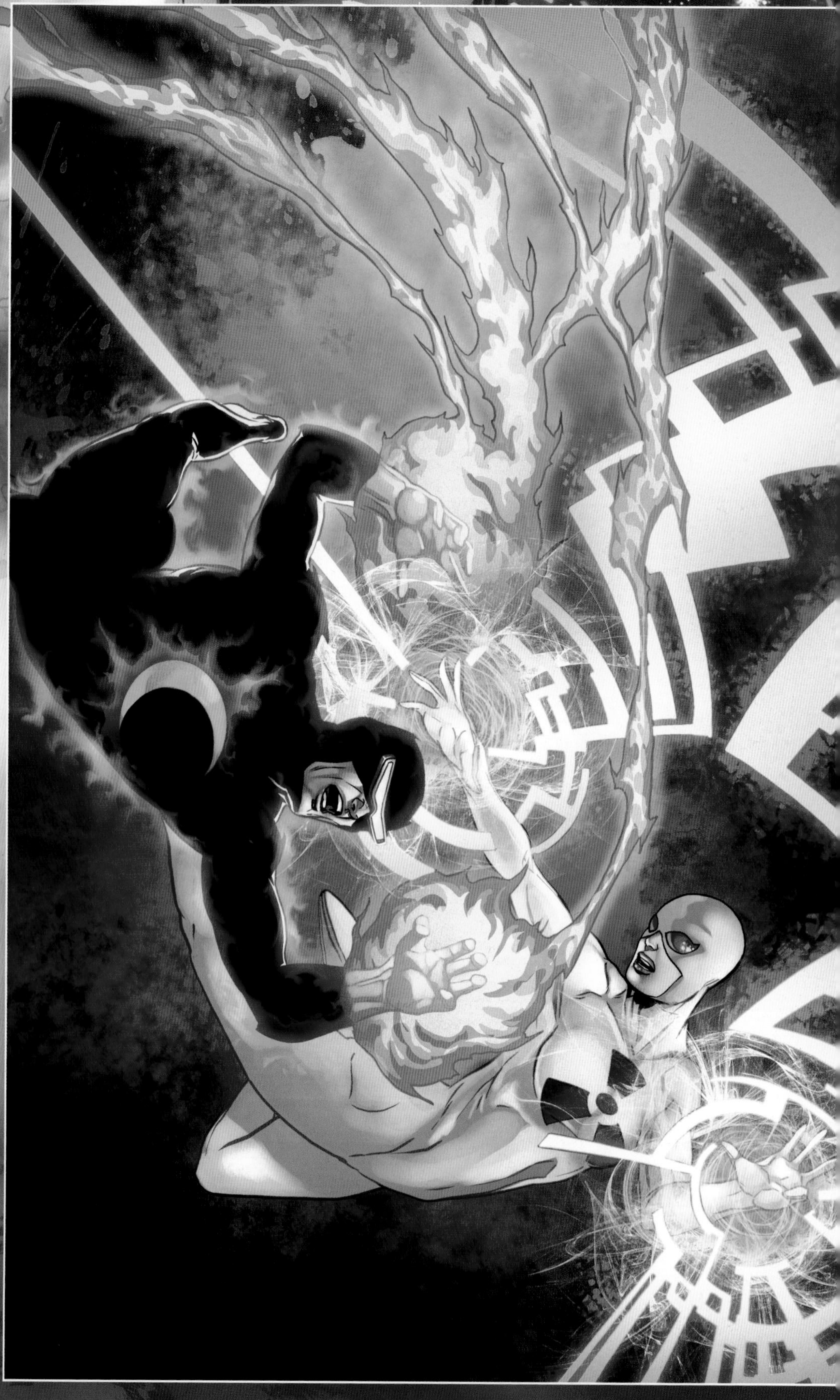

issue #12 cover by MARC LAMING
colors by IVAN NUNES

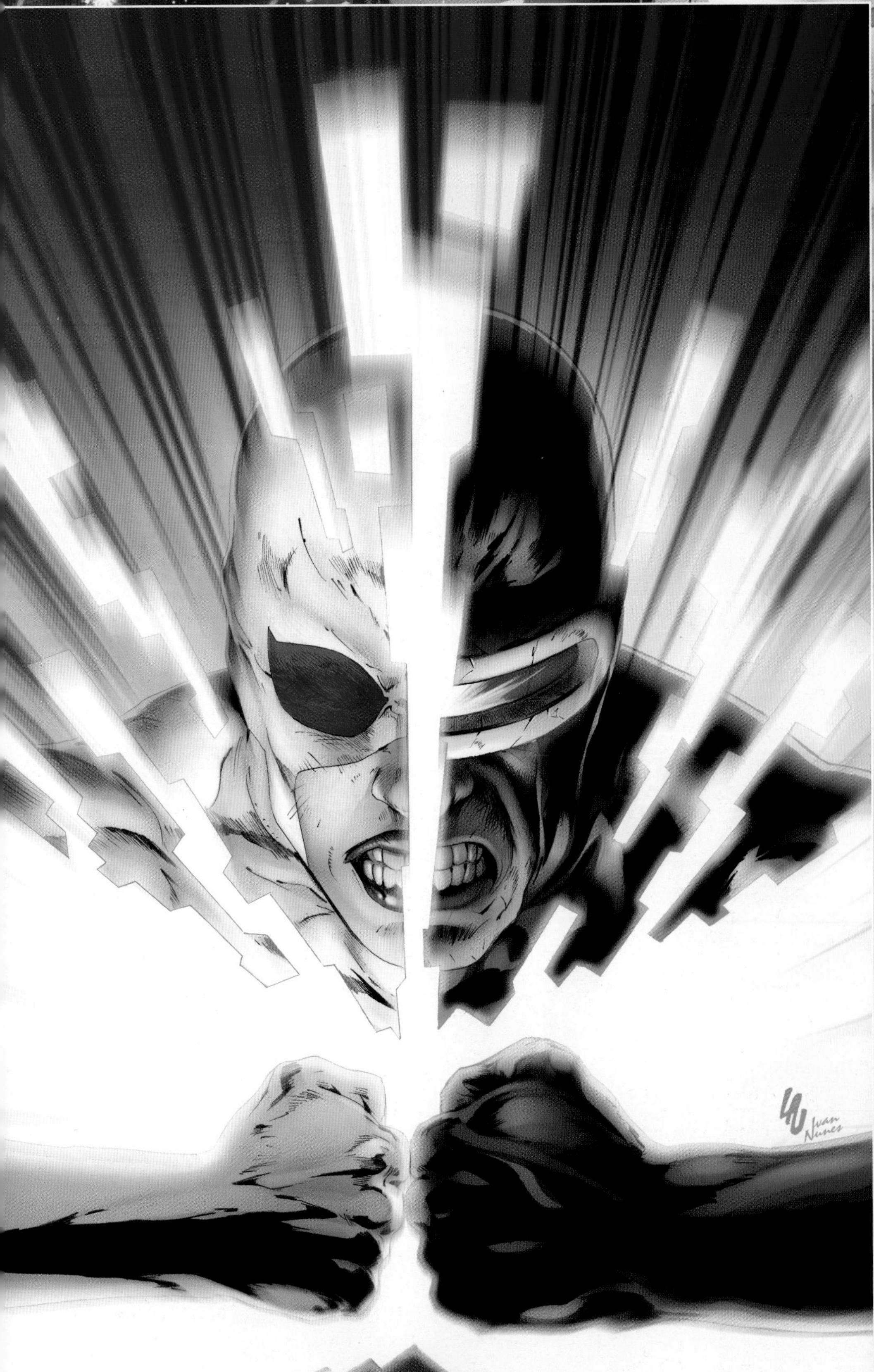
Ivan Nunes

issue #12 cover by JONATHAN LAU
colors by IVAN NUNES

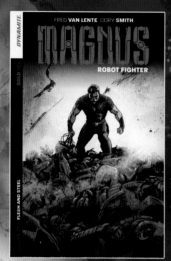

GOLD KEY: UNLOCK THE UNIVERSE

DYNAMITE
FRED VAN LENTE CORY SMITH
MAGNUS
ROBOT FIGHTER
GOLD KEY
FLESH AND STEEL

MAGNUS: ROBOT FIGHTER
VOL. 1: FLESH AND STEEL TPB

DYNAMITE
FRED VAN LENTE CORY SMITH
MAGNUS
ROBOT FIGHTER
GOLD KEY
UNCANNY VALLEY

MAGNUS: ROBOT FIGHTER
VOL. 2: UNCANNY VALLEY TPB

DYNAMITE
FRED VAN LENTE ROBERTO CASTRO JOSEPH
GOLD KEY
CRADLE AND GRAVE

MAGNUS: ROBOT FIGHT
VOL. 3: CRADLE AND GRAV

DYNAMITE
FRANK J. BARBIERE JOE BENNETT
SOLAR
MAN OF THE ATOM
GOLD KEY
NUCLEAR FAMILY

SOLAR: MAN OF THE ATOM
VOL. 1: NUCLEAR FAMILY TPB

DYNAMITE
FRANK J. BARBIERE JONATHAN LAU
SOLAR
MAN OF THE ATOM
GOLD KEY
WOMAN OF THE ATOM

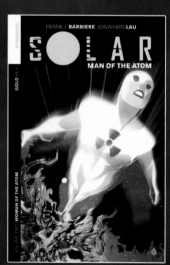

SOLAR: MAN OF THE ATOM
VOL. 2: WOMAN OF THE ATOM TPB

GOLD KEY: TRADE PAPERBACKS

GREG **PAK** · MIRKO **COLAK** · CORY **SMITH**

TUROK: DINOSAUR HUNTER
VOL. 1: CONQUEST TPB

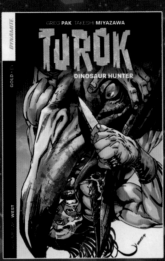

GREG **PAK** · TAKESHI **MIYAZAWA**

TUROK: DINOSAUR HUNTER
VOL. 2: WEST TPB

GREG **PAK** · PAUL **TOBIN**

TUROK: DINOSAUR HUNTER
VOL. 3: RAPTOR FOREST TPB

FRANK **BARBIERE** · JONATHAN **LAU**

SOLAR: MAN OF THE ATOM
VOL. 3: ECLIPSE TPB

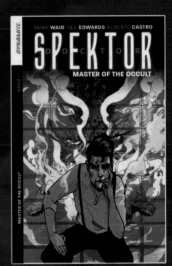

MARK **WAID** · NEIL **EDWARDS** · ROBERTO **CASTRO**

DOCTOR SPEKTOR
VOL. 1: MASTER OF THE OCCULT TPB

DYNAMITE®

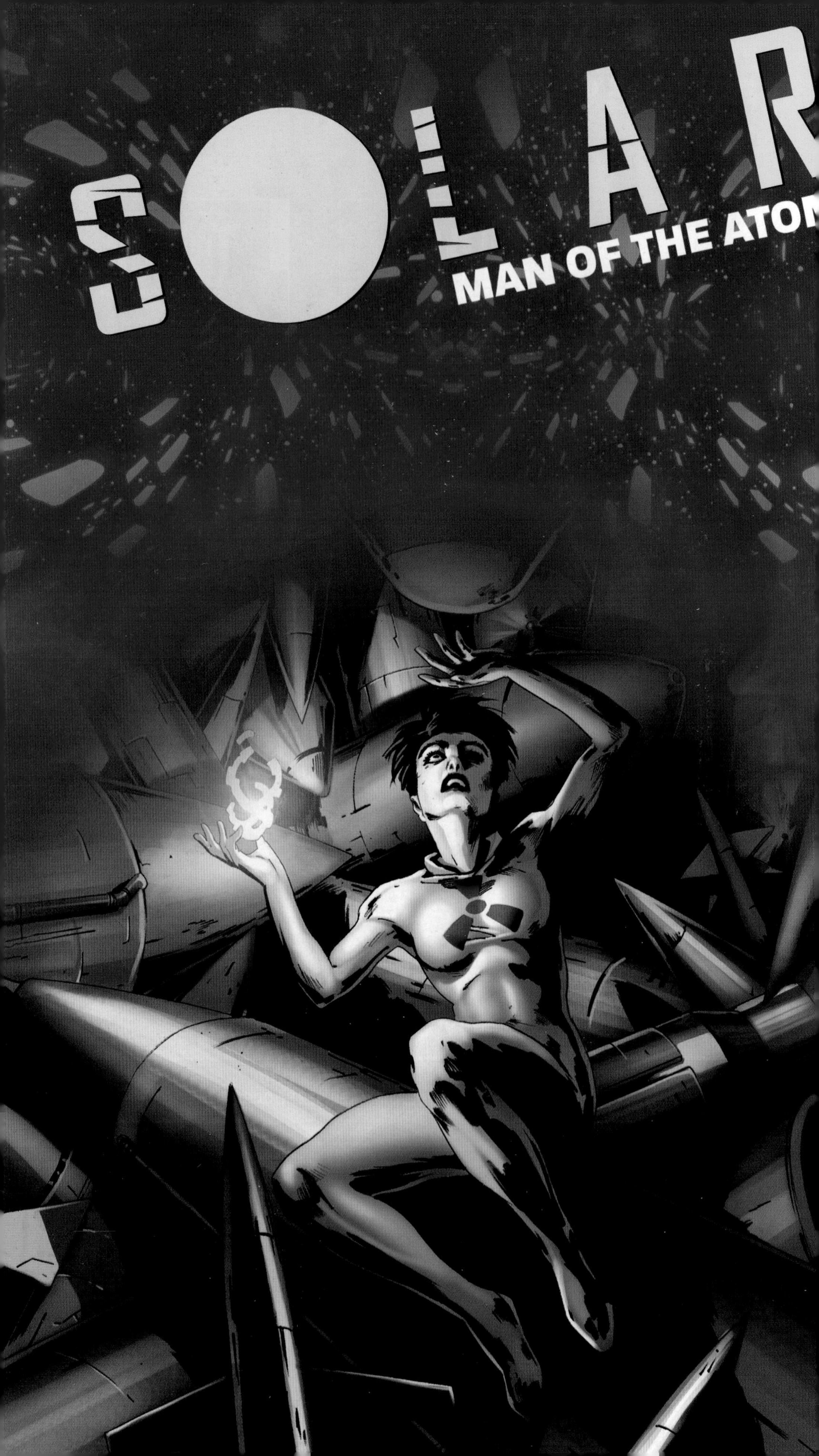

SOLAR
MAN OF THE ATOM